EAST EUROPEAN DISSENT

Volume 1
1953-64

EAST EUROPEAN DISSENT

Volume 1
1953-64

Edited and Introduced by Vojtech Mastny

Assistant Professor of History
Columbia University (New York)

FACTS ON FILE, INC. 169750 NEW YORK

EAST
EUROPEAN
DISSENT

Volume 1
1953-64

Library of Congress Catalog Card Number: 72-148185

ISBN 0-87196-196-2

9 8 7 6 5 4 3 2 1

PRINTED IN THE UNITED STATES OF AMERICA

CONTENTS

INTRODUCTION

IN COMMUNIST EASTERN EUROPE DISSENT serves a function quite different from its purpose in the West. The anecdotal Soviet visitor to the U.S., commenting about the freedom of expression here, has pinpointed the crux of the difference: "You in America can afford to let anyone speak as he wishes; you are accustomed to the cacophony and don't mind it. In our country, we would take it seriously." The significance of dissent under communism stems from the totalitarian aspirations of the regime. In a system striving to mold the citizens' opinions toward unanimity, any deviation from this however unattainable ideal qualifies as dissent.

For Communists in power—as for other advocates of totalitarianism—dissent is an altogether negative phenomenon in politics. It is to be prevented in order to forestall possible weakening of the state, rather than channeled for constructive purposes or at least tolerated as evidence of the regime's strength. But the lack of tolerance on the part of the members of the ruling oligarchy is not the result solely of their insecurity. Their attitude is also determined by the official Marxist ideology to which they subscribe. As a comprehensive and militant philosophy, embracing all aspects of human endeavor, Marxism leaves little room for alternative interpretations of the world. Particularly, the central doctrine of class struggle, which assumes implacable hostility by real or hypothetical enemies, interprets any accommodation to other viewpoints as the surrender of principle and the invitation to disaster.

Marxists hold a very high opinion of the power of ideas. Although they consider the material conditions of life primary and the ideological "superstructure" only secondary, they respect the impact of thought on society. Moreover, since ideas are for them not merely haphazard products of individual brains but manifestations of deeper social trends, all intellectual

1

activity has ultimately political implications. Thus, many acts
and ideas that would hardly qualify as dissent anywhere else
are a matter of serious concern in Communist countries. A lyric
poem or an abstract painting can be disruptive simply because
the regime—in its quest for uniformity—had prescribed certain
norms even for such seemingly unpolitical activities as writing
poetry or painting. Both the authorities and the public understand the significance of their violations very well. In Hungary
during 1956, the poetry enthusiasts of the "Petofi circles" gave
a vital impetus to a movement that culminated in fighting
against Soviet tanks in the streets of Budapest. In Czechoslovakia 12 years later, seemingly esoteric debates among
philosophers arguing about the humanistic content of Marxism
prepared the groundwork for another movement that
eventually provoked the Russian intervention. In the Soviet
Union of the 1960s—as in the tsarist Russia of the 19th century,
the greatest writers were also the most influential critics of the
contemporary regime.

Unlike the subtle intellectual deviations from the totalitarian norm, the often fierce disagreements within the ruling
group cannot be usually characterized as dissent, although their
consequences may be equally disruptive. The members of the
governing elite clash because of personal rivalries or different
opinions about tactics, but few of them question the wisdom
and desirability of totalitarian control. In the few instances in
which some of them challenged it—as did several spokesmen of
the Dubcek regime in Czechoslovakia in 1968—their voices
merged with those of genuine dissent. The ascendancy of such
dissenters in the Czechoslovak Communist Party aroused justified doubts about whether its new program could still be considered Communist in the accepted sense of the word. On the
other hand, it is certain that this very feature of the program
was the secret of its extraordinary popularity.

Although many east Europeans deeply dislike communism,
the extent and nature of their dissatisfaction defies simplistic
formulas. Political indifference is widespread—as in many
other parts of the world. Non-Communists often appreciate
positively, or at least take for granted, the accomplishments of
their governments in social welfare, in technological progress,
in the preservation of the cultural heritage. Yet the features of
the regimes that result from the totalitarian outlook of their

leading representatives are intensely unpopular. These include especially the restrictions against private initiative, individual self-improvement, the freedom of movement and the diversity of expression. Illustrative of the mass character of this kind of dissatisfaction is the phenomenon of defection.

Unlike previous mass migrations, the voluntary exodus of millions of persons from eastern Europe since World War II has been less a sociological and political than a psychological phenomenon. The refugees have been representative of all social groups—from the rich to the poor—and of all shades of political opinion—from the Fascist Right to the Communist Left. Although their individual motives for risking escape abroad have ranged from lofty idealism to sheer opportunism, their collective motives can be traced to revulsion against the arbitrary regimentation pervading life in their countries. The intensity of mass dissatisfaction cannot be measured by the outflow of refugees, which depends, rather, on the effectiveness of the physical barriers set up to prevent their departure. Yet the persistence of the exodus shows the magnitude of the revulsion. It proves the continued attraction of the Western ideal of freedom in eastern Europe despite decades of intensive indoctrination designed to eradicate it.

In the Soviet Union, the history of dissent dates back to the beginning of the Bolshevik regime in 1917. But although totalitarian features had always been inherent in the Leninist concept of party rule, the regime was more repressive than totalitarian during the 1920s. While suppressing political opposition ruthlessly, it tolerated a considerable diversity of nonpolitical opinion. Allowed enough freedom to experiment, the Soviet artists and writers of that period were not only creative and original but also overwhelmingly loyal to the state.

In the long run, however, the totalitarian tendencies of communism, nourished by the Russian tradition of despotism and manipulated by Stalin, prevailed. In the 1930s, Stalin inaugurated with skill and determination an era of unprecedented regimentation, later referred to euphemistically as the period of the "personality cult." Although he successfully eliminated any significant opposition by means of calculated terror, he magnified rather than solved the problem of dissent. Its repression became so much identified with the very foundations of the Soviet regime that any alternative policy amounted to a risky experiment. Among Stalin's successors, Nikita S. Khrushchev was the only one with enough imagination and courage to try it. Yet his denunciation of Stalinism in 1956 spurred rather than appeased dissent, precipitating disintegration in the Communist world.

After World War II, dissent under communism grew from a domestic Russian question into an international problem. Soviet-style regimes appeared in Yugoslavia and Albania as a result of indigenous revolutionary movements. In Rumania, Bulgaria, Poland, Hungary, Czechoslovakia and East Germany, the Russians imposed the Communist system of government. At first, the circumstances in these countries and the character of their new regimes differed considerably, suggesting that the introduction of the Soviet model was a matter of improvisation rather than of preconceived design. But from 1947—after decisive Western action against aggressive Soviet moves in Greece and the Near East—Moscow began to mold the area under its influence in a systematic fashion.

The "closing up" of eastern Europe in the late 1940s and early 1950s was a reenactment on the international scale of what Stalin had done in Russia in the 1930s. Before World War II, his drastic enforcement of rigid uniformity could have been inspired by the almost pathological fear generated by the danger of attack by Hitler's Germany. At the onset of the Cold War, which, however, was very much of Moscow's own making, Stalin used a similar approach to consolidate his new empire in the impending confrontation with the West.

The methods used to eliminate dissent in the east European "satellites" resembled closely those of the Great Purge of the 1930s, although significant regional differences existed. Paradoxically, the nations that had been most willing to accept Moscow's tutelage aroused Stalin's greatest suspicion. Thus, in the traditionally Russophile Czechoslovakia and Bulgaria, the purges assumed the most appalling features. More civilized in style was repression in the countries known to resent the Soviet domination most, particularly Poland and East Germany. Alone among the "satellites," these 2 nations were spared the proliferation of scandalous political trials with ludicrous forced confessions. Rumania and Hungary stayed in the middle between the 2 extremes.

Although the "Sovietization" of eastern Europe was never complete, Moscow succeeded in creating unprecedented uniformity and integration in a part of the world noted for diversity and fragmentation. Considering the traditional animosities of the many peoples in the area, the discipline enforced on them by the Russians was no mean achievement. Hardly less impressive was the profound political, economic and social transformation that brought about extensive equalization. The Communists destroyed the old class structure. Intensive industrialization and urbanization changed the demography and the physical appearance of all the countries. In the few more advanced areas, the standard of living usually declined or increased at a very moderate pace, while in the vast underdeveloped zone of eastern Europe it grew more rapidly.

Political and ideological uniformity was the most conspicuous feature of the new Soviet empire. Marxism became the only officially accepted pattern of thought. Other ideologies, particularly religious, were tolerated for reasons of expediency, but the Communist governments did not conceal their intention to phase them out. Although dissent persisted despite strict control of the public expression, it was on the decline between 1947 and 1953.

At the very beginning of its totalitarian consolidation of eastern Europe, in 1948, Moscow suffered a decisive setback. Yugoslavia successfully resisted integration into the Soviet bloc, then still in the process of formation, although it remained a Communist nation. Its defiance was initially less ideological than political and emotional. The Soviet leaders had themselves fanned it with arrogance and short-sightedness, rejecting many conciliatory gestures made by the Yugoslavs, who were anxious to forestall the break. The Balkan country has served ever since as the model for all nations dissatisfied with Russian predominance. The Soviet abuse of Yugoslavia during the Stalin era surpassed in virulence even the acrimonious verbiage aimed at the U.S.

Despite their break with Stalin, the Yugoslav leaders used Stalinist methods at home for several years after 1948. Under the impact of their rapprochement with the West, however, they gradually removed many restrictions on freedom of expression, while keeping power in the hands of the Communist party. Dissenters were allowed licenses unparalleled anywhere in eastern Europe except in Dubcek's Czechoslovakia during a brief period in 1968. The limitations of the Yugoslav dissent—as illustrated by the persecution of Milovan Djilas or Mihajlo Mihajlov—seem severe judged by Western standards. Yet for other east Europeans, these limitations appear insignificant compared with the freedoms actually granted. For this reason, too, the Yugoslav model has always fascinated the peoples of the Soviet bloc.

Dissent in eastern Europe appears on 2 levels. On the domestic scene, it is expressed in deviations from the totalitarian ideal of uniformity. On the international level, dissent takes the form of resistance to the Soviet efforts to impose uniformity in the area. There is, of course, an intimate connection between the 2 types, and often the 2 forms of dissent encourage each other.

Stalin's death Mar. 5, 1953 is a convenient point of departure for documentation on east European dissent. The elaborate and effective regimentation during his lifetime was so much his personal achievement that it could not continue without modification after the mastermind had disappeared. The inertia of the tightly organized apparatus was sufficient to prevent immediate and abrupt changes. Yet a reversal of the trend soon became evident: Whereas before Stalin's death dissent had been diminishing, afterward it began to increase.

In coping with Stalin's legacy, his heirs faced a formidable task: How could they, lacking his immense authority and skill, accommodate dissent without undermining the stability of the Soviet empire? The history of their efforts to solve the dilemma has been marked with both failures and accomplishments. Yet the problem remains unsolved till the present day. In 1970, its extreme urgency was underlined again in a book by a prominent Russian dissenter entitled: "Will the Soviet Union Survive Until 1984?"

This volume is a narrative record of facts as reported in the West from 1953 to 1963. The 2d volume will bring the material up to 1970. The narration itself aims at objective description—as accurate and comprehensive as possible—of the acts of dissent, rather than at the analysis and evaluation of the dissenters' ideas. As with most INTERIM HISTORY books, this volume consists largely of material that appeared in one form or another in previous FACTS ON FILE publications, supplemented by other necessary items adapted or digested from authoritative sources. The general introduction is included here as an essential explanation of the problem of east European dissent as a political and historical phenomenon. This interpretive analysis, obviously, mirrors the views of the editor. In the treatment of all factual material, however, great care was taken to present the narrative in the unbiased manner that is standard in all INTERIM HISTORY books.

—Vojtech Mastny

1953

The diffusion of power after Joseph Stalin's death Mar. 5 influenced decisively other developments within the Soviet bloc. For 10 days, Georgi M. Malenkov combined in his person all of Stalin's official functions. Afterwards, 4 other leaders shared supreme power with him. Each represented an important pressure group in Soviet politics and society: Malenkov as premier remained in charge of the government while Nikita S. Khrushchev assumed the highest party post as first secretary. Lavrenti P. Beria maintained strong influence as chief of the secret police. One of Stalin's closest collaborators, Vyacheslav M. Molotov, representative of the Bolshevik "Old Guard," held the post of foreign minister. The last of the 5, Defense Min. Nikolai A. Bulganin, spoke for the armed forces.

The absence of a single strong leader as Stalin's successor and the sharing of authority in the Kremlin, suggestive of a power struggle, created an impression of instability. This impression was further strengthened by Malenkov's "New Course." His policy cautiously de-emphasized austerity and regimentation, giving promise of a greater satisfaction of the economic needs of the population.

Against the background of apparently faltering Soviet power, the "New Course" enhanced among east Europeans the awareness of material plight and political oppression. As a result, serious disturbances broke out, spontaneously and independently of one another, in several countries of the Soviet bloc during the summer. A drastic currency reform precipitated riots in Czechoslovakia. In the Soviet Union itself, an unprecedented revolt of prisoners in a forced labor camp took place at Vorkuta in the Arctic. The most important insurrection was that in East Germany, touched off by workers' demonstrations in East Berlin. The hesitations of the regime in coping with the *crisis encouraged the spread of the rebellion throughout the entire country.*

All the revolts were eventually suppressed by force, in East Germany after a massive intervention by the Red Army. They had, however, serious repercussions for both the internal and the foreign policies of the Soviet bloc. The disturbances discredited the security apparatus, thus precipitating the dismissal and subsequent execution of its chief, Lavrenti P. Beria. His elimination implied the obsolescence of the Stalinist methods of police control, which he had personified. The suppression of the German uprising also meant the rejection of the concept, allegedly advocated by Beria, that East Germany was expendable as a bargaining item in a possible accommodation with the West. In the wake of the repressions within the east European bloc, Moscow took initiative to reduce its commitments elsewhere. In July, the Soviet Union used its influence to arrange for a truce in the Korean War.

The Moscow-Belgrade antagonism promoted Yugoslavia's diplomatic and military collaboration with the West. It culminated in a visit by Tito to London in mid-March and in an agreement on friendship and cooperation with Greece and Turkey, both members of the NATO, to which Italy was invited to adhere. In the meantime, however, Stalin's death had removed the main obstacle to better relations with Moscow. In summer, both sides began to move cautiously in order to prevent their further deterioration and prepare the groundwork for their improvement.

WORKERS' REVOLT IN EAST GERMANY

Strikes & Demonstrations

Demonstrations by East Berlin workers against labor conditions turned into major anti-Communist riots June 17. East German police opened gunfire, and a Soviet armored division moved into the eastern sector of the city. Press reports June 18 indicated that at least 16 demonstrators were killed—shot, or run down by Soviet vehicles—and more than 110 persons injured.

Several thousand construction workers, apparently encouraged by the more moderate "new course" after Stalin's death, had staged an 8-hour protest march in East Berlin June 16 against a recent 10% increase in individual production quotas. They shouted anti-Communist slogans and jeered officials who tried to appease them. The East German Politburo reacted by rescinding the increased work norms and making over-quota production "voluntary."

But leaders of the demonstration continued to urge a general strike, and 20,000-50,000 workers June 17 attacked public buildings. They tore down and burned Soviet flags, and only People's Police gunfire prevented the crowds from sacking government and Communist Party buildings.

West Berlin broadcasts encouraged people from all sectors of the city to join in the demonstration. 119 people injured in the riots were taken to hospitals in the Western sectors. Otto Nuschke, 70, East German deputy premier, was manhandled by demonstrators and taken into the U.S. sector. The riots, which centered in Potsdamer Platz, subsided only after Soviet troops arrived in tanks and armored cars, and the Soviet command declared martial law.

Premier Otto Grotewohl blamed the outbreak on "Fascist" agitators from the Western sectors, but allied officials in these sectors declared that the riots were spontaneous and showed the Germans' hatred for communism.

(The Soviet newspaper *Taegliche Rundschau* of East Berlin conceded June 13 that the Soviet Control Commission and East German Communists had erred in previous repressions of individual rights: these repressions had driven many people to the West as refugees and had "lowered morale" in those who remained. The statement praised the recent revocation of many repressive measures as "decisions of great international importance" that would facilitate movement toward "a united national German state." East German officials announced June 14 that 4,029 people jailed for trading with West Berliners and for other economic crimes had been freed since the government adopted a more moderate policy June 10.)

The Soviet and East German authorities combined repression and promises of leniency in an effort to regain control after the strikes and riots had spread into many East German cities.

Reports from Berlin June 20-21 mentioned disturbances and strikes in many vital industries throughout the country, including the southeastern uranium mines, and sabotage against Soviet military construction projects. Rioters in Magdeburg, Rathenow, the Saxony uranium-mining district and other localities were said to have lynched police and State Security officers.

The Soviet army reportedly also imposed martial law in Magdeburg, where several persons were killed in serious disorders. Five Germans accused of provoking attacks on authorities were tried and summarily executed, according to Soviet and East German announcements June 18-24. Additional thousands of persons were jailed during a nationwide roundup of demonstrators. Many others fled to West Berlin. The East German Socialist Unity (Communist) Party Central Committee acknowledged June 22 that resistance had not been entirely suppressed. Grotewohl admitted in a broadcast June 23 that the regime had made "mistakes" but said that the resignation of the government would be no "solution of the problem." Instead, a new program would be announced within 2 weeks to rectify "the consequences of its errors." The government promised June 24 to free most people arrested for rioting, return 40 nationalized factories to private owners and adopt a "new course" following—among other concessions—"public discussions" of complaints by factory workers.

Repression & Conciliation

Reports in West Berlin June 28 said the wave of anti-Communist outbreaks in East Germany had died down sufficiently for Soviet troops to turn back control to the People's Police in several trouble-centers. The East German government issued orders June 25 and 29 releasing large reserve supplies of food to the consumer market, apparently to placate workers who complained of food shortages.

Soviet authorities maintained martial law in East Berlin and guarded its borders with West Berlin but lifted a 10-day-old curfew June 30. The Soviet-sector commandant, Maj. Gen. P. T. Dibrova, rejected June 30 a demand from West-sector commandants that all restrictions on intersector travel be ended. He said East Germany must continue precautions to prevent "criminal elements from being sent into East Berlin again."

Soviet Amb.-to-U.S. Georgi N. Zarubin and Amb.-to-Britain Yakov A. Malik passed through West Berlin en route home July 1. Moscow was reported to have called its top officials in Germany and its ambassadors in major Western capitals to a Kremlin conference dealing mainly with outbreaks in eastern Europe.

Another wave of strikes in East Berlin and other East German cities was reported July 7-8. Workers on the Stalinallee luxury-apartment project in Berlin, where the June 17-18 disorders had originated, and important factory-worker groups were said to have stopped work because some colleagues were still in jail for previous demonstrations. The strikers were said to be reporting to their jobs but doing no work, avoiding street clashes with police and Soviet troops.

Despite the new passive resistance and martial law in East Berlin, the Communists July 9 removed all blockades to travel between eastern and western sectors of the city. Western newsmen who had toured East Berlin reported that damage done in the riots June 17-18 had been repaired. They said that they saw no street demonstrations but that sitdown-striking workers shouted insults at the police from the windows of factory buildings.

East German Pres. Wilhelm Pieck, 77, ill in a rest home in Russia, told his nation in a recorded speech July 2 to "carry out this new course [to appease the dissatisfied population] with increased vigor." Premier Grotewohl called on farmers July 5 to form guard units against the burning of crops and sabotage of farm machinery. The East German Federation of Trade Unions said July 6 that it would not permit increased worker-production quotas even if workers volunteered for higher norms.

The West Berlin *Telegraf* reported July 2 that 18 Russian soldiers had been executed by firing squad because they had refused to fire on workers storming a jail in Magdeburg to free political prisoners.

New strikes in East Berlin subsided July 9 after the government announced that most persons arrested for recent riots would be freed. The Soviet authorities lifted martial law July 12. Another sitdown strike by 14,000 workers in the Buna synthetic rubber factory near Halle for release of colleagues jailed for rioting was reported July 16.

5 persons from Westerhausen, Saxony-Anhalt were sentenced to one-to 4-year jail terms at Halle July 23 for rioting June 17.

The government announced July 21 that the Soviet Union had given it a $57 million credit for buying food during the rest of 1953. The agreement provided for 27,000 tons of butter, 10,000 tons of fat, 26,000 tons of vegetable oil and 20,000 tons of meat, plus 7,000 tons of textiles. The offer totaled 231 million rubles, bringing total Russian trade with East Germany in 1953 to 1.13 billion rubles (about $282 million), according to ADN (Allgemeine Deutsche Nachrichten), official East German news agency. East Germany was to pay with manufactured goods.

The authorities July 26 began a campaign to appease rebellious workers in the major industrial areas. In Magdeburg, the government announced that 520 tons of Russian butter would be distributed through ration-free stores at lower prices. Pay raises for 10,000 men in the Leuna synthetic gasoline works at Merseburg, 9 miles south of Halle, were disclosed. In Leipzig, 4 special commissions were set up to examine wage scales, and traditional annual vacations for workers, canceled June 1, were restored.

An extensive U.S.-supported underground was blamed for the June 17 uprising. The charge was made in a report issued July 28 by the Communist Party's Central Committee. Conceding that "about 5%" of East German workers had risen against the government June 17, the report said the riots showed the existence in East Germany of "a Fascist underground movement organized and supported by the Americans." Resistance groups representing varied political thinking, from dissident Communists to old Nazis, were listed. The report detailed changes in the 5-Year Plan to improve living standards and increase buying power in 1953 by 2 billion marks ($509 million), about $27 per person. Heavy industry was to be expanded only 6% in 1953 instead of the 13% previously planned. Light industry was to be enlarged by 10% instead of the planned 7.1% to increase production of consumer goods.

In a speech published in Berlin July 30, Communist Party leader Walter Ulbricht said the revised 5-Year Plan did not mean that the government was halting its collectivization movement and the creation of an army. He admitted that the program had been slowed as a temporary "new course." He said that conditions in East Germany must be "so improved that the living standard of workers ... in every way lies above that of West German workers." The "reactionary" influence of the church and the clergy on youth must be counteracted by a systematic education program emphasizing "questions of natural science," Ulbricht declared.

Rebellious mine workers were seriously crippling production in East Germany's only hard-coal field, Walter Buchheim, Communist Party first secretary in the Chemnitz area, revealed Aug. 13. Herbert Warneke, head of the labor federation, called for a purge of key unions Aug. 15 to weed out the anti-Communist underground. He rejected workers' demands for the election of new union officials and the release of workers held for the uprisings.

Strikes against bad working conditions by miners in Saxony were reported by the Free German Jurists Committee in West Berlin Sept. 8. The committee, which maintained an information underground in East Germany, had reported similar strikes Sept. 3 by foundry workers in Helbra and Hettstedt, Saxony-Anhalt. The East German press Sept. 7 published names of 100 workers in chemical and other industries fired for underground activity.

The government Oct. 26 announced extensive cuts in prices of food and other consumer items. Production goals for 1954-5 announced Dec. 19 promised increased supplies of shoes, autos and other consumer goods. The Soviet Union returned to East Germany Dec. 31 the last 33 industrial plants seized for World War II reparations.

7 East German Liberal Democratic Party leaders, tried in Dresden, were given prison sentences of 5 to 15 years for forming an underground organization, it was reported Dec. 25.

Party & Government Officials Purged

The ouster of Justice Min. Max Fechner for "activities hostile to the Republic" was announced July 15 by Premier Grotewohl. Fechner was replaced by Mrs. Hilde Benjamin, 51, chief deputy Supreme Court justice known for merciless punishment of "saboteurs" and "spies." (Fechner's ouster was linked by West Berlin observers to the purging of Soviet Internal Affairs Min. Beria. Fechner was a leader of Soviet-zone Social Democrats who had joined the Communists in 1945. He had been justice minister for 4 years.)

Mrs. Benjamin July 21 rescinded the right to strike, which had been granted to East German workers June 11 by Fechner. She said she would administer justice with "no mildness" toward "Fascist provocateurs." Lothar Markwirth, a photographer, was given a life sentence and 15 co-defendents were sentenced to prison in Dresden July 20 for a June 17 uprising in Niesky (on the Polish border).

The Communist Party newspaper *Neues Deutschland* July 19 denounced party agitators in factories who did not stand up against hostile workers during the recent disorders. A cabinet member, Bernd Weinberger and a party aide, Adalbert Hengst, were reprimanded for having left Rostock against party orders during disorders June 18. 6 Justice Ministry aides who had served under Fechner were reported arrested on Mrs. Benjamin's orders July 21.

Wilhelm Zaisser, 60, minister of state security and chief of police, was dropped from the government July 24 and ejected from the Communist Party Central Committee for "defeatism" July 27. No reason was given for the change although Zaisser, a Politburo member and the "Gen. Gomez" of the Spanish Civil War, was considered an appointee of the deposed chief of the Soviet secret police, Lavrenti P. Beria. He was replaced in the security post by Ernst Wollweber who was to work under the interior minister.

Removed from the Central Committee with Zaisser July 27 was Rudolph Herrnstadt, a candidate for Politburo membership and editor of *Neues Deutschland*. The Central Committee also expelled ex-Justice Min. Fechner from the Communist Party. 3 other prominent East Germans were dropped from the list of Politburo candidates: Mrs. Elli Schmidt, head of the Commission for Trade & Supply; her ex-husband, Acting Foreign Min. Anton Ackermann, and Hans Jendretzky, chief of the Communist Party in Berlin.

Bernd Weinberger was dismissed from the cabinet July 30 for "a capitulatory attitude" toward strikers in the June 17 riots. He was demoted to head of the reparations office. State Secy. for Coal & Power Max Fritsch was ousted from the government and was succeeded by Rolf Jaschonka, a veteran Communist.

Ackermann was dismissed as acting foreign minister Aug. 8, and Jendretzky was dropped as the party chief of Berlin Aug. 9 for appeasing workers in the June 17 riots. Several party leaders in Dresden, Halle, Magdeburg and Chemnitz districts were ousted Aug. 11.

The dismissal of Fritz Macher, 31, as labor minister was announced Dec. 9.

Western Response

U.S. Pres. Dwight D. Eisenhower said at his news conference July 1 that the U.S. planned no physical intervention in eastern Europe to aid anti-Communist uprisings. But he said that unrest in the Communist countries was of considerable importance and that all statements by U.S. leaders should assure repressed peoples that they had friends in the free world. He said in a message June 26 to West German Chancellor Konrad Adenauer that the East German riots had "stirred the hearts and hopes of people everywhere" and that the U.S. would "continue to strive for" free all-German elections.

Sen. Alexander Wiley (R., Wis.), U.S. Senate Foreign Relations Committee chairman, predicted in a Senate speech June 29 that the Chinese "will not long accept the domination of the Soviet." He said: "The pendulum of history is beginning to swing. Soviet control over its satellites is beginning to crumble." The Senate Foreign Relations Committee July 2 approved a resolution praising East Germans' "patriotic defiance of Communist tyranny" and calling for German unification on the basis of free elections.

Pres. Walter P. Reuther of the CIO (Congress of Industrial Organizations), addressing the International Confederation of Free Trade Unions congress in Stockholm July 7, said American unions were prepared to help victims of Soviet rule. He proposed an inquiry into East German conditons "which did so much to lead to the uprising." He and Pres. George Meany of the AFL (American Federation of Labor) jointly cabled Eisenhower urging that the U.S. press for negotiations for free German elections.

The Soviet Communist Party newspaper *Pravda* July 6 denounced Eisenhower and State Secy. John Foster Dulles for "slanderous fabrications and incendiary appeals" intended to stir trouble in eastern Europe.

Gen. Omar N. Bradley, retiring U.S. Joint Chiefs of Staff chairman, said July 6 that it was conceivable that unrest in Communist east European countries would cause Soviet leaders to start a war to stabilize control in satellite areas. Soviet "pressures" on the world had been lessened only a "little" by troubles in eastern Europe, Bradley asserted.

Ex-Czechoslovak Amb.-to-U.S. Juraj Slavik, in exile in the U.S., said July 5 that there was "no possibility" that anti-Communists in eastern Europe could throw off Soviet rule without "help from the outside."

Eddy Gilmore, ex-Associated Press bureau chief in Moscow, said on arriving in New York Aug. 5 that he didn't think "there's going to be any great revolution in Russia," and Premier Georgi M. Malenkov "has always given me the impression of a man who is very much in charge," Gilmore said.

Food Relief

Pres. Eisenhower promised June 20, in a letter to Adenauer, that the U.S. would send food to West Germany for distribution to the East zone "in the best available manner." The President repeated this pledge at his news conference July 22. (The first shipment left New York July 17.)

The Soviet Union demanded July 22 that West Berlin's distribution of free food to East Berliners be halted. Soviet High Commissioner Vladimir Semenov sent U.S. High Commissioner James B. Conant a note denouncing the American food program as an attempt to recruit "Fascist agents" against the East.

Mayor Ernst Reuter of West Berlin had announced July 19 that a coupon plan for distribution of food parcels to East Germans would go into effect July 27. The plan would give each East German applicant a monthly coupon for the purchase of 5 marks' worth of food. Reuter predicted new anti-Communist outbreaks. He scored businessmen in West Germany for expecting the U.S. to aid Berlin while they refused to help. (West Germans had cancelled many orders for

West Berlin manufactured goods after the June riots in East Berlin.)

More than 120,000 East Germans received free food in West Berlin July 27 and 28, the first 2 days of the West's relief food distribution program. Each food portion, received on presentation of an identity card, contained 1.5 pounds of lard, 2 pounds of flour, 4 small cans of condensed milk and 2 pounds of dried beans or peas. About 123,000 portions were distributed each day. Welfare officials estimated that the East Germans carried an average of 2 identity cards each. Food stations were doubled July 28 to avoid the long waiting which characterized the first day's distribution.

An attempt to disrupt the program was seen in the distribution July 28 of thousands of bogus newspapers promising free food for unemployed and pensioned West Berliners. The West Berlin government immediately denied the bogus newspaper promise. This was the 2d effort to upset the West's free food program. The West Berlin borough of Kreuzberg halted its distribution of food July 24 when forged food coupons appeared. Authentic coupons entitled the bearer to 5 West German marks' ($1.19) worth of food at any shop in Kreuzberg. Kreuzberg Mayor Willi Kressman, originator of the coupon plan, said the East Berlin government had "masterminded" the forgeries. He organized a new give-away plan July 25, distributing food to East Germans who showed unemployment or charity cards, in an effort to disprove Soviet High Commissioner Semenov's claim that there was no unemployment in East Germany.

A West German offer to sell East Germany $6 million worth of food was refused Aug. 7 by the East Berlin government, which said terms of the offer were unacceptable. The offer called for cash payment, although East-West trade generally was on a barter basis, because East Germany was delinquent in its regular barter pacts. East Germany also rejected as an "insult" an offer by U.S. High Commissioner Conant to recommend the release of blocked East German funds in the U.S. provided there were "adequate safeguards" that the funds would be used to buy food for East Germans.

Reports that Britain and France opposed continued distribution of free U.S. food to East Germans were described as "somewhat of an exaggeration" by a U.S. State Department spokesman Aug. 14. He said the British and French had made "suggestions" on the mechanics of distribution and "everybody is in complete agreement." British and French authorities in Germany had been reported Aug. 13 to oppose the program because they wanted a Big 4 conference while Russia still was in a "conciliatory" mood, thought further distribution of free food might stir up trouble.

The first phase of the food relief program ended Aug. 15 as all but 2 distribution stations in West Berlin were closed for reorganization. 2 stations were maintained for service to East Germans who had not yet received any food packages. Officials estimated that more than 2,600,000 parcels had been given out since July 27. The 2d round of distribution was to begin Aug. 27.

East German police continued border patrols against travel to West Berlin. East German newspapers printed names and pictures of East Germans caught with food parcels and assailed them as "weaklings."

West Berlin Mayor Reuter said Aug. 16 that the food program would not "be the last action with which we will help" East Germans.

Flow of Refugees to West Germany

West Berlin reported May 1 that 33,000 refugees had arrived there from East Germany during April. 42,000 were flown to the German Federal Republic during the month. A new influx of refugees, reported May 27, was attributed to measures depriving about 2 million persons of food rationing cards and a threat that East German farmers would suffer if they did not produce good crops in 1953. 467 People's Policemen fled to Western sectors during June.

20 East German soldiers and 17 People's Policemen sought refuge in West Berlin Aug. 5. They told Allied intelligence officers that discontent was spreading in the East German armed forces. A total of 1,675 soldiers and 880 policemen had fled to the West since Jan. 1.

(A Soviet Army transportation officer identified as Maj. Leonid N. Renzhin was reported Aug. 7 to have fled to West Germany last April.)

East German Deputy Premier Paul Scholz claimed Aug. 11 that almost 3,000 East Zone farmers who had fled to the West had returned within recent weeks to claim their abandoned farms. The West Berlin refugee office recorded more than 15,000 farmers from East Germany between Nov. 1952 and Feb. 1953. 27% of the 35,000 refugees registered between June 15 and Aug. 5 were known to have returned.

537 People's Policemen were reported Nov. 2 to have sought political asylum in October. This was a new monthly record.

The arrival of the year's 300,000th refugee was reported in West Berlin Dec. 9. 305,737 persons, more than 1.7% of East Germany's population, registered as refugees in West Berlin in 1953. The number ranged from a high of 48,724 in March to a low of 8,606 in December. The 1952 total was 120,000. The report said that a total of 617,200 had fled to the West in the past 5 years. 4,713 East German People's Policemen sought asylum in 1953, as against 2,300 in 1952.

UNREST SPREADS IN EASTERN EUROPE

Currency Reform Provokes Czechoslovak Riots

Reports of anti-government riots in Pilsen (Plzen), Bohemia and other Czechoslovak industrial cities, previously denied by the Czechoslovak government, were confirmed June 15 by Pres. Antonin Zapotocky. He said demonstrations against currency reform had been subdued but admitted that the reform had exacted "sacrifices" from the working class. Zapotocky called the reform an important step toward socialism.

The riots, described by Pilsen *Pravda* June 5 as a "counter-revolutionary putsch," began June 1 when employes of the Lenin Works (a former Skoda arms plant) in Pilsen staged a protest march. The demonstrators also were reported to have destroyed factory machinery, pillaged the town hall, trampled a Soviet flag and pictures of Communist leaders and waved a U.S. flag. Troops fired on the rioters and killed 6 persons. Demonstrations took place in the Moravian cities of Ostrava and Brno also, according to the Pilsen paper. Other reports received in Vienna described similar riots by workers at the

Vaclav and Sofie mines, the Bohumin Iron Works and the Stalingrad Iron Works in Liskovec, Moravia. "Sporadic firing" was reported as late as June 4.

Despite official denials that there had been riots, Pilsen *Pravda* reported June 5 that "anti-state demonstrations" by "some people not politically aware [who] let themselves be influenced by bourgeois elements" had occurred. "However," the paper said, "workers belatedly understood the nature of the conspiracy and they, with the aid of security units, are credited with the liquidation of the gang of rioters." Vice Pres. Zdenek Nejedly said June 7 the currency reform had "met with open resistance and condemnation in the first few days but the nation is beginning to understand that it means a good future." Zapotocky announced June 10 that Czechoslovak trade unions would be purged because of their resistance to the reform. He charged that the unions had hid "former entrepreneurs and bourgeois who inspired panic, unrest and hostile acts."

The Revolutionary Trade Union Movement (RTUM) ordered penalties for workers who participated prominently in the anti-government demonstrations, the Prague press reported June 22. The penalties were exclusion from trade unions and reduction or refusal of paid holidays, pensions, sickness compensation, canteen meals and family bonuses. No worker, whether or not he participated in the disturbances, was to be paid for work time lost as a result of the riots. Trade unions were ordered to send 4,000 of their best officials and workers into the Ostrava coal mines to halt the decline in coal output. The RTUM also resolved that "unions, to assure success of the currency reform," would reject any wage increase that would interfere with production.

Prague broadcasts June 30 indicated that the regime was trying to cope with a widespread passive resistance movement among workers who refused to report to their jobs. A week-old decree penalizing workers for absenteeism and job-changing was rescinded by the cabinet July 6 at request of the RTUM, which had recommended the decree June 19.

Prisoners Revolt in Vorkuta Camp

Sporadic strikes broke out among the inmates of the Vorkuta labor camp in the Komi Autonomous Region, located in the Arctic part of the Soviet Union in late July 1953 (July 21, according to the subsequent testimony of former captives). The initial wave of opposition came from a group of transfer prisoners from Karaganda, Kazakhstan, who had been promised considerably better conditions. When the word of the strike in Camp No. 7, which included the Karaganda group, spread, inmates in several other camps formed strike committees and refused to work.

Although distance and barbed wire prevented the prisoners from communicating and coordinating their efforts, their demands were similar. They requested especially the reduction of their prison sentences, the review of the cases of those convicted in political trials, improvements in the conditions of imprisonment (particularly the removal of barbed wire), and correspondence and visiting privileges for their families. The prisoners refused to deal with the local authorities presided over by Gen. Derevianko, and demanded the dispatch of a special representative from Moscow. An investigating team led by Gen. Maslennikov (allegedly a recipient of the Order of Lenin and twice a "Hero of the War for the Defense of the Fatherland") arrived in Vorkuta and promised substantial reforms. Subsequent testimony contended that the changes were limited and gradual. Nevertheless, the promise of reform combined with threats by the authorities caused most prisoners to abandon their strike, with little or no violence resulting.

Camp No. 29 was a notable exception. Its inmates not only refused to deal with the authorities but continued to press their demands while troops surrounded them. After the prisoners refused to adhere to an ultimatum, the troops opened fire, killing 64 prisoners and seriously wounding 200, many of whom subsequently died. This action effectively ended the Vorkuta revolt.

Hungary, Poland, Rumania & Albania

The Hungarian Communist Party announced June 30 that it had set up a 3-man secretariat consisting of Premier Matyas Rakosi (demoted from party secretary general), Lajos Acs and Bela Vec. The Orgburo (the Central Committee agency supervising party organization, jurisdiction and structural changes) was abolished and the Politburo cut from 17 to 9 members.

The regime July 4 replaced the cabinet of Rakosi, who had ruled the country as premier or from behind the scenes since 1945. Deputy Premier Imre Nagy, 57, also a veteran Communist, was advanced to the premiership. He promised to "liquidate" many "mistakes" made by the previous cabinet. Rakosi was assigned no office in the new government but remained a member of the new 3-man Communist Party secretariat. Nagy, a former economics professor, had been a minor official in Bela Kun's 1919 Communist regime but was exiled when the Red regime fell. He broadcast from Moscow during World War II. After returning to Hungary in 1944 he served variously as deputy premier, interior minister, agriculture minister and speaker of the Parliament. His daughter had meanwhile married and was the wife of a Calvinist pastor.

Nagy announced to Parliament a program similar to the recent "softening" of Communist rule in East Germany: the restoration of land to farmers; the remission of fines for non-fulfillment of crop quotas; less emphasis on the industrialization program because of a lack of "essential raw materials;" more stress on agriculture; price reductions and wage increases; a more liberal attitude toward private enterprise; the release of prisoners who did not endanger the state; a "patient" government policy on religion. Nagy said recent "disturbances in Berlin were a sign for us, and the other people's democracies must also follow our example."

Nagy's cabinet: *Deputy Premier and Interior Minister*—Erno Gero; *Deputy Premier and Agriculture*—Andras Hegedus; *Foreign*—Janos Boldoczy, ex-minister to Czechoslovakia; *Defense*—Maj. Gen. Istvan Bata, ex-chief of staff; *Finance*—Karoly Olt; *Justice*—Ferenc Erdei; *Smelting & Machinery*—Mihaly Zsofinyec; *Heavy Industry*—Istvan Hidas; *Light Industry*—Arpad Kiss; *Trade*—Joszef Tisza; *Building*—Lajos Szijarto; *Popular Culture*—Joszef Darvas; *Education*—Tibor Erdei-Gruz; *Health*—Sandor Zsoldos; *Transport & Postal*—Lajos Bebrits; *chairman of State Planning Office*—Bela Szalai. (All were Communists except Justice Min. Erdei and Culture Min. Darvas, both of the

National Peasant Party, and Trade Min. Bognar, Smallholders' Party.)

Hungary had elected a new 298-member Parliament May 17 by indorsing a slate presented by the Communist-led People's Front. The government said that 98% of the electorate had voted and that 98.2% of those voting approved the slate. Parliament July 3 reelected Istvan Dobi, ex-Smallholders' Party leader, as Hungarian president.

The Hungarian government reported Nov. 10 that 10% of its farm collectives had voted to dissolve under permission granted in July. The government had ordered price reductions on 10,000 consumer items Sept. 6.

West Berlin sources indicated June 30 that anti-Communist riots had occurred in 7 Polish cities June 17, the day that demonstrations had broken out in East Berlin. According to July 4 press reports, the disorders had persisted. Warsaw, Cracow and the Polish Silesian areas were rumored to be under martial law. Demonstrations were believed to have destroyed 17 tanks during a riot against a Soviet army unit in Chorzow. A huge crowd reportedly stormed the Cracow City Hall June 30 and hanged several officials.

The Polish government Nov. 14 announced 10%-40% price reductions on food and other consumer items.

Rumanian refugees in Yugoslavia claimed July 4 that peasants had looted cooperatives of food and machinery at 25 places in Rumania. The Rumanian government announced July 5 that it would release some food supplies from reserves and increase rations. Severe food shortages in Rumania had been reported for 6 months.

Albanian exile Apostol Taanefi, an anti-Soviet Communist ex-schoolteacher, was reported by *Paris Presse* Mar. 22 to be plotting in Yugoslavia to lead Albanian guerrillas in a revolt against the Enver Hoxha regime.

Defections

A 21-year-old Polish air force lieutenant, Franciszek Jarecki, flew a MIG-15 jet fighter to the Danish Baltic island of Bornholm Mar. 5 and applied for political asylum. Poland Mar. 6-9 delivered 3 notes to Denmark demanding the return of the plane, the first MIG ever to fall intact into the hands of a

Western country. Poland also interned 6 Danish fishing vessels and 23 crewmen in Danzig Mar. 8 but released them Mar. 11. The MIG was shipped to Copenhagen Mar. 8. Another Polish air force lieutenant, Zdzislaw Jazwenski, 21, landed a MIG-15 on Bornholm May 22.

6 Czechs escaped to the U.S. zone of Germany Mar. 24 by seizing a Czechoslovak Air Lines DC-3 plane with 23 other persons aboard and flying it to an American airfield near Frankfort-on-the-Main. The pilot and 5 passengers remained behind when the others returned to Czechoslovakia Mar. 31. Helmut Cermak, a mechanic at the Skoda arms plant in Pilsen, said he had worked for 2 years to plan the escape and was aided by pilot Miroslav Slovak. Dr. Jan Papanek, president of the American Fund for Czechoslovak Refugees, said in New York Mar 26 that the 6 had been granted aid from MSA (Mutual Security Administration, the U.S. agency administering the Marshall Plan) funds for Iron Curtain exiles.

Capt. Jan Cwiklinski of the Polish liner *Batory* was revealed June 23 to have jumped ship and asked for political asylum in Britain. (It was on his vessel, which quit calling in New York because of a dock labor boycott against it, that the East German Communist leader Gerhart Eisler had escaped from the U.S. in 1949.) The ship had been in Hebburn, England for 6 weeks for refitting.

A Czech mechanic, Vaclav Uhlik, 32, ran through the Czechoslovak-German border July 25 in a home-made armored car, carrying his wife, 2 children and 4 other persons with him. He said he had filched scrap metal for 2 years to fashion the vehicle. He brought out Mrs. Libuse Cloud, 32, wife of U.S. Army veteran Lennart Cloud of Sioux City, Ia., who had been forced to leave Czechoslovakia 3 weeks after they were married in 1949.

Ivan Smirnov, 18, of Stalingrad (later Volgograd), who identified himself as a former mechanic in the Soviet Army's 17th Storm Sapper Brigade, surrendered to U.S. Immigration authorities in New York Oct. 6 and asked for asylum. He said he had deserted in East Germany and smuggled himself to the U.S. with the aid of 2 French sailors on an unidentified ship.

YUGOSLAV DEVIATION

Tito-West Links & Balkan Pact

Yugoslavia moved cautiously to improve its relations with Western countries after Moscow had expelled the Yugoslav Communist Party from the Cominform, had severed diplomatic and economic relations and had mounted a hostile propaganda campaign against the Balkan giant. Yugoslavia received from the West economic and military aid; U.S. assistance amounted to $106,750,000. Tito's efforts to strengthen the links with the West reached a climax Mar. 16. The Yugoslav president arrived in London aboard the Yugoslav naval training ship *Galeb* on the first visit ever paid Britain by the head of a Communist state.

Tito was welcomed by Prime Min. Winston Churchill, Foreign Secy. Anthony Eden and the Duke of Edinburgh. Tito said on his arrival that Britons should regard Yugoslavs as "staunch allies" and that both peoples were "striving toward the same ends." He lunched with Queen Elizabeth II Mar. 17 and conversed with Churchill and Eden about the new Soviet premier, Malenkov, with whom Tito last had personal dealings during a conference with Stalin in Moscow in 1946.

Britain took heavy precautions in London to shield Tito from hostile acts by pro-Soviet Communists, Roman Catholics and followers of exiled King Peter II, who was living in London. The Vatican radio Mar. 10 expressed regret over Tito's visit to London and said he must be counted "among present-day persecutors of religion and of the Church."

(Meanwhile, Col. Gen. Peko Dapcevic, Yugoslav army chief of staff, had arrived in Washington Mar. 12 for a 2-week tour of American military installations to study U.S. Army organization and training methods.)

Tito ended his visit to Britain Mar. 21 with the declaration that it would result in closer "collaboration" between Yugoslavia and Britain. A communique on Tito's talks with British leaders Mar. 20 said they would not regard "aggression in Europe" as a "local" matter. This was considered an implied British promise to help Yugoslavia if it were attacked by Cominform countries. Churchill was said Mar. 19 to have declined to formalize commitments to Yugoslavia pending further efforts to settle the Yugoslav-Italian dispute over

Trieste. The British disclosed Mar. 21 that Tito had promised to liberalize his regime and try to settle its differences with the Roman Catholic church.

Tito said on his return to Belgrade Mar. 31 that he had received Churchill's promise: "If our ally, Yugoslavia, is attacked, we will defend her too." Tito said his trip showed that Yugoslavia "has won respect in the world." He said he believed that the new Malenkov regime in Russia was more "moderate" than Stalin's and would not risk a shooting war but would rely instead on "cheaper" cold-war strategy.

Speaking at celebrations commemorating the Yugoslav air force anniversary May 21, Tito denied that his country's relations with the Cominform had improved since Stalin's death or that Yugoslavia would ever rejoin the Soviet bloc. "On the frontier, still," he declared, "their rifles are shooting at our guards. Their press is slandering us. If the USSR has softened its propaganda, that is not enough for our country to change its attitude and fall into the arms of those who have so badly harmed us. Any changes must be demonstrated by deeds, not words." Tito praised the U.S., Britain and France for their aid to Yugoslavia and called them "peace-loving countries" that he would never desert. Foreign Secy. Koca Popovic added May 26 that Yugoslavia was "ready to undertake negotiations" to settle disputes with Soviet-bloc countries but had little hope of restoring "normal and bearable relations with all our neighbors."

Yugoslavia Mar. 23 ratified a treaty of friendship and cooperation with Greece and Turkey that had been negotiated Feb. 28. This "Balkan Pact" became effective May 29 when Turkey deposited its ratification document in Belgrade.

Internal Reforms

Soon after initiating a *rapprochement* with the West, the Yugoslav regime began to depart from rigid Marxist policies in domestic affairs. Vice Pres. Edvard Kardelj announced Mar. 29 that peasants would be allowed to choose whether they wanted to remain on collective farms, join Western-type cooperatives or become independent farmers. A decree published Mar. 30 said the plans would take effect after the 1953 harvest. Parliament Mar. 24 approved an amnesty for persons imprisoned for violation of previous agricultural regulations. The price of bread, subsidized since 1952, when a summer drought had caused a grain shortage, was raised Mar. 23 to 12¢ (from 9¢) for a 2-pound loaf. The government reported Mar. 28 that the relaxation of control in many enterprises had caused unemployment totaling a record 92,284 (up 20,000 since January) during the "transition to the new economic system."

Kardelj said Apr. 7 that Yugoslavia would stress payment of workers on the basis of merit and skill and de-emphasize government planning of salary levels. He indicated that the regime was ready to do away with an "accumulation" system whereby it siphoned off quotas of the profits of Yugoslav enterprises.

Vice Pres. Aleksander Rankovic, an ex-interior minister, was quoted by the *N.Y. Times* Apr. 12-13 as saying: there were about 7,000 political prisoners in Yugoslavia, of whom 4,500 were pro-Soviet Communists; the government was preparing to let more Yugoslavs, including opponents of the regime, leave the country as emigrants and tourists. (5 members of a Yugoslav soccer team who refused to go home from Vienna had been granted asylum by Austria Apr. 11.) Arrests of 171,731 Yugoslavs, many "without reason," during 1948-52 were acknowledged Sept. 7 in a government report promising judicial reforms. Dr. Radenko Stankovic, 73, one of 3 prewar regents, in 1953 partly paralyzed, was released Aug. 29 after 8 years in prison for German collaboration.

A "freedom of religion" law passed without opposition by Parliament May 22 provided that (1) Yugoslavs could worship where and how they pleased, (2) they must not be intimidated into joining a church and (3) church activities must be restricted to religious worship. The law denied Roman Catholics the right to operate religious schools for general education. It required a civil ceremony to legalize a marriage, did not recognize a church ceremony alone. Clergymen were brought under the social security program for workers. The law was said to have the indorsement of the Serbian Orthodox Church, which represented 47% of the Yugoslav population (36% Roman Catholic, 11% Moslem). But Rankovic charged in a speech to Parliament that the Vatican meddled in Yugoslav public affairs and refused to reach an agreement on church-state relations. He said 161 priests were in prison and those released were taking part in government-sponsored priests' associations.

Parliament May 22 adopted (with one dissenting vote) an agrarian reform program that limited private land holdings to 10 hectares (about 24.7 acres) instead of 30 as provided in a 1945 law. The new measure would add 300,000 hectares to the land pool of 200,000 already held by the government. The pooled land was to be used entirely by cooperatives, collectives and industrial enterprises making use of the particular area's product. None was to go to individual landless peasants. The number of collective farms, however, dropped from 6,797 in 1951 to 1,258 at the end of 1953.

USSR Moves Toward Reconciliation

The renewal of full diplomatic relations between Yugoslavia and Russia, at the request of the USSR, was announced June 14 by Marshal Tito. Vasily Alexeevich Valkov, 49, Soviet ambassador to Holland in 1945-9, was accepted by Yugoslavia June 15 as the new Soviet ambassador to Belgrade.

The Yugoslav president said the Soviet bid to exchange ambassadors represented "a great victory" for Yugoslavia in its feud with the Cominform (since June 1948). (The Soviet Union had recalled its ambassador from Belgrade and ousted the Yugoslav ambassador to Moscow in 1949.) Tito said the move was not a Soviet-Yugoslav reconciliation and would not weaken his ties to the West. He denounced "ill-intentioned propaganda" in Western countries that the Yugoslavs would "jump back into Russia's open arms" when the Kremlin "smiled on us." He said that he could never "believe 100% in the Soviet Union" and that the Russians' words "mean nothing." Frontier incidents with the satellites are double these days what they were during the Stalin regime," Tito noted. But he pointed out that many countries hostile to each other maintained full diplomatic relations.

Neighboring Soviet bloc countries thereafter relaxed their former hostility toward Yugoslavia. Yugoslavia and Hungary agreed Oct. 23 to set up commissions on border incidents.

Yugoslavia announced Dec. 21 that it had accepted an Albanian offer to resume diplomatic relations. An agreement on the settlement of frontier disputes had been announced Dec. 11.

1954

After the upheavals of 1953, the east European regimes tried to consolidate their domestic position under Soviet guidance. They acted to eliminate some of the causes of the popular grievances, especially the shortage of consumer goods. Combined with the intimidating effect of the earlier reprisals, this policy barred further manifestations of discontent.

Extensive purges of the party and government apparatus left excluded from power many discredited officials who had been closely identified with the Stalinist excesses. The purges were reflected in the higher incidence of defections by prominent personalities. These included diplomats and personnel of the intelligence and of the internal security services.

In Yugoslavia, the rapprochement with the West created acute tension as the prospects of reconciliation with Moscow improved. The Western orientation generated desire for relaxation of internal controls. At the same time, the changes in Moscow's attitude encouraged the many remaining pro-Soviet elements in the Yugoslav party. The latent controversy about the extent of liberalization led to an open break between Tito and Vice Pres. Milovan Djilas. Djilas subsequently became a leading east European critic of Communist totalitarianism.

UNREST CONTINUES

Opposition in East Germany

Continued unrest in East Germany was reported Jan. 3 by a U.S. State Department official who said the government was "still practicing terrorism with one hand and making seemingly conciliatory gestures with the other." Geoffrey W. Lewis, head of the Office of German Affairs, wrote in the State Department *Bulletin* that political arrests continued but "so, reportedly, do sitdown strikes and stoppages in mines and factories of greatest value" to the Soviet Union. He said that "thousands" of East Germans had been sentenced to long jail terms for taking part in the June 1953 uprising (an unofficial estimate was 12,000) and that "several thousand participants," including women and children, were "seen loaded aboard trains headed for the Soviet Union." (German prisoners of war returning from Russia said Jan. 1 that "many" East Germans were being held in Soviet prisons.) Other victims included religious dissenters. The number of imprisoned Jehovah's Witnessess was raised to 1,343 by the jailing of 9 more, it was reported Aug. 14.

Wilhelm Prinz, ex-chairman of the Hamburg Communist Party, told reporters in Hamburg Aug. 25 that he had fled East Germany to escape "Communist brutality." He said he had gone to a party meeting in Feb. 1953 in Loewenberg, East Germany, where he had been picked up by security police. Prinz charged with having worked for the Western powers, was kept in solitary confinement until Apr. 1954.

Personnel Changes in the Bloc

The East German Communist Party Jan. 23 expelled ex-State Security Min. Wilhelm Zaisser and Rudolph Herrnstadt, ex-editor of *Neues Deutschland,* from party membership for opposing its leaders after the June 1953 uprisings. Other disciplinary actions in connection with the June events: ex-Acting Foreign Min. Anton Ackermann was ousted from the Central Committee; ex-Politburo member Franz Dahlem was barred from party posts; Mrs. Elli Schmidt, ex-head of the German Democratic Women's League, and Hans Jendretsky, ex-Berlin Communist Party chairman, were reprimanded. Georg Dertinger, deposed in Jan. 1953 as East German foreign minister, was reported June 8 to have received a 15-year prison sentence for plotting to overthrow the regime.

Hungary announced Mar. 13 that Lt. Gen. Gabor Peter, who as chief of political police had assembled the cases against Jozsef Cardinal Mindszenty, Robert A. Vogeler (vice president of the International Telephone & Telegraph Co. and its chief representative in Budapest before his arrest on espionage charges late in 1949) and Hungarian officials purged in 1947-9, had been sentenced to life imprisonment for anti-state crimes. Ex-Justice Min. Guyla Decsi received a 9-year sentence.

The appointments of N. T. Kalchenko as premier and ex-Premier D. S. Korotchenko as Parliamentary Presidium president in the Ukraine were announced Jan. 15. Other provincial government shifts: Georgian First Deputy Premier Vilian Zodelava was replaced by M. I. Kuchava Jan. 17. (Tiflis radio reported Feb. 21 that the Georgian Communist Party had expelled 3,000 members in the past 17 months and chosen V. P. Mzhavanadze as new party leader.) Kazakh SSR party leader Shumabay Shayakhmetov was replaced by ex-USSR Culture Min. P. K. Ponomarenko Feb. 7; Shayakhmetov was ousted on charges of favoritism to friends and relatives. Zinovi Timofeevich Serdyuk of Ukraine was made party leader in Soviet Moldavia Feb. 7. USSR Health Min. Andrei F. Treyakov, physician in charge of treating Stalin at the time of Stalin's death, was replaced Mar. 2 by his woman deputy, Dr. Maria D. Kovrygina.

Pres. A. Aroyan of Soviet Armenia's Supreme Court was dismissed for unannounced reasons, it was reported in the Armenian party paper *Communist* (which arrived in Moscow Aug. 16).

The Supreme Soviet approved a reorganization of the Soviet Council of Ministers (cabinet) by Premier Georgi M. Malenkov Apr. 27. At least 12 new ministries were created, and the cabinet's membership was fixed at 55 (as against 73 under Stalin and 32 in Mar. 1953 when the Malenkov government was formed). State and internal security functions, combined in 1953 into a single Internal Affairs Ministry under the late Lavrenti P. Beria, were again separated. External state security matters were assigned to a Committee of State Security under the chairmanship of Col. Gen. Ivan A. Serov, veteran secret police official. Domestic security remained under Internal Affairs Min. Sergei N. Kruglov.

Other new ministers included: Radio Manufactures Min. V. D. Kalmykov, Ferrous Metals Min. A. N. Kuzmin, Nonferrous Metals Min. P. F. Lomako, Meat & Milk Products Min. S. F. Antonov, Power Stations Min. A. S. Pavlenko, Electrical Goods Min. I. Skidanenko, Shipbuilding Min. I. I. Nosenko, Transport Machine Construction Min. S. Stepanov, Heavy Machinery Construction Min. N. Kazakov, Building & Road Machinery Min. Y. S. Novoselov, Autos, Tractors & Agricultural Machinery Min. S. Skopov, Machine Tools & Instruments Min. P. I. Parshin, Timber Min G. M. Orlov, Paper & Wood Products Min. F. D. Varaksin, Construction of Metal & Chemical Plants Min. D. Y. Raizer, Construction Industry Min. N. A. Dygai, State Bank Chairman V. F. Popov.

Author-journalist Konstantin Simonov replaced poet Alexander T. Tvardovsky as editor-in-chief of *Novy Mir (New World)*, Soviet literary magazine, in a shake-up announced Aug. 17 by *Literaturnaya Gazeta (Literary Gazette)*, official organ of the Union of Soviet Writers. The union's Presidium denounced *Novy Mir* and Tvardovsky for contradicting Communist Party "instructions" and "principles" and demanded a new code for publications.

High Officials Escape to West

Yuri Alexandrovich Rastvorov, 34, 2d secretary of the Soviet mission to Japan, was reported Feb. 1 to have been granted asylum by American authorities in Japan. Officials of the mission, which remained in Tokyo in defiance of Japan's peace treaty with the other Allies, had said Jan. 29 that Rastvorov had disappeared Jan. 24 after a "nervous breakdown." The Russians then charged Feb. 1 that he had been kidnapped by U.S. "espionage" agents.

The U.S. revealed Aug. 13 it had granted political asylum to Rastvorov. He said at a Washington news conference arranged by the State Department Aug. 13 that (1) he had been a lieutenant colonel in the Soviet Internal Affairs Ministry (MVD, headed by Beria until his execution in late 1953), (2) he had been sent to Japan in Jan. 1946 as a 2d secretary in the Foreign Affairs Ministry but in reality had served as an espionage agent, (3) he had sought U.S. asylum because he "wanted to live like a decent human being." Rastvorov had been flown to the U.S. "almost immediately" after his defection in January. The Justice Department said Rastvorov had been granted temporary entry into the U.S. at the Attorney General's discretion. Although his wife and 8-year-old daughter were still in Russia, Rastvorov said, he had decided not to return because the Communists had turned the land into a concentration camp. He said there was an effective Soviet spy system in the U.S. but he knew no details since he had worked exclusively in Japan.

State Department press officer Henry Suydam told reporters that Soviet Amb.-to-U.S. Georgi N. Zarubin had been asked to come to the State Department to confer with Undersecy. Walter Bedell Smith early Aug. 13. The Soviet embassy replied that Zarubin was ill and no other member of the embassy available. The State Department then informed the embassy that Rastvorov had received U.S. asylum and was available for an interview with Zarubin. In a note to the U.S. State Department Aug. 23, Zarubin charged that U.S. intelligence agents had taken Rastvorov from Japan in violation of elementary standards of international law. The 6-month delay in revealing that Rastvorov was in the U.S. proved that American agents had influenced him against his country, the note said.

A Soviet secret police officer, Evgnevich Khokhlov, 32, sent to West Germany to kill an anti-Communist figure, had surrendered to U.S. security agents and requested political asylum, American authorities in Bonn revealed Apr. 22. He had been assigned to kill Georgi Sergeevich Okolovich, an official of the anti-Soviet refugee group *Natsionalny Trudvoi Soyuz* (NTS). 2 German Communists, recruited in Berlin, had preceded Khokhlov to Frankfurt. Khokhlov then arrived in Frankfurt Feb. 17 and told Okolovich of the plot Feb. 18. Okolovich arranged Khokhlov's meeting with U.S. agents Feb. 20, when Khokhlov requested asylum and persuaded his 2 German associates to surrender. (U.S. authorities later pointed out that Khokhlov's MVD superiors had been executed in 1954 as Beria men. They expressed some doubt over his motives in seeking asylum.)

Khokhlov said that his wife, Yanina, 32, a Moscow engineer, had persuaded him to desert to the West. He appealed to Pres. Eisenhower and Pope Pius XII Apr. 27 for aid in saving her and their 21-month-old son from Soviet revenge.

American agents found ingenious murder weapons left for Khokhlov in the Frankfurt railroad station: 2 dummy cigarette cases concealing silenced pistols and 2 electrically-fired miniature pistols, all equipped with poison pellets.

The official East German Party newspaper *Neues Deutschland* Apr. 24 ridiculed Khokhlov's surrender. It said he was an emigre Russian whose story had been devised by the U.S. to wreck the Geneva Conference.

The U.S. protested to the Soviet Union Apr. 23 against the "outrageous and uncivilized" plot revealed by Khokhlov. The U.S. also charged that Dr. Alexander Truchnovich, West Berlin head of the NTS, who had disappeared Apr. 13, had been "brutally kidnapped" by Soviet agents. Moscow rejected a British protest over Truchnovich Apr. 27. West Berlin offered a $25,000 reward Apr. 22 for aid in finding Truchnovich or his kidnappers. The East German government, however, said that Truchnovich had come East voluntarily after realizing the "futility" of the emigre resistance movements. It announced Apr. 26 that another anti-Communist leader, Josip Krutij, head of a Ukrainian Nationalist group in Munich, had entered East Germany illegally and had surrendered to Communist authorities.

The Soviet Union severed diplomatic relations with Australia Apr. 23 over Australia's refusal to return self-exiled Soviet diplomat Vladimir Petrov and his wife. Australia Apr. 25 rejected Soviet charges that Mrs. Petrov had been kidnapped. (The Soviet Union also claimed that Petrov had stolen Soviet funds.)

The U.S. disclosed Sept. 28 that Jozef Swiatlo, 39, a former deputy department chief of the Polish State Security Ministry, had been in U.S. custody since fleeing to West Berlin Dec. 5 and had been granted asylum. At a news conference in Washington Sept. 28 Swiatlo gave these details of the fate of Noel, Herta and Hermann Field, Americans missing 5 years: Swiatlo had personally arrested Hermann Field at Warsaw airport in Aug. 1949 when Field was en route to Prague in search of his brother Noel, an ex-U.S. State Department official who had vanished there. Hermann was imprisoned near Warsaw with no news of his wife and children. He went on hunger strikes and tried to commit suicide in 1951. Hermann, Noel and Herta (Mrs. Noel) Field, believed in the U.S. to be Communist sympathizers, were accused in Warsaw and Budapest of Titoism and of being "American imperialist spies." The Noel Fields were imprisoned in Budapest. (Noel's adopted daughter, Mrs. Erika Glaser Wallach, disappeared in East Berlin in Aug. 1950.) The U.S. sent notes to Hungary and Poland Sept. 28 demanding release of Hermann, Noel and Herta Field, but Swiatlo said Sept. 29 that he suspected all 3 were dead. (Poland freed Hermann Field from prison Oct. 26, and the Hungarian government said Nov. 16 that Noel and Herta Field had been released.)

Yugoslavia Between Liberalization & Repression

Vice Pres. Milovan Djilas called Jan. 4 for an end to strict discipline and dogma in the Yugoslav Communist party (officially: the Yugoslav League of Communists). He said party discipline necessary during revolution had become outmoded.

Djilas, 42, was ousted from all party offices Jan. 17 by the Central Committee for having advocated less party discipline and more individual expression. Pres. Tito, to whom Djilas had been a top-ranking political aide and potential successor, rebuked him for having caused "unrest" and having tried to "achieve liquidation of the League of Communists, restoration of capitalism and Western democracy and anarchy." (Djilas, in published articles, had also accused wives of some Yugoslav leaders of snobbery, charging that they shunned Vilena Vrajakova, bride of Gen. Peko Dapcevic, the army chief of staff, because she had not been a World War II partisan. He assailed the morals of some of the other wives.) Djilas said after a 2-day party trial that he accepted the criticism. Tito promised a purge by "mild" methods of other party members guilty of Djilas' line of thinking. (Djilas was reported Apr. 21 to have resigned his party membership.)

Tito was unanimously reelected as president by the Federal Assembly (parliament) Jan. 29. He pledged that his government would continue its independent policy despite renewed invitations to rejoin the Soviet bloc. Tito said he was confident that efforts to "normalize" relationships with the countries of the bloc, particularly in regard to trade, would not affect

Yugoslavia's ties with the West. Before his election (he was the only candidate), Tito had emphasized the need for "a resolute struggle" against "very dangerous counter-revolutionary" elements. He said he had abandoned Soviet methods because compulsion itself could not create a "free Socialist community," but he said he thought the use of force against counter-revolutionaries was essential.

Tito was sworn in Jan. 30 for a 4-year term. (His past term was one year.) Also inaugurated were 4 vice presidents: incumbents Eduard Kardelj and Aleksander Rankovic, ex-Economy Min. Svetozar Vukmanovic-Tempo, ex-Cultural & Scientific Affairs Min. Rodoljub Colakavic. The latter 2 replaced Mosa Pijade, 66, who was elected president of the Federal Assembly Jan. 28, and Milovan Djilas, who had resigned as Federal Assembly head and had withdrawn from "all public work" after being expelled by the party Central Committee.

A Greek-Yugoslav-Turkish plan for a full military alliance "strengthening peace and collective security under the UN Charter" was announced in Athens June 5 at the conclusion of a visit there by Tito and Foreign Secy. Koca Popovic. The agreement was signed in Bled, Slovenia (Yugoslavia) Aug. 9 by Popovic, Greek Foreign Min. Stefan Stephanopoulos and Turkish Foreign Min. Fuad Koprulu.

The Yugoslav government reported Mar. 21 that it held 158 Christian clergymen (124 Roman Catholics) in prison, mostly as wartime pro-Nazis or post-war foes of the Tito regime. It said 101 priests had been released in 1953. The district court in Cetinje July 29 imposed a 11½ year prison sentence at hard labor on Bishop Arsenije Bradvarevic, 71, Orthodox metropolitan of Montenegro, after his conviction on charges of opposing the government and plotting to overthrow it.

Yugoslav athletes Gavra Budisin, 28 and Julko Jost, 24, asked Portugal for political asylum Mar. 21 after their team won a volleyball tournament in Lisbon. Tennis player Mirko Tusukovic, 20, sought Italian asylum Mar. 22 in Genoa.

1955

Differences about the means to be used to consolidate the bloc after the disruptions of 1953 continued to divide the Soviet leadership. The original coalition of 5 individuals, established in the wake of Stalin's death, crumbled, until Khrushchev emerged as the most powerful man in Moscow. In January, Malenkov lost the premiership to Bulganin, although effective power was concentrated in Khrushchev's hands. The changes in the Kremlin were followed by further purges of ex-Stalinists throughout eastern Europe.

Khrushchev diverted attention from internal problems by initiating an active foreign policy intended, in turn, to give greater stability to the Soviet bloc. His new slogan of "peaceful coexistence" actually referred to aggressive diplomacy short of war. Exploiting the insufficient flexibility of U.S. foreign policy at that time, Khrushchev profited from bold diplomatic moves calculated to promote the image of the Soviet Union as a peaceful power, especially among the non-aligned nations. Moscow consented to the neutralization of Austria and withdrew all Soviet troops from the country. The Soviet Union established diplomatic relations with West Germany. At the same time, however, the Russians reaffirmed interest in the East German state by transferring to it vestiges of formal sovereignty. Khrushchev's pragmatism, along with his "folksy" approach to politics—so different from Stalin's—were interpreted in eastern Europe as evidence of strength rather than weakness and discouraged domestic opposition for the time being.

Khrushchev's most spectacular foreign initiative was the formal reconciliation with Yugoslavia, accomplished during his trip to Belgrade in January. In exchange for the promise of Tito's diplomatic support, Khrushchev paid the heavy price of recognizing Yugoslavia's independence and its "revisionist" *deviations. The rapprochement with Moscow resulted in a setback for the Yugoslav advocates of Western orientation and internal liberalization. 2 of them, Milovan Djilas and Vladimir Dedijer, were tried and jailed.*

POLICY OF CONTROLLED LIBERALIZATION

Advent of Khrushchev Era

Several leading Soviet government and political posts changed hands early in 1955, and these changes indicated a shift in the center of power.

Anastas I. Mikoyan, who had stressed consumer production, was relieved as Soviet trade minister (reportedly at his own request), but he remained a deputy premier, Tass reported Jan. 24. Dimitri V. Pavlov, advocate of more heavy industrial production, became trade minister.

The Soviet government removed Georgi M. Malenkov from the post of premier Feb. 8 and renounced his policy of stressing consumer rather than heavy industry. Marshal Nikolai A. Bulganin, 59, was advanced from defense minister to premier. Nikita S. Khrushchev, 60, first secretary of the Communist Party's Central Committee, emerged as the strongest political figure. Marshal Georgi K. Zhukov, 59, previously Bulganin's first deputy, was named defense minister Feb. 9.

In a Georgian SSR cabinet shakeup disclosed Jan. 23 by the Communist Party newspaper *Zarya Vostoka (Dawn of the East),* Justice Min. Georgi Vassili Kishvardovich Mamaladze was replaced by Mikhail Karamonovich Limidze; Commerce Min. Josif Dimitrovich Kotchlamazishivili was replaced by Chalva Ilyitch Sabanadze and the heads of the Georgian state-owned bread and grocery chains—L. I. Zhordaniya and A. L. Lalakhivili—were dismissed by Central Committee decree Jan. 20 (it was reported Jan. 26) for failure to check speculative buying.

State security (counter-espionage) chiefs of the various Soviet republics received cabinet rank under a decree ratified by the Supreme Soviet Feb. 7. Col. Gen. Ivan A. Serov was named chairman of the National Committee of State Security. The Soviet government announced Feb. 11 that 6 of the 70 members of the Supreme Court had been replaced Feb. 7—3 for reasons of health.

U.S. State Secy. John F. Dulles said in a speech in New York Feb. 16 that the "last act of the drama" in Russia's change of premiers "has not yet been played" and that the changes might indicate a conflict between the Soviet Communist Party and government. He predicted that Russians "of stature" eventually would rebel against subordinating national interests to international Communist objectives.

The Supreme Soviet Presidium Mar. 1 announced further cabinet changes. The trade specialist Mikoyan, the fuels and power administrator Mikhail G. Pervukhin and the economic planning expert Maksim Z. Saburov were elevated to first deputy premierships. The production administrators V. A. Kucherenko, Pavel P. Lobanov, Col. Gen. A. P. Zavenyagin and Lt. Gen. Mikhail V. Khrunichev were made deputy premiers; Zavenyagin was designated also as medium machine-building minister (believed responsible for atomic production). Replacement of State Farms Min. Alexei Ivanovich Kozlov with Ivan A. Benediktov and Coal Industry Min. Aleksandr Fyodorovich Zasyadko with A. N. Zademidko was announced by Premier Bulganin Mar. 2.

The resolution of Soviet political problems permitted the Kremlin's new leaders to turn their attention to bloc affairs.

Hungary announced Apr. 18 that Premier Imre Nagy had been expelled from the government and from his Communist Party posts Apr. 14 because he "represented ideas ... controversial to the interest" of the country. He was succeeded Apr. 18 by Deputy Premier and former Agriculture Min. Andras Hegedus, 40. The party newspaper *Szabad Nep (Free People)* had labelled Nagy a "Titoist" Apr. 9 and had said he had "wandered from the only correct road for the establishment of communism after [according to] the example of the Soviet Union and [had] propagated his own Hungarian version." (Nagy, like ex-Soviet Premier Malenkov, had stressed the production of consumer goods over the development of heavy industry.) The Hungarian Communist Party also dropped 2d Secy. Mihaly Farkas from party positions for supporting Nagy's policies.

Yugoslav-Soviet Reconciliation

Ex-Vice Pres. Milovan Djilas and Vladimir Dedijer, official biographer of Marshal Tito, were found guilty in Belgrade Jan. 25 of waging propaganda against the government. (Djilas, with Dedijer's support, had said in an article for the newspaper *Borba* and in a statement to the foreign press that there should be more political freedom in Yugoslavia.) Djilas was given an 18 month prison sentence and Dedijer a 6-month sentence, but both were released on terms of probation running 3 and 2 years, respectively.

Khrushchev and Bulganin visited Yugoslavia May 26-June 3 for talks on closer cooperation between the USSR and Yugoslavia. Arriving May 26 at Belgrade's Zemun Airport, they were met by Tito, who greeted them in a bemedalled sky-blue marshal's uniform. The 6-man Soviet "good will" party, its members wearing business suits, included Dmitri T. Shepilov, editor *Pravda*. (Soviet Pres. Klementi Voroshilov sent "sincere congratulations" on Tito's 63d birthday May 25. This was the first such greeting since Tito was expelled from the Cominform in 1948.)

Tito listened impassively and made no reply to an 11-minute arrival speech read in Russian May 26 by Khrushchev, who led the Soviet group from a 2-engine Convair-type transport plane and apparently outranked Bulganin in importance. Khrushchev addressed himself to "dear Comrade Tito ... dear comrades and citizens" and recalled the "ties of long brotherly friendship and the joint struggle against the (Nazi German) enemy." He said "we sincerely regret" that "these good relations were destroyed" and asserted that his group "resolutely" rejected the Kremlin-Tito rupture. He added: "We ascribe without hesitation the aggravations to the provocative role that Beria, Abakumov and others—recently exposed enemies of the people—played in the relations between Yugoslavia and the USSR." (Lavrenti P. Beria, ex-Soviet Internal Affairs Min., was executed in 1953. Viktor S. Abakumov, an aide to Beria, was executed in 1954.)

Khrushchev said: The Soviet leaders had "studied assiduously the materials on which had been based the serious accusations ... against the leaders of Yugoslavia. The facts show that these materials were fabricated by enemies of the people, contemptible agents of imperialism who, by deceptive methods, pushed their way into the ranks of our party." "We are profoundly convinced that this period of the deterioration of our relations has been left behind us. For our part we are ready to do everything necessary to eliminate all obstacles standing in the way of complete normalization of relations between our states...."

Speaking as a Soviet Communist Party representative, Khrushchev said that "the strongest ties" were created among those countries "where the leading forces are parties that base their activities on the teachings of Marxism-Leninism." He added: "We would not be doing our duty to our peoples and to the working people of the whole world if we did not do everything possible to establish mutual understanding" between the Soviet and Yugoslav Communist parties. Khrushchev said the USSR, "following the teachings of ... Lenin," based its relations with other countries "on principles of the peaceful coexistence of states, on principles of equality, nonintervention and respect for sovereignty and national independence, on principles of nonaggression and ... the impermissibility of some states encroaching upon the territorial integrity of others." Khrushchev expressed hope that the strengthening of USSR-Yugoslav friendship "will contribute to improvement of relations among all countries" and "to consolidation of peace in general."

After 2 days of talks in Belgrade, Tito and Khrushchev led their respective delegations May 29 to Brioni Island, in the Adriatic Sea off Pula, where the talks continued at Tito's villa. Daily communiques gave no details of the discussions, except for references to talks about "future Soviet-Yugoslav relations."

American press reports from Belgrade May 27-28 said Tito had resisted Khrushchev's efforts to get the Yugoslav Communist party to rejoin the Cominform and bring the country back to the Soviet political bloc. Tito was said to have (a) told the Russians that Yugoslavia must retain its present independence and (b) insisted on the settlement of economic questions, including Yugoslavia's contention that Russia owed $200 million for broken trade pacts.

The talks ended in Belgrade June 2 as Bulganin and Tito signed a declaration halting the Moscow-Belgrade feud and supporting UN membership for Communist China and its claim to Formosa. (Khrushchev took a side seat at the signing ceremony; this was the first time he did so since his arrival.) The joint statement called for arms reduction, an atomic arms ban, the establishment of "a general system of collective security, including a system of collective security in Europe based on a treaty, and the use of nuclear energy for peaceful purposes." The statement said: "Through such efforts, an atmosphere would be created" making possible a peaceful solution of "such urgent problems of the first importance as ... an agreed settlement of the German question on a democratic basis in conformity both with the wishes and interests of the German people and in the interest of general security and the satisfaction of the legitimate rights of [Communist China] to Formosa."

The Soviet-Yugoslav statement favored strengthening "the role and the authority of the UN" by giving Communist China "the representation to which it is entitled." It said the talks had "started from the following principles": (1) "Respect for sovereignty, independence, integrity and for equality among states in their mutual relations"; (2) "recognition and development of peaceful coexistence among nations, regardless of ideological differences"; (3) "noninterference in internal affairs for whatever reason, whether of an economic, political or ideological nature, because questions of internal organization, or difference in social systems and of different forms of Socialist development, are solely the concern of the individual countries"; (4) removal of factors "which impede the exchange of goods and hamper the development of productive forces"; (5) approval of aid programs "through the appropriate UN bodies, as well as in other forms" in accordance with UN principles, for national economies and the economically underdeveloped areas; (6) elimination "of every form of propaganda and misinformation, as well as of other forms of conduct which create distrust or in any other way impede the establishment of an atmosphere conducive to constructive international cooperation and to the peaceful coexistence of nations"; (7) "condemnation of all aggression and of all attempts to subject other countries to political and economical domination"; (8) "recognition that the policy of military blocs increases international tension, undermines confidence among nations and augments the danger of war."

The conferees agreed to make "necessary arrangements" for the development of economic and cultural relations between the USSR and Yugoslavia and to establish "normal treaty conditions which will provide a base" for cooperation in other fields. They also agreed to take steps to conclude a treaty regarding the citizenship and repatriation of nationals of one country residing in the other and to "assist and facilitate cooperation among the social organizations of the 2 countries through the establishment of contacts, the exchange of Socialist experiences and a free exchange of opinions" so that people of both countries can "become better acquainted and achieve better mutual understanding."

Although Khrushchev spoke of "mutual understanding" between the Soviet and Yugoslav Communist parties on his arrival in Belgrade, the final statement did not mention relations between the 2 parties. *Pravda* said June 3 that the joint declaration had "tremendous significance." It underlined the section dealing with noninterference in internal affairs.

During a factory-inspection tour in Zagreb June 1, Khrushchev told Yugoslav Communist party and workers' representatives that the USSR might "make use of some of your experience in worker self-management." He said that "there may be things ... which we can borrow from Yugoslavia ... just as we are ready to borrow from the Americans." Leaving a Belgrade reception that lasted into the early hours of June 3, Tito acted as interpreter as Khrushchev first referred to waiting Western newsmen as "dangerous" and then invited Frank Kelley of the *N.Y. Herald Tribune* to visit Moscow. Khrushchev's own interpreter took over to add: "And you can have your visa tomorrow if you wish. You can all have them. You can all get in."

Khrushchev, Bulganin and First Deputy Premier Mikoyan stopped in Sofia June 3 and Bucharest June 4 before returning to Moscow by air June 5. (Andrei A. Gromyko, first deputy foreign minister, Pavel N. Kumyikan, a deputy foreign trade minister, and Dmitri T. Shepilov, editor of *Pravda,* flew home via Budapest.) In Sofia, Khrushchev said at a street rally June 3 that "the period of bad relations" between Moscow and

Belgrade was "ended" and that "the road toward the development of friendly relations between the USSR and the peoples' democracies on one side and Yugoslavia on the other side has been opened." He added: "We have seen that Yugoslavia did not abandon her sovereignty but maintained her independence before the imperialists."

In Bucharest next day, Khrushchev said at a mass party rally: "Bad relations between the Soviet Union and Yugoslavia were in the interest of imperialist powers"; the Soviet bloc was "not weakening in our power." While in Bucharest, the Soviet leaders met with Hungarian and Czechoslovak government and party leaders, and a communique issued in Bucharest June 5 expressed hopes of "friendly cooperation" with Yugoslavia so as to strengthen "the cause of peace and socialism." A Sofia communique that day expressed similar hopes.

But the *N.Y. Times* quoted official Belgrade sources as saying June 5 that Yugoslavia would not join the Warsaw military alliance. Yugoslav officials also were said to be annoyed at post-Belgrade statements by Khrushchev that they felt were designed to embarrass Yugoslavia with the West.

Other Developments

Rumanian anti-Communist exiles seized the Rumanian Legation building in Bern, Switzerland Feb. 15 and held it by force of arms until Feb. 16, when they surrendered to Swiss police. 3 of the original group of 6, who vowed to hold the legation until imprisoned resistance leaders in Rumania were released, gave up when threatened with tank fire. 3 escaped but one was later arrested. The legation chauffeur was killed when the building was seized.

Valery Lysikov, a Soviet lieutenant colonel's son who had fled to West Berlin Mar. 22, voluntarily returned to the East Apr. 9 with his parents, who picked him up at U.S. High Commission Headquarters in Berlin. A U.S. official said the youth "dwelt constantly on what might happen to his parents and finally decided he would return home."

Hugo Hanke, who had been appointed premier of the Polish government-in-exile by the exile-government Pres. August Zaleski in London, was named by Warsaw radio Sept. 10 as one of the Soviet-bloc refugees who had heeded the east

European "come home" campaign. Warsaw radio broadcast a speech by Hanke urging others to follow his example. Polish exiles said in London that they had not known where Hanke was; he had been seen last in Rome Sept. 5.

The head of the Soviet program for the return of refugees, Gen. Nikolai F. Mikhailov, was quoted in Warsaw Sept. 20 as saying that no records had been kept on the number of refugees returning to the USSR but that 250 had returned through Berlin since April.

The Communist east European states issued during the spring a series of amnesties to refugees who wished to return to their countries and "integrate themselves in the constructive work" of their homelands.

(The USSR Sept. 18 announced an amnesty for Russians who had collaborated with the Germans during World War II. The amnesty provided for the immediate release of minor collaborators, the reduction of sentences for major collaborators and the immediate liberation of persons convicted of serving in German military or police units. *Izvestia* said one reason for the amnesty was the ending of the state of war with Germany. This was achieved in agreements between the Soviet Union and West Germany Sept. 13 to establish diplomatic relations and between the Soviet Union and East Germany Sept. 18 to confer sovereignty on the Pankow regime.)

East German party chief Walter Ulbricht had acknowledged June 10 that youths were reluctant to serve in the country's militarized police. He warned that "youth [must] understand that future military service of 2 to 3 years must be planned." His report to the party was made after the flight to the West of record numbers of East German youths fearing conscription. The 4th congress of the Communist-controlled Free (East) German Labor Union Federation was urged in East Berlin June 15 to contribute to "fully armed defense forces" to counter West German forces. The congress June 20 approved a statute effectively barring strikes by 5 million East German unionists so that "the national economic plan" would be carried out with "Socialist work discipline."

The 2d anniversary of the 1953 East German revolt passed quietly June 17. East and West Berliners met in front of the West Berlin city hall to hear speeches by West German political leaders (including Social Democratic leader Erich Ollenhauer),

who opposed proposals for internationalizing Berlin and
pledged the restoration of Berlin as capital of a unified
Germany.)

West German officials reported Dec. 31 that 271,000
persons had fled East Germany in 1955. This was the largest
number of refugees since 1953.

1956

The increased international prestige that the Soviet Union gained because of its strategy of peaceful coexistence created favorable conditions for a new departure in domestic policy. In an attempt to dissociate the Soviet system from the outrages of the Stalin era, Khrushchev strongly denounced the Stalinist "cult of personality." His condemnation of the Stalinist police terror, delivered at a secret session of the 20th congress of the CPSU in February, accelerated the rehabilitation—often posthumous—of many of its victims, at least those from the ranks of the Bolsheviks. The Soviet leadership repudiated Stalin's legacy by abolishing the Cominform (Communist Information Bureau)—Moscow's instrument to impose uniformity on the foreign Communist parties—and by dismissing Foreign Min. Molotov, the chief architect of Stalin's foreign policy. Both measures facilitated further improvement in relations with Yugoslavia.

The opening of the "de-Stalinization" campaign was apparently a result of impulsive decision-making rather than of careful preparation. The leakage of Khrushchev's secret speech and its subsequent publication created embarrassment for the Soviet government. The fervor of his attack on Stalin evoked malaise in the east European party establishments, long accustomed to clear direction from Moscow. They became demoralized at the very time the Soviet Union, proclaiming the desire for partnership rather than mere subordination, hoped to promote their self-reliance as well as their solidarity with Moscow. Moreover, revelations about the scandalous treatment of foreign Communists under Stalin inspired patriotic indignation, especially in Poland and Hungary. And the apparent Soviet approval of the Yugoslav deviation further encouraged the trend toward "national communism" in these countries. In the

Soviet Union itself, unrest among the non-Russian nationalities, workers and students increased.

The first large-scale outbreak of popular discontent was
the June revolt of Polish workers at Poznan. It was initially
suppressed with the use of methods reminiscent of 1953. But the
incident generated ferment within the Polish Communist party
and brought to power Wladyslaw Gomulka, a prominent victim
of the Stalinist purges. His extensive concessions to the pressure
for greater political freedom—concessions that had strong anti-
Russian overtones—precipitated a confrontation with
Khrushchev and a threat of Soviet armed intervention. Several
factors combined to prevent the catastrophe: the Poles' confidence in Gomulka, his ability to assert authority over both the
"liberals" and the "Stalinists" in the party, his unswerving
loyalty to Moscow despite his Polish nationalism, and the
Chinese warning to the Russians to desist from military
intervention—the first important repercussion in eastern
Europe of the nascent Sino-Soviet rift.

The Polish developments dramatized the problem of control in the "de-Stalinization" process, the limits of which
Khrushchev had probably never defined with clarity. The
growing attractiveness of the Yugoslav model of "national
communism" among the nations of eastern Europe put in question the relative benefits of the Soviet rapprochement with
Yugoslavia for the Kremlin. By the middle of the year Soviet-
Yugoslav relations had deteriorated again, despite Khruschev's
2d visit to Belgrade.

The example of Poland—where popular upheaval compelled the regime to grant substantive freedoms and forced the
Russians into a partial retreat—precipitated revolt in Hungary
late in October. The pattern of Poland repeated itself, but at an
accelerated pace and with greater intensity. The first disturbances provoked brutal repression, immediately followed by
attempts at appeasement. Unlike its Polish counterpart, the
Hungarian party was severely divided within itself. After
repression had fanned further disturbances, the "national
Communist" government of Imre Nagy tried to control the
popular movement by assuming its leadership. By that time,
however, the revolutionary development had gained a momen-
tum far beyond that in Poland. The vicinity of the West generated hopes for outside assistance. Under strong pressure from

below, Nagy agreed to withdraw Hungary from the Warsaw Pact and to seek Hungary's neutralization.

Unlike the Gomulka regime, the Nagy government took measures that threatened to upset the Cold War balance of power in central Europe. These measures provoked the Soviet leaders into intervening militarily, although only after considerable hesitation. Their growing panic amidst the catastrophic consequences of "de-Stalinization" helps explain the reversion to Stalinist tactics during the suppression of the uprising. Yet unlike their Soviet predecessors in the solution for East Germany in 1953, the Kremlin leaders of 1956 did not restore the discredited Stalinist officials to power in Hungary. Janos Kadar, a former victim of the purges because of alleged "nationalist" deviations, became the head of the new government. Owing his power over an intensely hostile people exclusively to the Red Army, he had initially little choice but to implement the policy of counterrevolutionary terror dictated by the Soviet Union. Despite sporadic resistance lasting until the end of the year, the terror was effective. The Kadar regime remained firmly in power.

DESTALINIZATION CAMPAIGN

20th Congress of Soviet Communist Party

An attack on one-man rule begun by Soviet Communist Party First Secy. Nikita S. Khrushchev Feb. 14 was carried forward by First Deputy Premier Anastas I. Mikoyan at the 20th Soviet Communist Party Congress in Moscow Feb. 16. They and other Soviet leaders strongly criticized the "cult" of "individual" and of "personality" that had prevailed under Stalin. (Mikoyan's speech, containing a long and detailed indictment of Stalin's policies, was not published until Feb. 18.) After a succession of other party and government leaders had discussed the policies laid down by Khrushchev in his speech, the Congress unanimously voted Feb. 20 to indorse them.

Khrushchev had said in his keynote address to the Congress Feb. 14: The Communist Party Central Committee had "vigorously condemned the cult of the individual as being alien to the spirit of Marxism-Leninism and making a particular leader the hero and miracle-worker." The "cult of the individual tended to minimize the role of collective leadership ... and at times resulted in serious drawbacks" in the work of the Communist Party. The "working collective of leaders" set up since Stalin's death in 1953 was based "on ideas and principles permitting neither mutual forgiveness nor personal antagonism." The Central Committee had sometimes "found it necessary to correct some people who introduced confusion in certain clear issues which the party had settled long before."

Mikoyan assailed both Stalin's dictatorship and his interpretation of the USSR's early history. Mikoyan said in his speech Feb. 16: "The main feature which characterizes the work of the Central Committee and its Presidium during the past 3 years is the fact that, after a long interval, collective leadership has been created in our party." It had developed into "a strongly welded leading collective whose strength lies not only in the fact that it consists of comrades who have become a team in the course of many years of revolutionary struggle ... The most important thing is that this collective, guided by Lenin's ideas and Lenin's principles of the structure of the party and party leadership, has within a short space of time achieved the restoration of Lenin's forms of party life, from top to bottom. The principle of collective leadership is elementary for the proletarian party ... of the Lenin type." For "about 20 years we, in fact, had no collective leadership. The cult of personality, condemned already by Marx and ... Lenin, flourished, and this, of course, could not but exert an extremely negative influence ..." With collective leadership in "the past 3 years," the "entire fruitful influence of Lenin's methods of leadership can be felt." This has given "a fresh strength to our party."

Mikoyan also called for revision of current textbooks (prepared during Stalin's regime) on the USSR's early history to correct their mistakes about "allegedly subversive activity of some former party leaders who many years after the events described were wrongly declared enemies of the people." He said that Ukrainians Vladimir Antonov-Ovseenko, a military leader under Lenin and diplomat under Stalin, and Stanislav V. Kossior (or Kassier), Ukrainian Bolshevik leader, had been falsely accused in the Stalinist purges in the 1930s. Mikoyan said also that the Stalinist *Short Course of the History of the Party* no longer was adequate as a textbook.

Deputy Premier Georgi M. Malenkov, in his first major speech since he had stepped down as premier in 1955, told the Congress Feb. 17 that one-man rule had led to "arbitrary, irrevocable decisions," "high-handedness" and serious abnormalities." He said enemies of the USSR who hoped for internal dissension would be disappointed. The Paris newspaper *France-Soir* said June 11 that Khrushchev, in a talk at a meeting of Soviet leaders in Moscow, had charged Stalin with "erotomania," keeping a harem of young girls and having shot and strangled his 2d wife (Nadezhda Alliluyeva, who had been rumored to have committed suicide Nov. 8, 1932.)

Khrushchev's Secret Speech

Reports from U.S. diplomats and news correspondents in Moscow Mar. 15-19 gave accounts of a speech in which Khrushchev, at the 20th party Congress Feb. 24, had indicted Stalin for barbarously criminal misrule. Khrushchev was said to have charged the late dictator with: (1) murders of 70 of 133 members of the Soviet Communist Party Central Committee in 1937 to consolidate his personal power; (2) wanton killing of thousands of other people following purge trials and during forced collectivization of peasants in the 1930s; (3) the unjustified execution of Marshal Mikhail N. Tukhachevsky and other Red Army leaders during the 1937 purge, with the result that the Soviet Union was almost overrun by the Germans in 1941 for lack of skillful military leadership; (4) reluctance to believe that Hitler had broken his Soviet alliance and had attacked the USSR in 1941, and personal cowardice in leaving Moscow when it appeared that the Nazis would capture the city; (5) personal responsibility for the Cominform's break with Tito in 1949; (6) fabrication of charges against Nikolai A. Voznesensky, Politburo member and State Planning Commission chairman, who was shot in 1949, and against several Leningrad leaders who had disappeared in 1949. Khrushchev was said to have wept as he told how he had lived in fear of liquidation on Stalin's whim during the last years of the dictator's life. (Khrushchev had become a Communist Party Central Committee secretary under Stalin in 1949.) Khrushchev's Feb. 24 speech was said to have been kept secret for fear of adverse reaction in the USSR and satellite states, pending the clarification and interpretation of the de-Stalinization campaign.

The U.S. State Department June 4 released a 26,000-word text of the 4-hour Khrushchev speech. The State Department affirmed that "this version is understood to have been prepared for the guidance ... of a Communist Party outside the Soviet Union." Washington dispatches June 5 reported rumors that the text had been made from a copy sent to Tito about Mar. 15. The United Press reported from Washington June 6 that Khrushchev's text had been obtained by the State Department early in May through sources in Poland, one of the countries where Communists had received confidential copies from Moscow. The text omitted some parts of the speech dealing with Stalin's handling of foreign policy and methods employed in blood purges during his regime. Acting U.S. State Secy. Herbert Hoover Jr. issued orders June 2 for the publication of the text after an investigation had apparently established its authenticity.

Excerpts from the Khrushchev speech:

"After Stalin's death the Central Committee ... began to implement a policy of explaining concisely and consistently that it is impermissible and foreign to the spirit of Marxism-Leninism to elevate one person ... into a superman possessing supernatural characteristics akin to those of a god. Such a man supposedly knows everything, sees everything, thinks for everyone, can do anything, is infallible ... Such a belief ... about Stalin was cultivated among us for many years.

"The objective of the present report is not a thorough evaluation of Stalin's life and activity.... The role of Stalin in the preparation and execution of the Socialist revolution, in the civil war and in the fight for the construction of socialism in our country is universally known." "At the present we are concerned with ... how the cult of the person of Stalin ... became at a certain specific stage the source of a whole series of exceedingly serious and grave perversions of party principles, of party democracy, of revolutionary legality."

The "classics of Marxism-Leninism denounced every manifestation of the cult of the individual. In a letter to the German political worker Wilhelm Bloss, Marx stated: 'Because of my antipathy to any cult of the individual, I never made public during the existence of the [First] International the numerous addresses from various countries which recognized my merits and which annoyed me.... Engels and I first joined the secret society of Communists on the condition that everything making for superstitious worship of authority would be deleted from its statute....'"

Lenin "always stressed the role of the people as the creator of history, the directing and organizational role of the party as a living and creative organism, and also the role of the Central Committee." Lenin "mercilessly stigmatized every manifestation of the cult of the individual, inexorably combated the foreign-to-Marxism views about a 'hero' and a 'crowd' and countered all efforts to oppose a 'hero' to the masses and to the people ... stressing that the guiding principle of party leadership is its collegiality.... During Lenin's life the Central Committee of the party was a real expression of collective leadership ... Lenin never imposed (by force) his views upon his co-workers. He tried to convince; he patiently explained.... Party congresses and the plenary sessions of the Central Committee took place at the proper intervals."

Lenin "detected in Stalin ... those negative characteristics which resulted later in grave consequences." Lenin's "testament" letter to the Soviet Communist Party Congress in Dec. 1922 said: " 'Stalin is excessively rude, and this defect, which can be freely tolerated ... in contacts among us Communists, cannot be tolerated in one holding the position of the party secretary general. I propose that the comrades consider the method by which Stalin would be removed from this position' " in favor of a man of " 'greater tolerance, greater loyalty, greater kindness and more considerate attitude toward the comrades, a less capricious temper, etc.' "

"The party congress should become acquainted with 2 new documents": (1) a letter Dec. 23, 1922, from Nadezhda Konstantinovna Krupskaya (Lenin's wife) to Politburo head Lev B. Kamenev protesting that she had been the target of Stalin's " 'rude interference with my private life and ... vile invectives and threats' "; (2) a letter from Lenin to Stalin Mar. 5, 1923 saying: " '...I consider as directed against me that which is being done against my wife. I ask ... whether you are agreeable to retracting your words and apologizing or whether you prefer the severance of relations between us.' "

"These negative characteristics of [Stalin's] developed steadily and during the last years acquired an absolutely insufferable character." He demanded "absolute submission to his opinion. Whoever opposed this concept or tried to prove his viewpoint ... was doomed to removal from the leading collective and ... moral and physical annihilation."

Stalin played a "positive role" in the 1920s in the Communist Party's "serious fight" against Trotskyists, Zinovievites, Bukharinites [purported followers of Stalin's earlier rivals Leon Trotsky and Grigory E. Zinoviev or of Nikolai I. Bukharin, party moderate—all 3 murdered or executed by 1942] and other "anti-Leninist" factions, but in this "ideological fight ... extreme repressive measures were not used against them." They were "long since defeated politically" when, in the 1935-37-38 period, the Stalinist "practice of mass repression through the government apparatus was born"—first against ideological "enemies of Leninism," then "against many honest Communists." Stalin "originated the concept 'enemy of the people' " under which it became "unnecessary that the ideological errors of a man or men engaged in a controversy be proven" and "the most cruel repression ... against anyone who in any way disagreed with Stalin" was practiced. "In the main ... the only proof of guilt used ... was the 'confession' of the accused himself; and, as subsequent probing proved, 'confessions' were acquired through physical pressures...."

Lenin's attitude toward errant party workers was reflected in a hitherto "unpublished" note to the Communist Party Politburo in 1920 in which he said that " 'an effort should be made to quiet [and] explain' " to such persons and find for them tasks " 'for which they are psychologically fitted.' " But Stalin relied on "administrative violence, mass repressions and terror," and his "arbitrary behavior ... encouraged and permitted arbitrariness in others." Whereas Stalin employed "mass arrests and deportations of many thousands of people, execution without trial and without normal investigation" against personal rivals and deviating Communists, Lenin would have had such methods "resorted to only against those people who had in fact committed criminal acts against the Soviet system."

Prior to the Oct. 1917 revolution, the party's Central Committee members Kamenev and G. E. Zinoviev "declared themselves against Lenin's plan for an armed uprising" and "published ... a statement ... declaring that the Bolsheviks were making preparations for an uprising and that they considered it adventuristic." They "thus disclosed to the enemy the decision ... to stage the uprising...."

"This was treason," and Lenin asked the Central Committee to consider their expulsion from the party. Yet, after the revolution, "they carried out most responsible party tasks" under Lenin. They "committed ... other serious errors ... during Lenin's life," but he "did not pose the question of their arrest and certainly not their shooting."

Many Trotskyists eventually "broke with Trotskyism and returned to Leninist positions. Was it necessary to annihilate such people?"

"Lenin without hesitation used the most extreme methods—however, only against actual class enemies and not against those who blunder, who err.... Lenin used severe methods only in the most necessary cases when the exploiting classes were still in existence and were vigorously opposing the revolution." But "Stalin ... used extreme methods and mass repressions at a time when the revolution was victorious [and] the exploiting classes were already liquidated." Stalin often acted in the name of the party Central Committee without the approval or knowledge of other members.

Lenin always upheld "the principles of collegiality [collective leadership] in the direction of the party and the state." He "considered it necessary regularly to convoke [party] congresses [and] plenary sessions of the Central Committee" during "the most difficult period" of the revolution and its aftermath—1918-21. Stalin observed this practice "during the first few years after Lenin's death," but later, "when Stalin began ... to abuse his power, these principles were brutally violated." "Was it a normal situation when 13 years [1939-52] elapsed between the 18th and 19th party congresses?" Not even a Central Committee meeting was held during World War II; Stalin would not meet with Central Committee members when they tried to hold a session in Oct. 1941.

A party commission was set up after Stalin's death to investigate the cause of "mass repressions against the majority of the Central Committee members and candidates elected at the 17th [1934] Congress. In "NKVD archives" and "other documents" it found "many facts pertaining to the fabrication of cases against Communists ... which resulted in the death of innocent people.

... Many party, government and economic activists who were branded in 1937-8 as 'enemies,' were actually never enemies, spies, wreckers, etc. but were always honest Communists. Often, no longer able to bear barbaric tortures, they charged themselves ... with all kinds of grave and unlikely crimes."

"The commission found: "Of 139 members and candidates of the party's Central Committee who were elected at the 17th congress, 98 persons, *i.e.* 70%, were arrested and shot—mostly in 1937-8." However, inasmuch as 80% of the voting delegates in the 17th Congress had joined the party before and during the revolution, plus the fact that 60% of the delegates were "workers," it was "inconceivable that a congress so composed would have elected a Central Committee, a majority of whom would prove to be enemies of the party." The commission also found that 1,108 of 1,966 voting or advisory members of the 17th Congress eventually "were arrested on charges of anti-revolutionary crimes."

The increase in "mass repressions" after the 17th Congress was due to the fact that Stalin—having liquidated the Trotskyite, Zinovievite and Bukharinite groups—"thought that now he could decide all things alone and all he needed were statisticians.... After the criminal murder of Sergei M. Kirov [a party Politburo member], mass repressions and brutal acts of violation of Socialist legality began." On Dec. 1, 1934 [the date of Kirov's death], Stalin on his own authority had Abel S. Yenukidze, a party Central Committee presidium secretary, issue a directive that " 'investigative agencies ... speed up the cases of those accused of the preparation or execution of acts of terror,' " that " 'judicial organs ... not ... hold up the execution of death sentences of crimes of this category in order to consider the possibility of pardon,' " and that " 'organs of the Commissariat of Internal Affairs ... execute the death sentences ... immediately after the passage of the sentences.' " In subsequent "fabricated court cases" against purge victims, "the accused were charged with 'the preparation' of terroristic acts" and this—under the Yenukidze directive—"deprived them of any possibility that their cases might be reexamined, even when they stated before the court that their 'confessions' were secured by force, and when ... they disproved the accusations against them."

The investigation of Kirov's murder had shown that circumstances surrounding it were "inexplicable and mysterious" and that the killer, Leonid V. Nikolayev, was aided by one of Kirov's guards, who himself was killed next day "in a car 'accident' in which no other [riders] were harmed."

Stalin and the late Andrei A. Zhdanov (a party secretary who later dealt with cultural affairs and championed "Socialist realism") sent a telegram Sept. 25, 1936 to Stalin's brother-in-law Lazar M. Kaganovich, Foreign Min. Vyacheslav M. Molotov "and other members of the Politburo" warning that the NKVD had fallen 4 years behind in "unmasking the Trotskyite-Zinovievite bloc" and that NKVD head Henryk G. Yagoda had been found incompetent and replaced by Nikolai I. Yezhov. "This Stalinist formulation that the 'NKVD is 4 years behind' ... directly pushed the NKVD workers on the path of mass arrests and executions." The acceptance of the policy was "forced on" the Socialist Unity (Communist) Party Central Committee at its meeting in Feb.-Mar. 1937, even though the Trotskyite-Zinovievite opposition was long since defeated and had polled "only about 4,000" votes in

1927 as against "724,000 for the party line." Stalin tried to justify the mass terror in saying at the 1937 Central Committee session that "class war must allegedly sharpen," but Lenin had taught that "revolutionary violence" was necessary only "when the exploiting classes existed and were powerful." In Jan. 1920, when the Red Army had defeated Anton I. Denikin, "Lenin instructed [Felix E.] Dzerzhinsky [OGPU head] to stop mass terror and abolish the death penalty."

At the Feb.-Mar. 1937 Central Committee plenum many "questioned the rightness of the established course," and "Comrade [Pavel P.] Postyshev most ably expressed these doubts" when he said: " 'I have philosophized' " that after years of party struggle " 'members who have lost their backbones have broken down or have joined the camp of the enemy' "; but he could not believe that his friend, Ukrainian party Central Committee worker Karpov, could withstand the early troubles " 'and then, in 1934, join the Trotskyites. It is an odd thing.' " But it was "Stalin's formulation ... that the closer we are to socialism the more enemies we will have," and this accounted for the fact that "arrests based on charges of counterrevolutionary crimes had grown 10 times between 1936 and 1937."

Stalin "brutally abused" a party statute on rules for the expulsion of party leaders passed by the 17th Congress. He "kept retractions of forced confessions from Politburo members."

"An example of vile provocation, of odious falsification and of criminal violation of revolutionary legality" was the case of Robert I. Eikhe, candidate for the Politburo and a party member since 1905, who "was arrested Apr. 29, 1938 on the basis of slanderous materials" and "forced under torture to sign" a confession. On Oct. 1, 1939 he "denied his guilt and asked for an examination of his case." A 2d Eikhe declaration, sent to Stalin Oct. 27, 1939, told how, under torture by "Ushakov and Nikolayev" (presumably NKVD men), he had signed a confession of membership in a Bukharinite net and implicated V. I. Mezhlauk. In court Feb. 2, 1940, Eikhe denied guilt, but "on Feb. 4 Eikhe was shot." He "has been posthumously rehabilitated."

Railroads Commissar Jan E. Rudzutak, Central Control Commission chief and candidate for the Politburo, "retracted in court the confession which was forced from him" and asked to be permitted to write to the party Central Committee. "This declaration ... was ignored" and "sentence was pronounced on him in 20 minutes and he was shot." Rudzutak also "has been rehabilitated posthumously."

Comrade Rozenblum, arrested in 1937 by the Leningrad NKVD, revealed during examination of the rehabilitation of the Bolshevik leader Komarov in 1955 that on arrest "he was subjected to terrible torture," then taken to Leonid Zakovsky, who offered him freedom on condition he make "a false confession" implicating Chudov, Ugarov, Smorodin, Pozern, Shaposhnikova (Chudov's wife) and others. "Even more widely was the falsification of cases ... in the provinces." The Sverdlovsk Oblast NKVD accused the party Central Committee member Kabakov of leading the "so-called 'Ural uprising staff.' "

"The vicious practice was condoned of having the NKVD prepare lists of persons ... whose sentences were prepared in advance." "In 1937-8, 383 such lists containing the names of many thousands of party, government, Komsomol [Communist Youth Union], army and economic workers were sent to Stalin. He approved these lists." Since 1954, "the Military Collegium of the Supreme Court has rehabilitated 7,679 persons, many ... posthumously." "It would be a display of naivete to consider this [the 1937-8 purges] the work of Yezhov [NKVD chief] alone. It is clear that these matters were decided by Stalin."

"Stalin was a very distrustful man, sickly suspicious.... He could look at a man and say: 'Why are your eyes so shifty today,' or, 'Why are you turning so much today and avoiding to look me directly in the eyes?' Everywhere ... he saw 'enemies', '2-facers', 'spies'."

A coded telegram from Stalin to secretaries of *oblasts, krais,* central committees and NKVD units Jan. 20, 1939 defended "physical pressure in NKVD practice" because "all bourgeois intelligence services" used pressure against Socialist representatives. The investigative Judge Rodos, "a vile person, with the brain of a bird and morally completely degenerate," who handled the cases of Politburo members Stanislav V. Kossior and Vlas B. Chubar, who vanished in 1938, and of Komsomol Secy. Alexander A. Kosaryev, purged in 1938, told the Central Committee Presidium that " 'I was told that Kosior and Chubar were people's enemies and for this reason, I ... had to make them confess that they are enemies.' He could do this only through long tortures ... receiving detailed instructions from Beria."

In many "novels, films and historical 'scientific studies'," Stalin's World War II role "appears to be entirely improbable. Stalin had foreseen everything." It was represented that the Soviet Army, using Stalin's "active defense" tactics, "allowed the Germans to come up to Moscow and Leningrad," then "turned to the offensive and subdued the enemy." "During [and] after the war Stalin put forward the thesis that the tragedy [of] the first part of the war was the result of the 'unexpected' attack of the Germans.... But, Comrades, this is completely untrue."

Hitler had openly said he would liquidate communism. "Documents which have now been published show that by Apr. 3, 1941 Churchill, through his Amb.-to-the-USSR [Stafford] Cripps, personally warned Stalin "of German intent to attack the USSR." "Churchill stressed this repeatedly in his dispatches of Apr. 18 [1941] and in the following days. However, Stalin took no heed of these warnings [and] ordered that no credence be given to information of this sort, in order not to provoke the initiation of military operations." Warnings from the Soviet military attache in Berlin, Capt. Vorontsov, May 6, 1941; from the deputy military attache in Berlin, Khlopov, May 22, 1941; from the Soviet embassy in London June 18, 1941, were ignored and "the necessary steps were not taken to prepare ... for defense."

The USSR had the industrial capability to prepare for the war, but little was done to organize mass production of weapons, particularly tanks, anti-aircraft and even rifles. "I recall that in those days I telephoned Comrade [Georgi M.] Malenkov from Kiev and told him: 'People ... demand arms, you must send us arms.' Malenkov answered me: '... We are sending all our rifles to Leningrad and you have to arm yourselves.' "

"On the eve of the invasion of the ... Soviet Union," a German citizen crossed the border and "stated that the German armies had received orders to start the offensive...June 22. Stalin was informed, [but] as you see, everything was ignored." As a result, "in the first hours and days the enemy had destroyed ... a large part of our air force, artillery" and "disorganized our military leadership..."

"Very grievous consequences ... followed Stalin's annihilation of many military commanders and political workers during 1937-41." Many victims of the repression, despite "severe tortures," fought heroically: Marshal Konstanty Rokossovski, Col. Gen. Aleksandr V. Gorbatov, Marshal Kirill A. Meretskov, Podlas (who died at the front)—"many others."

At the start of the war, "Stalin thought that this was the end" and lamented in a speech: " 'All that Lenin created we have lost forever.' " Stalin "for a long time actually did not direct the military operations and ceased to do anything whatever." He "returned to active leadership" at the insistence of Politburo members, but his "nervousness and hysteria" continued to harm army operations. He lacked "real understanding" of developments at the front and "never visited any section of the front or any liberated city except for one short ride on the Mozhaisk Highway during a stabilized situation at the front."

An incident that Marshal Ivan K. Bagramyan, who " is present at this [20th] congress ... can corroborate": In an "exceptionally serious situation for our army in 1942 in the Kharkov region, we had decided to drop" an encirclement operation. Khrushchev learned from Marshal Aleksandr M. Vasilevsky that "Stalin refused" to concur. "I telephoned Stalin" but "Stalin informed me through Malenkov that I should speak to Malenkov ... although he [Stalin] was only a few steps from the telephone. After 'listening' in this manner to our plea, Stalin said, 'Let everything remain as it is'." The encirclement failed, the Germans "surrounded our army concentrations, [and] we lost hundreds of thousands of our soldiers."

After the war, "Stalin began to downgrade many of the commanders [and] tell all kinds of nonsense about Zhukov" including a false tale that Zhukov had decided when to attack by smelling the earth. Stalin spread through films, novels and histories the legend that victory was due "to the courage, daring and genius of Stalin and of no one else."

Although the USSR was "considered a model of a multinational state," Stalin during the war caused "monstrous ... mass deportations from their native places of whole nations, together with all Communists and Komsomols without any exception"—an action "not dictated by any military considerations." This fate befell: "all of the Karachai" and "the whole population of the Kalmyk Autonomous Republic" in Dec. 1943; the Chechen & Inguish people, whose republic was "liquidated," in Mar. 1944; the Balkars of the Kabardino-Balkar Autonomous Region (renamed Kabardanian Autonomous Region) in Apr. 1944. The Ukrainians escaped "only because there were too many of them...."

Just as the party "came out of the Patriotic War tempered, hardened and unified ..., the so-called 'Leningrad affair' " was fabricated. Those who innocently lost their lives included Comrades Nikolai A. Voznesensky, a Politburo member and planning expert, Leningrad party leader A. A. Kuznetsov, Russian Republican Premier Mikhail A. Rodionov, Leningrad party figure Petr S. Popkov and others.

After the war, "Stalin became even more capricious, irritable and brutal; in particular, his suspicion grew. His persecution mania reached unbelievable dimensions. Many workers were becoming enemies before his very eyes, [and] everything was decided by him alone."

"This unbelievable suspicion was cleverly taken advantage of by the abject provocateur and vile enemy, [Lavrenti P.] Beria, who had murdered thousands of Communists and loyal Soviet people. The elevation of Voznesensky and Kuznetsov alarmed Beria" and he " 'suggested' " the Leningrad "fabrication." The party Central Committee, after an investigation, had "rehabilitated" innocent victims, and "honor has been restored to the glorious Leningrad party organization. Abakumov and others who had fabricated this affair ... received what they deserved."

Stalin dictated party Central Committee resolutions in Nov. 1951 and Mar. 1952 to purge Georgia of an alleged Mingrelian nationalist organization. Actually, "there was no nationalistic organization" in Georgia, but "thousands of innocent persons fell victim ... under the 'genial' leadership of Stalin, 'the great son of the Georgian nation.' "

The Soviet Communist Party Central Committee's July plenum studied the reasons for the Soviet-Yugoslav break and found: "It was a shameful role which Stalin played here...." Yugoslav leaders also were at fault, but Stalin once told Khrushchev, " 'I will shake my little finger—and there will be no more Tito. He will fall.' We have dearly paid for this 'shaking of the little finger.'... No matter how hard Stalin shook, not only his little finger but everything else that he could shake, Tito did not fall.... Tito had behind him a state and a people who had gone through a severe school of fighting for liberty and independence."

In "the 'Affair of the Doctor Plotters' " in 1953, "there was no 'affair' outside of the declaration of the woman doctor [Lydia F.] Timashuk, " in a letter to Stalin, that "doctors were applying improper methods of treatment." But "such a letter was sufficient for Stalin," who said that academician V. N. Vinogradov, a leading Soviet physician accused in the "plot", "should be put in chains" and who told ex-State Security Min. Semyon D. Ignatiev: " 'If you do not obtain confessions from the doctors we will shorten you by a head.' " Stalin told the investigative judge in the case to "beat, beat and,once again, beat." All of the doctors survived and were "rehabilitated."

"In organizing the various dirty and shameful cases, a very base role was played by the rabid enemy of our party, an agent of a foreign intelligence service—Beria, who had stolen into Stalin's confidence [and] had climbed up the government ladder over an untold number of corpses." Among incidents involved:

● Immediately after Health Commissar Kaminsky told a party Central Committee plenum in 1937 that Beria "worked for the Mussavat intelligence service ... Kaminsky was arrested and then shot."

● According to Comrade Snegov, a Transcaucasian party member who had been rehabilitated after 17 years in prison camps, Central Committee member Kartvelishvili-Lavrentiev, a Transcaucasian party secretary, refused in Oct. 1931 to accept Stalin's nomination of Beria as 2d secretary of the Transcaucasian Krai Committee. But Beria received the post 2 days later, and Kartvelishvili was slated to be "deported from the Transcaucasus."

● Lenin's friend Mikhail Kedrov, Goluviev and Baturnia, "who wished to inform the Central Committee concerning Beria's treacherous activity," were "shot without any trial."

● The "old Communist Comrade Kedrov," protesting his innocence of spy and terror charges, wrote that he was threatened "with more severe, cruel and degrading tortures." He was "found innocent by the Military Collegium" but "was shot at Beria's orders."

● Politburo member Stalin "allowed the liquidation" of the brother of Grigori K. Ordzhonikidze, an avowed foe of Beria, "and brought Ordzhonikidze himself to such a state he was forced to shoot himself."

Stalin, "using all conceivable methods, supported the glorification of his own person." "Dissolute flattery [and] loathsome adulation" characterized his short biography of 1948, some of which he "added in his own handwriting to the draft text." He deified the "theme of the Stalinist military genius," claimed authorship of the *Short Course in the History of the Communist Party,* recognized a national anthem praising himself, authorized erection of massive statues of himself while people still lived in wartime huts. He "loved to see the film 'The Unforgettable Year of 1919' in which he was shown ... vanquishing the foe." Actually, "I [Khrushchev] probably will not sin against the truth when I say that 99% of the persons present [at the 20th Congress] heard and knew very little about Stalin before the year 1924...."

Stalin's conceit "gave birth to many flatterers and specialists in false optimism and deceit." Because of his repressions, "many workers began to work uncertainly ... feared their own shadows. ..." He refused to support measures to solve "the difficult situation in agriculture" because he "did not know the actual situation in the provinces"; "the last time he visited a village was in 1928." He proposed in 1952-3 that kolkhoz taxes "be raised by 40 billion rubles," although the kolkhozes' entire revenue in 1952 "for all their products ... sold to the government" had totaled only 26.28 billion rubles.

"Some comrades may ask us: Where were the members of the [Politburo]? ... Initially, many of them backed Stalin." Later, "attempts to oppose ... resulted in the opponent falling victim of the repression [as with] Comrade Postyshev." Bulganin once told Khrushchev: "'It has happened sometimes that a man goes to Stalin on his invitation as a friend [and] does not know where he will be sent next, home or to jail.'" Because Stalin never convened the party Central Committee and seldom the Politburo in his last years, it was "difficult ... to take a stand. ..." Stalin deprived [Klimenti] Voroshilov [currently the Soviet head of state] "of the right of participation" in Politburo sessions and "toyed also with the absurd and ridiculous suspicion that Voroshilov was an English agent." He "also separated" Andrei A. Andreyev from the Politburo. After the 19th party Congress in 1952, Stalin suggested that V. M. Molotov and Anastas Mikoyan "were guilty of some baseless charges. It is not excluded that, had Stalin remained at the helm for another several months, Comrades Molotov and Mikoyan would probably not have delivered any speeches at this [20th] Congress. Stalin evidently had plans "to finish off the old members" of the Politburo.

"Comrades: ... We must correct" the custom of naming communities, industries and institutions for living individual Soviet leaders. "We must abolish the cult of the individual," return to the thesis of the people as the creators of history, restore Leninist norms of "collective party leadership," uphold "Socialist legality" under the USSR Constitution.

Rehabilitations & Purges in Satellites

Khrushchev's speech seemed to be the signal for bloc-wide activity toward a historical revision of Stalin's era as depicted by Stalin's chroniclers and toward the rehabilitation of Stalin's victims from the Communist parties of eastern Europe. Hungarian, Polish and Bulgarian party and government leaders were quicker with gestures of adjustment toward the new scheme of things than were those of Czechoslovakia, Rumania and Albania. Among developments in these 3 countries:

Hungary—Bela Kun, Hungarian Communist leader executed as a Trotskyite in the USSR in the 1930s, was discussed favorably by Hungarian-born economist Eugene S. Varga in *Pravda* Feb. 21 (70th anniversary of Kun's birth). The article described Kun's friendship with Lenin and apparently restored his name to favor. Kun had not been mentioned in the latest volume of the *Soviet Encyclopedia,* published in Sept. 1955.

First Secy. Matyas Rakosi of Hungary's Communist party announced Mar. 29 the posthumous rehabilitation of ex-Foreign Min. Laszlo Rajk and "other comrades" tried and executed with him in 1949 on charges of Titoism and treason. Rakosi also said that "former Social Democrats who have been condemned" were being freed after review of their cases by a special commission of the Justice Ministry appointed in 1955 to study the Rajk trials. A Mar. 29 Belgrade dispatch said that the Rajk's co-defendant Lazar Brankov had been released.

The Viennese paper *Kleines Volksblatt* said Mar. 24 that Archbishop Joseph Groesz of Kalocsa had been freed by the Hungarian government. The Hungarian MTI news agency reported May 12 that Groesz, 68, pardoned May 11 after imprisonment since 1951 for treason, had agreed to cooperate for "good relations between the Catholic Church and the state."

Reports in Vienna May 12 said that ex-Hungarian Pres. Zoltan Tildy had been freed from house arrest imposed in 1948 and that ex-Pres. Arpad Szakasits, Social Democratic leader who succeeded Tildy and later was arrested, had been free for several weeks.

First Deputy Premier Erno Gero succeeded Matyas Rakosi July 18 as party first secretary. Rakosi, 64, blamed poor health for his resignation but admitted in a letter to the Central Committee that he had committed serious mistakes "which resulted from the cult of personality and were opposed to the laws of socialism." Gero, in a speech to the Central Committee July 18, asked that the party "be forgiven for past slanders" against Yugoslavia. But the Central Committee July 22 expelled Gen. Mihaly Farkas, a former defense minister and supporter of ex-Premier Imre Nagy, for "breaches of Socialist legality."

A new Hungarian cabinet announced July 30 by Premier Andras Hegedus included: *First Deputy Premier*—Istvan Hidas; *Deputy Premier*—Gyorgy Marosan; *Foreign Minister*—Imre Horvath; *Coal & Power Industries*—Sandor Czottner; *Chemical Industry*—Gergely Szabo; *Food Industry*—Rezso Nyers; *Education*—Albert Konya.

Hungarian leaders, including Pres. Istvan Dobi and Premier Hegedus, attended state funerals Oct. 6 for the exhumed bodies of Rajk, Communist Party Central Committee members (Maj. Gen.) Gyoergy Palffy and Tibor Szonyi and the party organizer Andras Szalai, all executed in 1949. 200,000 marchers filed past the coffins at the Kossuth mausoleum, in Budapest's central cemetery, in ceremonies watched by ex-Premier Nagy and relatives of the executed men.

Poland—The Warsaw Yiddish paper *Folksstime* Apr. 4 confirmed Soviet liquidation of Polish and Soviet Jewish leaders, writers and scholars in purges during the 1930s and 1948-52. The report, reprinted in the New York *Jewish Daily Forward* and the U.S. Communist Party's *Freiheit,* suggested the possible rehabilitation of Polish Jewish labor leaders Victor Alter and Henryk Erlich, reportedly executed in the USSR for treason in Mar. 1953. Listed as victims of the purges of the 1930s: Ester Frumkin, S. Dimanshtein, Rachmael Weinshtein, Moishe Litvakov, Izi Kharik, Moishe Kulbak, H. Duniets, Mikhail Levitan, Yankel Levin, Herschel Brill, Max Erik and Yasha Bronshtein. Among those on the list identified as literary figures: Samuel Halkin (reported alive in Leningrad), Aaron Kushnirov, Lipe Reznik, Ezra Finenberg, Hersh Orland, Noah Lurie, Itzik Kipnis and Note Lurie. Jewish writers listed as purged in the 1948-52 period: Col. Itsik Feffer, David

Bergelson, Perets Markish, Leib Kvitko, David Hofshtein, Isaac Nusinov, Elijah Spivak, Froyim Kahanovitch, S. Persov and Benjamin Suskin. The *Folksstime* report said that the Jewish Anti-Fascist Committee in Moscow had "been liquidated and its leaders sentenced to destruction." The death of actor Solomon Mikhoel, committee president, previously had been listed as due to an automobile accident. Mikhoel and Col. Feffer had toured the U.S. during World War II on behalf of the USSR's war effort.

Polish State Council (cabinet) changes announced Apr. 27 included the following appointments: Ex-Foreign Min. Stanislaw Skrzeszewski as cabinet secretary; ex-Cabinet Secy. Marian Rybicki as prosecutor general; Jan Domanski as a cabinet member; Kazimierz Mikhail as local government minister to replace Wladyslaw Baranowski, new Polish party education department chief. Rybicki succeeded Stefan Kalinowski, ousted as prosecutor Apr. 20 with State Farm Min. Stanislaw Radkiewicz and Chief Military Prosecutor Gen. Stanislaw Zarakowski. Warsaw Radio said Apr. 6 that Edward Ochab, named party first secretary Mar. 20, had announced the exoneration and release of ex-party Secy. Gen. Wladislaw Gomulka, ex-Deputy Premier Marjan Spychalski, ex-Deputy Defense Min. Waclaw Komar and others jailed in 1951 and 1953 on charges of Titoism.

The ouster of Polish Justice Min. Henryk Swiatkowski and Culture Min. Wlodzimierz Sokorski (replaced by Karol Kurylek) was announced Apr. 21.

The government said Apr. 22 that an amnesty was in preparation for 70,000 political and criminal prisoners (30,000 to be freed and given full rights). An announcement Apr. 28 said full rights and pensions would be given veterans of Gen. Tadeusz Bor-Komorowski's Polish Home Army, which had been aligned with the West and had staged the Warsaw uprising during World War II.

Bulgaria—Vulko Chervenkov, 55, reputed to be pro-Stalinist and anti-Titoist, resigned Apr. 16 as Bulgarian premier (his post since 1950). Parliament in Sofia accepted his resignation, then elected Anton Yugov, 52, chief of the Bulgarian Communist Party Politburo whom Chervenkov had demoted from interior to industry minister in 1950, as new premier Apr. 17. The Central Committee disclosed Apr. 16 that it had exonerated the late former deputy premier and Communist Party Secy. Traicho Kostov, who was deposed and executed in 1949 on charges of Titoism and treasonable alliances with U.S. and British spies.

Czechoslovakia — Prague radio broadcast Apr. 25 that Deputy Premier and Defense Min. Alexej Cepicka, son-in-law of the late Pres. Klement Gottwald, had been "relieved of his posts because of mistakes and shortcomings" and that Bohumil Lomsky had been named defense minister. Premier Viliam Siroky said Apr. 13 that "certain manifestations of anti-Semitism" and Titoism had been wrongly introduced into the 1952 trial of Rudolf Slansky and 13 others but that the main charges against Slansky and ex-Foreign Min. Vladimir Clementis still stood. Siroky said that ex-Deputy Foreign Min. Artur London, Vavro Hajdu and ex-Deputy Foreign Trade Min. Evzen Loebl, all tried with Slansky, were being released and that a pardon was being studied for Israeli citizen Mordecai Oren. The trade union paper *Prace* said Apr. 25 that a wave of officially-initiated anti-Semitism had followed the Slansky trial, that World War II veterans of Western armies had faced discrimination and that huge police political dossiers had followed Czechoslovak citizens "almost to the grave."

Prague reports June 23 said Party First Secy. Antonin Novotny had told a Communist Party national conference: The party's pre-"liberation" line was "correct [and] we have carried it out"; many "incorrect views" had been expressed since the February Soviet Communist Party congress; a 5-man commission under Interior Min. Rudolf Barak was reviewing the case. Novotny told the Central Committee Mar. 31 that the Communist Party had created a "cult of the individual" in memorializing Gottwald.

Rumania—The Communist party in Rumania, the final location of the soon-to-be abolished Cominform, had actually done nothing to reform itself as a de-Stalinized organization beyond adopting Mar. 30 a resolution to the effect that Stalin's guidance had led it into error. The resolution spoke of "incorrect tactical decisions" made by the Rumanian Workers' (Communist) Party in the former period and the party's failure strictly to observe Lenin's principles on Communist party democracy. (Gheorghe Gheorghiu-Dej, the party's first secretary, pledged at the same Central Committee session that the Central Committee's plenums would take place more frequently and said that several members of Rumania's security police would face punishment for grave illegalities.)

Rumania announced May 7 that Dimitru Petrescu had been relieved of office as a deputy premier but did not reveal whether he remained as finance minister.

Appeasement of Tito Continues

Yugoslavia and Czechoslovakia Feb. 11 signed an economic agreement reported to give Yugoslavia $100 million in damages for the disruption of economic relations during the Tito-Cominform dispute.

A Yugoslav-Soviet agreement on cultural cooperation calling for the exchange of scientists, students and cultural workers was initialed in Belgrade Mar. 30.

Vyacheslav Molotov's resignation as Soviet foreign minister was announced without explanation June 1 in Moscow. Dmitri Trofimovich Shepilov, 50, editor of *Pravda* since 1952, was named as his successor in the Foreign Ministry. Molotov remained a first deputy premier.

The USSR's change in foreign ministers, which preceded a visit to Moscow beginning June 2 by Pres. Tito, was generally interpreted in Yugoslavia and the West as a conciliatory Soviet gesture toward Tito as well as a symbol of change in Soviet diplomatic tactics. Tito had frequently implied during the past 8 years that he regarded Molotov as a major Soviet foe of the Yugoslav regime. Molotov and Stalin had signed letters to Tito that led to the Yugoslavic's break with the Cominform in 1948. When Molotov criticized Tito in a speech to the Supreme Soviet in Feb. 1955, Tito issued a sharp reply that was published in *Pravda*.

Tito received an elaborate welcome when he arrived in Moscow June 2 for a 3-week visit to the USSR and talks with Soviet leaders on the restoration of friendly Yugoslav-Soviet relations. The entire Soviet Communist Party Presidium and chief cabinet members, formally led by Soviet Pres. KlimentiYe. Voroshilov and including Molotov, greeted his train at Kievsky Station. Tito acknowledged the welcome with a speech in Russian in which he said: "Something unheard of and tragic took place between us" to cause the Yugoslav-Cominform break; he

had believed that "the time would come when everything sepa-
rating us would be overcome," and "this time has come." (Tito
had conferred with Italian Communist Party leader Palmiro
Togliatti in Belgrade May 29 before leaving for Moscow.)

Tito and Khrushchev were surrounded by excited crowds
when they strolled informally on Gorky St. in Moscow June 4.
They retreated into an ice cream parlor when the swarm of
admirers became too dense. Tito visited the Lenin-Stalin
mausoleum in Red Square June 4 and left a wreath inscribed
only to Lenin. He said at a luncheon hosted by Premier Bulganin June 5 that Soviet "initiatives ... in the last few years
have contributed substantially to the lessening of tension in the
world." He praised Russia's announced plan for reduction of its
armed forces but said disarmament eventually must be achieved
within the framework of the UN. (Bulganin, in a message to
the Yugoslav people May 29, had asserted that the USSR
sought friendship without "interfering in the internal affairs of
other states.")

Tito told reporters at a Yugoslav embassy reception for
Soviet government leaders in Moscow June 18 that ties had
been resumed between the Yugoslav and Soviet Communist
parties, and that his Kremlin talks had brought "general agreement about future cooperation, not in the framework of any
general organization, but in the form of bilateral cooperation."
He noted that he had seen a "real change" in the USSR. Tito
refused to comment on Moscow rumors that he had sought
licenses to build MIG jet fighters in Yugoslavia. He had visited
the Black Sea resort of Sochi June 13-17 and said in a speech
there June 17 that "I feel at home in the Soviet Union because
we are part of the same family—the family of socialism."

Tito, speaking in Dynamo Stadium in Moscow June 19,
blamed "the sad thing that happened in 1948" on "evil slander
and distortion." He said that he and the current Soviet leaders
at last had "easily found a common language and mutual
understanding." Khrushchev, in a speech to the same crowd,
said that the Yugoslav-Soviet break had been "temporary" and
that "no power on earth is capable of dividing the Socialist
countries."

A joint declaration of renewed relations between the
USSR and Yugoslav Communist parties was signed in Moscow
June 20 by Khrushchev and Tito. It proclaimed that "the con-

ditions of Socialist development are different in different countries" and said that the 2 parties "have agreed" on cooperation in "complete freedom of will and equality." The agreement rejected as "alien to both sides any tendency of imposing one's own views in determining the ... forms of Socialist development." It called for "the free and comradely exchange of experiences and views" as a "component part of all contacts with other Communist and workers[,] ... Socialist and other progressive movements." It outlined a plan for maintaining relations through personal contact, exchanges of delegations and joint meetings of party workers.

The statement and the text of a pact on Soviet-Yugoslav government relations, signed in the Kremlin June 20 by Bulganin and Tito, were made public by Yugoslavia's Tanjug news agency. The agreement between the 2 governments called for: UN membership for Communist China; a solution of the Formosa dispute; further world arms reductions and a ban on atomic arms; unity talks between East and West Germany; UN aid to underdeveloped areas; Soviet-Yugoslav trade and cultural, scientific and atomic exchanges.

Soviet Defense Min. Georgi K. Zhukov said June 20, on receiving the Yugoslav Order of Freedom from Tito, that "Soviet and Yugoslav military forces fought shoulder to shoulder against German fascism" and that "should war be imposed upon us, we will struggle shoulder to shoulder for the good of mankind." Moscow reports June 20 related that Tito, who later received the USSR's Order of Suvorov, had nodded approval at Zhukov's words and had grasped his hand.

Yugoslav State Foreign Affairs Secy. Koca Popovic said at a Moscow news conference June 20 that "we hope there will be no war" and "consider that ... cooperation with other countries can only serve to remove any danger of war." (Washington sources said June 20 that, despite a review of U.S. aid for Yugoslavia, Eisenhower Administration officials did not feel Tito had been drawn into the Soviet orbit.)

Tito left Moscow by train June 20, stopped in Kiev June 21 and arrived June 24 in Bucharest, where he opened talks with Rumanian Workers' (Communist) Party First Secy. Gheorghe Gheorghiu-Dej, a leader in Cominform denunciations of Tito in 1948-50. According to Bucharest reports June 24, Rumanian party leaders told Tito they would welcome direct contacts with

Western Socialist parties. Joint agreements on relations between the Yugoslav and Rumanian parties and governments were signed June 25 in Bucharest by Tito, Gheorghiu-Dej and Rumanian Pres. Chivu Stoica.

Tito, returning to Belgrade June 26, said that "it is logical that we should have good relations with countries that are building socialism" but "we do not intend to" "harm our relations with the West." According to Belgrade dispatches June 29, Tito had privately expressed to U.S. Amb. James W. Riddleberger his discomfort at Soviet leaders' anti-Western statements in his presence.

(Vice Pres. Svetozar Vukmanovic-Tempo, Yugoslav economics chief, said in an interview with the Belgrade and Zagreb newspaper *Borba* July 14 that Yugoslav production had gained only 4% in the first 5 months of 1956 and that Yugoslavia would need long-term credits from both East and West to balance its international trade deficit and cope with admittedly serious shortages in food and consumer production.)

Soviet First Deputy Premier Anastas I. Mikoyan arrived on the island of Brioni for a day of informal talks with Tito July 22 after an unannounced trip from Hungary. Yugoslav sources had said July 21 that Mikoyan had solicited the invitation, and some Western observers regarded the visit as a deliberate Soviet move to compromise Tito while Yugoslav aid bills were before the U.S. Congress.

Communist Parties Assert Independent Line

The dissolution of the Cominform (Information Office of the Communist and Workers' Parties) was announced simultaneously Apr. 17 in statements issued by the Central Committees of the Bulgarian, Hungarian, Italian, Polish, Rumanian, Soviet, Czechoslovak and French Communist parties. The statements said that, in view of "the modifications that have taken place in the international situation in the past few years," member parties "recognized that the office as constituted in 1947 has exhausted its uses" and "should cease its activities, and the Information Office organ, *For a Lasting Peace, For a People's Democracy,* should cease publication."

The Italian Communist Party newspaper *L'Unita* quoted the dissolution order as saying the move was undertaken to overcome "splits in the working class" and reinforce "working class unity." It said that the ex-Cominform members would battle "according to the particular national conditions of their own countries" and would "find new useful methods of establishing links with each other."

(Moscow dispatches said Apr. 16 that the Cominform dissolution reportedly had been demanded by Tito in return for a reconciliation with the Soviet bloc. Tito had attacked Stalin's domination of Cominform policies and had been ousted from the group in 1948. Immediately after the break, Cominform headquarters had been shifted from Belgrade to Bucharest.)

The British, French, Italian and U.S. Communist parties, acting immediately after the conclusion of Tito's visit to Moscow, issued a series of declarations June 21-26 asserting independence of Moscow's control and questioning Khrushchev's denunciation of Stalin. Actions by Soviet satellite Communist parties continued to reflect policy changes announced by the Soviet party.

According to Washington reports June 26, American experts on the USSR differed in their appraisal of developments—some believing that criticism of Soviet leaders by non-Soviet Communist parties had been directed from Moscow, and others contending that statements issued by Western and satellite Communist parties proved that the USSR had lost control of the anti-Stalin campaign. Among actions by Western Communists:

Britain —The British Communist Party's Political Committee June 21 demanded an analysis "of the causes of degeneration in the functioning of Soviet democracy." It asked for "a more adequate estimate of the role of Stalin" and said the British Communist Party had been forced to rely on "enemy sources" for the text of the Khrushchev speech (which the U.S. State Department had made public). The London *Daily Worker* June 18 printed anti-Stalin extracts from the New York *Daily Worker* and *L'Unita* in Rome. The London *Worker* commented: "Only the leaders of the Soviet Communist Party ... can and ought to elucidate further."

France—The Central Committee June 22 approved a June 18 French Politburo statement asserting that it was "not just" to blame Stalin for "all that was negative in the activity of the Communist Party of the Soviet Union." The Politburo had called for a "profound Marxist analysis" of the growth of Stalinism. It said that "explanations given up to now ... are not satisfactory" and asked for copies of the Feb. 24-25 Khrushchev speech. A 3-man delegation that included Waldeck Rochet, reportedly leader of opposition to French Communist Party Secy. Maurice Thorez, left for Moscow June 25 for talks "concerning the 2 parties and the whole international workers' movement."

Italy—Communist Party Secy. Gen. Palmiro Togliatti told his Central Committee June 25 in Rome that the Feb. 24 Khrushchev speech implied "co-responsibility on the part of those who today denounce the errors." He asked the USSR for "guarantees against the repetition of similar errors" and said the Italian Communist Party must seek "an Italian way of development toward socialism." Togliatti urged "full autonomy for individual Communist movements and parties [and] bilateral relations between them." He told the Central Committee meeting (called June 22 to prepare an Italian Communist Party congress) that on a 1951 trip to Moscow he had successfully blocked Stalin's plan for him to quit the Italian Communist Party and head the Cominform. Leftwing Italian Socialist Pietro Nenni June 23 attacked the Khrushchev analysis and the "Soviet system" for a lack of "political liberty."

United States—The U.S. Communist Party's National Committee said June 25 it had been "deeply shocked" by Khrushchev's revelations concerning Stalin and did not "share the view that the questions dealt with ... are exclusively the affair of the Communist Party of the Soviet Union." The statement refused to accept an "analysis" that attributed "such profound mistakes" to "a single individual." It asked for "a basic analysis of how such perversions of Socialist democracy ... were permitted to develop and continue unchecked for 20 years." The American Communist Party leaders said they represented an "independent Marxist party of American workers dedicated to socialism"; they had been "deeply disturbed by ... information coming from Poland that organs and media of Jewish culture were summarily dissolved and their leaders executed." "Khrushchev's failure to deal with these outrages and the continuing silence of Soviet leaders requires an explanation." The statement noted the lack of "a whiff of self-criticism by the leadership of its own errors."

A Soviet Communist Party Central Committee resolution July 2 attempted to answer foreign Communist criticism of the role played by the current Russian leaders under the Stalin regime. It said that the drive to uproot Stalinism had created "firm guarantees" of continued collective leadership and "that in the future phenomena similar to the personality cult can never appear in our party." The resolution repeated criticisms of Stalin found in Lenin's "testament" and said that "certain of our friends abroad have not got to the bottom of the personality cult and its consequences." Singling out Togliatti's critique of the Russian interpretation of Stalin's rule, the Soviet Communist Party statement said: "One cannot, in particular, agree with Comrade Togliatti when he asks whether Soviet society has not reached certain forms of degeneration."

"Indisputably," the statement said, "the personality cult has inflicted serious harm on the cause of the Communist Party and Soviet society," but in spite of this, "it could not change and has not changed the nature of the social order." "Even Stalin was not big enough to change the state."

The Central Committee repeated July 2 that Stalin's consolidation of power and popularity, backed by the "agent of international imperialism, Beria," had "made the struggle against the lawless deeds perpetrated at the time more difficult." The Central Committee conceded that "it might be asked why" the corps of leaders emerging during the war, often bypassing Stalin, "did not take an open stand [and] remove him from leadership?" "This," it said, "could not be done." There was no "lack of personal courage" among party leaders, but "it is obvious that anyone who had acted in that situation against Stalin would not have received support from the people. Moreover, such a stand would in these conditions have been regarded as a ... blow against the unity of the party and the whole state, extremely dangerous in the presence of capitalist encirclement." "One should also bear in mind that many facts" about Stalin "became known only in recent times, after his death."

Togliatti, writing for the leftist Rome newspaper *Paese Sera* July 3, professed "unreserved approval" of the Soviet Communist Party analysis and made mention of his "incorrect" criticisms. Togliatti said that the statement was a "clarification of questions that have been raised" in the international Communist movement, but he asked for further "frank discussion" of "differences [in] judgment." In an earlier July 3 edition of *Paese Sera,* Togliatti had refused to reconsider his past statements on the anti-Stalin campaign and Western Communist party autonomy and said he had not seen the Soviet resolution text.

The New York *Daily Worker* editorialized July 3 that the Soviet party resolution would satisfy "many Marxists," but that "many will feel that the discussion must continue."

U.S. Communist Party Secy. Gen. Eugene Dennis had said in a New York *Daily Worker* article June 18 that "the crimes that sullied the latter period of Stalin's leadership are unforgivable." He asked Soviet leaders: "Why did these things happen? Were they inevitable?" *Pravda,* the first Soviet newspaper to mention Khrushchev's speech, explained to its readers June 27 that the Dennis article referred to "materials published by the U.S. State Department and entitled 'Report by Khrushchev at the 20th Party Congress'." The Dennis article, as quoted by *Pravda* June 27, asked: "Did some of [the current Soviet leaders] try to bring about changes before the last 3 years? Could the past evils have been checked earlier? How big and serious are the changes now ... ?" Dennis' criticism was also carried by the Polish Communist Party's *Trybuna Ludu* (Warsaw) June 28.

New York *Daily Worker* foreign editor Joseph Clark said July 3, however, that the June 27 *Pravda* reprint had deleted Dennis' references to Soviet liquidation of Jewish cultural leaders in East Europe and that, "if the charge was untrue, all *Pravda* had to do was deny it." Clark added July 3 that "an explanation is long overdue from the Soviet leaders about the physical annihilation of the top Soviet Jewish writers and poets" in the 1940s.

De-Stalinization Encourages Dissent

Among instances of east European unrest apparently stemming from the blocwide program of de-Stalinization:

Soviet Union—Reports of student demonstrations Mar. 7-8 at the University of Tiflis, Georgia in defense of Stalin were confirmed Mar. 23 by Georgian publications reaching Moscow. They denounced recent "hooliganism" at the university and described Communist Party activities in Georgia (Stalin's native province) to indoctrinate the public on the current anti-Stalin campaign. *Zarya Vostoka (Dawn of the East),* official Georgian Communist Party organ, announced Mar. 24 (disclosed Mar. 26 in Moscow) that Sergei M. Dzhorbenadze had been dismissed as Communist Party secretary for the University of Tiflis for "failure in party political work." *Zarya Vostoka* Mar. 23 rebuked Viktor D. Kupradza, rector of the university, for having failed to give a satisfactory explanation for lack of discipline among students.

Soviet First Deputy Premier Anastas I. Mikoyan, on a tour of India, said in New Delhi Mar. 27 that there was "natural" opposition to the new evaluation of Stalin but that the Stalinist "cult of personality" would be overcome. He termed the disclosures of Stalin's shortcomings "criticism," not "attacks."

The Defense Ministry newspaper *Krasnaya Zvezda (Red Star)* May 9 defended one-man military command and attacked the ministry magazine *Voyenny Vestnik (Army Bulletin)* for having charged World War II army losses and unpreparedness to the Stalinist cult Apr. 24.

According to Vienna reports Apr. 30, 200 political prisoners were killed in April after riots and the seizure of 3 Siberian labor camps (Vereshchagino, Verkhne Imbatskoe and Mirnoe) 600 miles north of Tomsk.

Viennese diplomatic sources reported June 7 that 100 persons had been arrested in Tiflis in May after the appearance of posters proclaiming "an independent Georgian Republic."

The Frunze newspaper *Sovietskaya Kirgizia* reported May 19 that the deported Karachai and Balkar peoples had been settled in the Kirghiz SSR and were regaining minority rights and the use of their languages. Settlement of the Chechen and Inguish peoples in the Kazakh SSR was said to have been reported in the USSR in 1954.

The Central Committee organ *Partiinaya Zhizn (Party Life)* Apr. 28 urged "the widest freedom of discussion" despite a drive against "anti-party statements." *Pravda* July 6 rejected any move to form opposition parties or political groups in the USSR as contrary to Leninist ideology. An editorial took the position that "mass meeting democracy" of the workers must be subordinated with "iron discipline" to the will of one person, "the Soviet leader at work." *Pravda* declared that "some people abroad are interested in having in the USSR artificially created non-Communist parties financed by foreign capital and serving its interests." "As for our country, the Communist party has been and will be the only master of minds and thoughts, the spokesman, leader and organizer of the people in their struggle for Communism."

Khrushchev, attending a July 4 U.S. embassy reception in Moscow, told Columbia University Prof. Philip E. Mosely that there was room in the Soviet Communist Party for differences among leaders and that when "we disagree ... we take a vote." In a June 28 article in *Pravda,* French Sen. Leo Hamon had noted Soviet efforts at collective leadership and said that "an important part ... could be played by a well-informed parliament where opinions were voiced publicly" and whose action would "exercise control" over the government "to prevent rash actions."

Various diplomatic and press reports from Moscow in November and December mentioned unrest among students and workers. Western diplomatic accounts cited by the *N.Y. Times* Dec. 1 told of a sitdown strike in the Kaganovich ball-bearing plant in Moscow. The Soviet press disclosed Dec. 4 that several prominent Kiev writers and Leningrad student leaders had been rebuked for deviations on ideology and art. A *France Soir* (Paris) dispatch from Stockholm Dec. 19 carried the report that the Putilov factory in Leningrad, as well as Moscow's Kaganovich plant, had been tied up by a strike for higher pay and better working conditions. Reports from French and British diplomatic sources Dec. 20 affirmed that Moscow University students recently had refused to hear a speech by Khrushchev. Washington diplomatic sources disclosed Dec. 20 that strikes had occurred in industries in the Ural Mountains and Don River valley. The Moscow newspaper *Sovetskaya Rossiya (Soviet Russia)* Dec. 22 denounced "demagogic" speeches made recently by students of the Urals Polytechnic Institute in Sverdlovsk.

Czechoslovakia—Students in Prague were permitted May 20 to revive a traditional May Festival parade lampooning officials with whose work they found fault. Complaints were demonstrated against housing, food, textbooks, and courses of study. The students criticized the practical application of Marxism in their country. A May 27 *N.Y. Times* report said demands drafted by the Czechoslovak Youth Union of the Prague Institute of Pedagogics had requested full press coverage of events, access to foreign periodicals and broadcasts and an end to the index of prohibited books.

Education Min. Frantisek Kahuda June 26 rejected demands for academic freedom, ordered restoration of "class selection" of university students and urged party indoctrination of youth.

REVOLT IN POLAND

Poznan Riots

In the midst of the worldwide Communist policy upheaval, workers in Poznan June 28 struck, rioted and began a 3-day armed rebellion against depressed living conditions, the continued presence of Soviet forces and the Communist regime. The disorders, which were witnessed by many Westerners attending the Poznan International Fair, were the most severe in eastern Europe since the uprising by East German workers in June 1953.

Polish and West German dispatches June 28-29 said that strikers, led by Zispo (Stalin) Engineering Plant workers protesting their bonus system, blocked Poznan streets June 28 chanting "Bread, bread!" and "We want freedom!" The crowds then attacked the Security Police Headquarters and jail, the United Workers (Communist) Party building and a foreign-broadcast jamming station.

Firing reportedly began June 28 after strikers drew arms from Zispo plant guardrooms and Polish Army forces entered the city. Western observers said the first infantry and tank units to arrive fraternized with the rebels and at least one tank crew joined the strikers and opened fire on Security Police

Headquarters. Poznan was surrounded June 28 and a military curfew imposed. Fighting was said to have continued sporadically through June 29 and early June 30 until it ended in suppression of the revolt.

Warsaw Radio said June 30 that 48 persons had been killed in Poznan. Another Polish broadcast said July 2 that 424 wounded had been treated at hospitals and aid stations. Western businessmen and correspondents, in Poznan for the 25th Poznan International Fair June 17-July 1, estimated the death toll at 200 to 300. Berlin dispatches said July 1 that 1,000 strikers had been arrested.

(Poznan [population 327,192 by 1950 estimate], lies 155 miles east of Berlin. It was developed by West Slavs as a port city on the Warta River before the coming of Christianity in the 10th century. It passed to Prussia in 1793 and became a German city known as Posen until reincorporated into Poland when the country was formed anew after World War I. Nazi Germany reoccupied it during most of World War II. Poznan's International Fair was established in 1922.)

Press accounts June 28-July 1 gave no indication of a spread of the revolt to other Polish cities and despite the extension of armed patrols and security precautions to Warsaw July 1. A private West German intelligence service, however, said July 3 that troops and aircraft had inflicted heavy losses on a rebel band driven from a forest 50 miles north of Poznan, and travelers arriving in Berlin July 3 reported "a center of agrarian discontent" at Ostrow-Kalisz, 70 miles southeast of Poznan.

Other eastern European governments warned of action they would take to prevent similar revolts. The East German Socialist Unity (Communist) Party newspaper *Neues Deutschland* said June 30 that "the workers and peasants state can be of steel-hard rigor." Prague Radio said June 30 that "anybody who raises his hand against the regime will have his hand chopped off." A Budapest newspaper reportedly said June 30 that "the Poznan provocation is bound to fail," and "we are not going to deviate from our adopted path."

The Polish news agency PAP, in a June 28 communique entitled *Events in Poznan,* blamed "imperialist agents" and "underground reactionaries" for the uprising and said that the rebels would be punished "with all severity of the law."

Premier Jozef Cyrankiewicz, who was reported to have visited Poznan June 28-30, said in a statement broadcast June 29 that "provocateurs" had taken advantage of "the undoubtedly existing dissatisfaction in a number of industrial enterprises" caused by "mistakes" which "must and will be immediately corrected." Cyrankiewicz promised trials for "those found with arms in their hands," but said that the outbreak would not stop "the process of democratization of Poland's political life." The *Gazeta Poznanska* editor Lech Jestka said July 1 that 300 persons had been arrested and would be tried by military or civilian courts. Berlin reports said July 3 that trials of "secondary" rebel leaders had begun and that "political trials" would follow for revolt ringleaders.

Reports via Berlin July 1 said that a bulletin given visitors at the Poznan International Fair had said that the Polish government "was carefully distinguishing between provocateurs" and "the workers of Poznan, who filed justified demands and protested against unjustified cuts of their wages." German correspondents said July 2 that Polish officials had told them the uprising was instigated by "the Gehlen organization," a private intelligence agency commanded by ex-Wehrmacht Lt. Gen. Reinhard Gehlen.

Warsaw Radio said July 1 that Radio Free Europe leaflets had been found on some rebels, who were said to have come from "many towns," indicating mobilization of "the entire Polish underground" for the Poznan outbreak.

July 2 a Soviet Communist Party Central Committee resolution criticized Stalin and also asserted that "the anti-people's demonstrations in Poznan were paid [for] from" an American "appropriation of $25 million for subversive activity, which is cynically being called 'an encouragement of freedom beyond the Iron Curtain.'" The resolution denounced "American monopolist capital" for "appropriating large sums for intensifying subversive activity in the Socialist countries" and "trying to activize the 'cold war.'" It said the U.S. Congress had provided $100 million during the cold war, "in addition to funds being spent unofficially," to support "subversive activity in the countries of people's democracy and the Soviet Union."

The U.S. State Department said July 2 that the Soviet charges were "wholly false" and that the riots were a "surge of pent-up bitterness on the part of an oppressed and exploited people." The State Department emphasized that "the whole world is watching closely the ... treatment of the people of Poznan." A U.S. Senate resolution July 2 lauded the Poznan rebels for "courage in resisting ... tyranny." A U.S. House of Representatives resolution July 3 asked that Pres. Eisenhower bring the issue of the revolt before the U.N.

U.S. Acting State Secy. Herbert Hoover Jr. June 30 asked the American Red Cross to conduct inquiries on whether a U.S. surplus food gift would be accepted by Poland to relieve the "reported hunger and distress of the Polish people."

The Yugoslav League of Communists' newspaper *Borba* June 30 called the revolt "reactionary and destructible" and said it had been directed by Stalinists against the "democratization" of Poland. The Italian leftist newspaper *Paese Sera* said June 30 that the outbreak proved that the road to Socialism is "steep and full of obstacles" and that "men cannot be asked to make excessive sacrifices." Rome's Left Socialist *Avanti* denounced dealing with provocateurs by machine-gunning the people of Poznan.

French Foreign Min. Christian Pineau said in Lille June 29 that the Poznan uprising proved the existence of basic changes in the Communist world and the "need for us to reexamine our approach to East-West relations." British diplomats were reported June 29 to feel that the disorders stemmed from local industrial grievances, rather than from widespread political unrest.

Government Reprisals

Reports carried to Berlin by travelers from Poland said July 4 that a "liberal" faction headed by Premier Cyrankiewicz favored leniency toward persons arrested for the uprising, while a "Stalinist" group under Polish Party First Secy. Edward Ochab wanted "firmness" toward the prisoners (estimated at 500 to 2,000 in reports July 5). The Polish government, answering July 7 a British Labor Party appeal for "restraint in dealing with ... Poznan," said it would not be guided by "any feeling of revenge" but that "those responsible" must "be brought to justice." Reports July 5 said that a party committee headed by Edward Gierek, party secretary and a Sejm parliament member for Poznan, had begun "a long and exhaustive" investigation to ensure that "innocent people or people involved accidentally" did not suffer.

Auto & Tractor Industry Min. Julian Tokarski was dismissed July 8 and the ministry was incorporated into the Engineering Ministry under Electric Power Min. Boleslaw Jaszczuk. Engineering Min. Roman Fidelski became Jaszczuk's deputy July 8. Tokarski had been responsible for negotiations with a delegation of Poznan workers in Warsaw the week preceding the revolt. The government July 5 had distributed 1.2 million zlotys to Zispo Locomotive Plant workers in Poznan as the first of 4 installations to repay excessive taxes conceded to have been collected in 1953-56.

Warsaw Radio said July 4 that the Polish Red Cross had rejected the U.S. offer of surplus food but stated that Poland was prepared "to buy grains and foodstuffs ... on a basis of equality." Polish Amb.-to-U.S. Romuald Spasowski July 6 protested U.S. "interference in Polish internal affairs" in connection with State Department statements following the rebellion.

Trials began Sept. 27 in Poznan, for 3 youths (aged 18-20) charged with participation in the mob murder of a security policeman and for 9 persons accused of stealing arms and attacking civil and security police buildings during the June 28-30 riots. 200 spectators, including representatives of Western embassies, Western newsmen and 3 Western lawyers, attended the murder trial, at which State Prosecutor Alfons Leman conceded Sept. 27 that police had used "active violence" on suspected rioters, that 10 policemen were facing trial and that 4, including the Poznan police chief, had been dismissed. The court Sept. 29 barred the use of pretrial statements obtained from the accused under duress. Defense counsel said Oct. 2 that the riots had marked "a turning point in the political and social life of Poland." (Pres. Eisenhower called upon the Polish government Sept. 26 to give "tangible evidence" that Stalinist methods had been corrected through "fair and open" Poznan trials "with *bona fide* legal counsel" for the defense.)

The court Oct. 8 convicted the first group of defendants. Trial Judge Wieslaw Celinski sentenced Jozef Foltynowicz, 20, Jerzy Sroka, 18, and Kazimierz Zurek, 18, to from 4 to 4½ years in prison for participating in the fatal beating of the security policeman June 28. Celinski said that the prosecution had not proved charges of murder and that he had considered only statements made in the courtroom, where "the accused could talk freely."

Jules Wolf, trial observer for the Belgian League for the Rights of Man, told reporters in Poznan Oct. 8 that "the Poznan trials are an example for Polish tribunals and those of other countries." Wolf said the conduct of the trials would "accelerate the new course in Poland," but he criticized the presumption of guilt of the accused and the practice of holding prisoners without legal counsel "at the mercy of the prosecutor."

The 2d group of Poznan defendants consisted of the other 9 youths accused of stealing arms and attacking civil and security police buildings. Their defense counsel, a former head of the lawyers' guild in Poznan, invoked Marxist principles Oct. 9 to link the June 28 outbreak with conditions prevailing in Poland. The state prosecutor Oct. 8 had demanded the death penalty for all 9.

A 3d group of rioters, 10 men aged 18 to 25, went on trial Oct. 5 on charges of stealing arms and attacking secret police headquarters.

(Judge Franciszek Wrobleski, president of Poznan's courts, said Oct. 7 that 4 new trials originally scheduled for the next 10 days had been postponed. He said the 3 trials under way had taken longer than planned.)

Deputy Foreign Trade Min. Roman Fidelski and Foreign Trade Undersecy. Edward Dobrynowicz were suspended Sept. 29 from their posts pending inquiry into their role in labor unrest. Action against Fidelski was for his part in the strike of the Stalin plant workers that preceded the revolt.

Gomulka Appointed Party Secretary

Radio Warsaw Oct. 9 announced the resignation of Hilary Minc as a first deputy premier and party Politburo member. Minc, 51 and reportedly a leukemia victim, blamed ill health for his resignation, but Warsaw reports Oct. 9 linked it to the expected restoration of former Polish Party First Secy. Wladyslaw Gomulka to his party posts. Gomulka, who had opposed Minc's drive for rapid collectivization of the peasantry in 1947-9, had been rehabilitated.

A new Politburo was elected Oct. 21. It pledged commitment to the development of greater internal freedom and a Polish communism independent of Soviet control. The new body was headed by Gomulka. Polish Marshal Konstanty K. Rokossovski was dropped from membership. The election of the Politburo followed (a) a flying trip to Warsaw by a Soviet Communist Party delegation led by Khrushchev Oct. 19-20 and (b) reports of a clash between Polish and Soviet troops on the Polish-East German frontier near Stettin (Szczecin) Oct. 19.

Key figures in the Polish shift were Gomulka and Rokossovski. Gomulka, who became first secretary of Polish United Workers' Party Oct. 21, was considered a symbol of opposition to Russian domination. Imprisoned in Aug. 1951 for rightist and nationalist deviation, he had been released in Dec. 1954, reinstated in party Aug. 4, 1956 and reelected to the Polish party Central Committee Oct. 19. Born Feb. 6 1905 in Krosno, Rzeszow Province, Gomulka had started work as a blacksmith at 14, joined in organizing Communist youth and labor groups after World War I. Imprisoned repeatedly by the government during the 1920s and 1930s, he was in Lodz jail when World War II began but joined in the defense of Warsaw as a member of a workers' battalion. Following the defeat of Poland in 1939, Gomulka crossed into Soviet-occupied territory and later settled in Lodz. He worked in the Communist resistance organized in Lodz and Warsaw after the German invasion of Russia in 1941, became a Polish Workers' Party secretary in 1943 and joined the Lublin Committee of National Liberation in 1944. Elected vice premier and party first secretary following World War II, Gomulka had advocated an early form of "national communism." He was dismissed as Polish United Workers' Party (PUWP) first secretary Sept. 5, 1948, at the height of the campaign against Titoism, was dropped from the cabinet Jan. 21, 1949 and was ousted from the party Nov. 14, 1949.

Rokossovski, excluded from the new Politburo Oct. 21, had been named to the Central Committee (CC) Nov. 14, 1949 at the same meeting at which the CC expelled Gomulka. He became defense minister and marshal of the army Nov. 7, 1949 after being "placed at the disposal of the Polish government" by the USSR. Rokossovski entered the CC Politburo May 11, 1950. His supporters had justified his entry into Polish political life after a career as a high Soviet army officer on the grounds of Polish citizenship (adopted in 1944) and of birth (allegedly in Warsaw in 1896). Rokossovski had begun his army career as a Russian military school cadet, had entered the Czarist armies during World War I and had reached rank of major. In 1917, according to Soviet sources, he joined the Red Guards and took part in the Bolshevik Revolution, civil war and the 1919-20 Russo-Polish campaign. He reportedly joined the Soviet Communist Party in 1919 and attended Frunze Military Academy as a specialist in air and tank warfare. Reports of his imprisonment during Stalin's 1937-41 purges of the Soviet Army were substantiated by Khrushchev in his speech to the 20th party Congress. Rokossovski reportedly was released for service at the front on the intercession of the then Soviet army chief of staff Boris N. Shaposhnikov after a June 1941 German invasion of Russia. He entered the war as a colonel, was credited with leading the defense of Smolensk (1941), Moscow and Orel (1941-2) and offensives at Stalingrad (1942-3) and Warsaw (1944). Rokossovski was married to a Russian.

The PUWP Central Committee had met Oct. 19 to act on Gomulka's reinstatement and the selection of a new Politburo. The old Politburo, headed by Ochab, resigned, and the Central Committee readmitted Gomulka, Gen. Marjan Spychalski, former Vice Defense Minister, Vice Justice Min. Zenon Kliszko and Col. Ignacy Loga-Sowinski, all ousted with Gomulka in Poland's 1949-50 Titoist purges.

According to reports by Warsaw correspondent Sidney Gruson, appearing in the *N.Y. Times* Oct. 21, a motion then was presented for election of a new Politburo including Gomulka and his "liberal" supporters, Ochab and Cyrankiewciz, but excluding the pro-Soviet "Natolin faction"* led by Marshal Rokossovski and the current Politburo members

* Named for the Warsaw suburb where the pro-Soviet Politburo bloc had caucused.

Zenon Nowak and Frantisek Jozwiak-Witold. Action on the
motion was halted by Ochab's announcement that the
Khrushchev mission had arrived in Warsaw. The Central
Committee adjourned to permit Gomulka, Ochab and the current Politburo to open talks with the Russians.

Polish-Soviet Confrontation

Khrushchev landed in Warsaw Oct. 19 with a Soviet
Communist Party delegation including First Deputy Premiers
Vyacheslav M. Molotov, Anastas I. Mikoyan and Lazar M.
Kaganovich, Warsaw Pact Commander Ivan Konev and,
reportedly, Defense Min. Georgi K. Zhukov. Polish sources said
Khrushchev presented the Poles with an ultimatum demanding
retention of their old Politburo and a slowdown in democratiza-
tion. Khrushchev reportedly threatened intervention by 2
Soviet divisions said to be moving toward Warsaw.

Ochab was reported to have told Khrushchev Oct. 19 that
"if you do not stop them [the Soviet troops] immediately, we
will walk out of here and break off all contact. ... Don't think
you can keep us here and start a *putsch* outside." Ochab was
said to have told the Russians that the "party and our workers
have been warned and they are ready."

Khrushchev reportedly called Gomulka a "traitor" and
accused him of wanting "to sell the country to the Americans
and the Zionists" after "the [Soviet] soldiers shed their blood
here" during World War II. Nevertheless, the Soviet troops
were said to have been ordered to halt Oct. 19.

The Russian and Polish delegations met for a 2d series of
talks late Oct. 19 after the Polish party had convened to discuss
the Soviet ultimatum. Polish informants said that, in talks
lasting into Oct. 20, the Soviet mission accepted a proposed list
of new Polish Politburo members. (Following the conclusion of
the 2d meeting, the Khrushchev mission left for Moscow early
Oct. 20.)

The Polish party Central Committee was convened immediately after the meeting Oct. 20 to hear members' views on the
political crisis and a 2½-hr. speech by Gomulka.

Excerpts from Gomulka's address:

● "When I was speaking 7 years ago, I thought that I was speaking for the last time to the Central Committee of the party."

● "The leaders of the national economy did not manage to do their job properly. The whole nation had to pay for the erroneous economic policy."

● "The key to the solution lies in the hands of the working class. The future depends entirely on the attitude of the working class, and that attitude depends on the party policy."

● "The working class taught the government a painful lesson. The Poznan workers, demonstrating in the streets, called with a loud voice: 'Enough of this, one cannot live like this, we must return from the wrong way.' They did not do it lightheartedly." "It was a great mistake to picture the Poznan tragedy as a work of agents and *provocateurs*. The causes of the Poznan tragedy lie in us, the party, the government."

● "There would be no Poznan riots if the leadership of the party would not conceal the truth. There would be no bloodshed if the leadership of the party would candidly reveal the truth."

● "It is not enough to change the people in the government to improve the situation. It is necessary to make changes in the system of government. All bad parts in our model of socialism must be exchanged for better ones." "The impatience of the working class comes from the poor living conditions ... Even if we change the whole membership of the party, nothing will change [in our economy]."

● We "must tell the workers the truth: The situation does not allow us to make any considerable increases of pay. The string has been stretched to the breaking point." We must "produce more, cheaper and better ... The insufficient amount of building materials could be overcome by resorting to private enterprise."

● "The imbecility of the agricultural policy in the past period brought ruin to many an individual farmer ... The quotas should be revised in favor of the farmers."

● "The roads to socialism may be various, such as in the Soviet Union, in Yugoslavia and possibly some [other countries]. Every country has the right to be independent and sovereign [or] I would say it begins to be so."

● "In the Soviet Union, the place of discussion within the party has been taken by the cult of personality ... The cult of personality" extended to "every [Soviet-bloc] country," and "even the party" became "totally subjugated ... In such conditions, could the relations between [the Communist parties of eastern Europe and the USSR] be based on the principle of equality? It is clear they could not."

● Party "leaders should set up a commission with the task of examining" past purges of members and ending "matters connected with the activities of the Polish Berias." The most powerful trend "sweeping the country" is the call "for democratization of our life and demands for liquidation of ... the cult of personality."

● The party must fight those who aim at "weakening our friendship with the Soviet Union." The differences with the USSR are "of the past."

● "In order that the party [may] be equal to its tasks [it must] be compact and monolithic ...,,not govern [but] only lead ... The personal composition of the government must be reduced to the actual needs of the country."

● "The truth told to the nation shall become the [people's] source of strength ... It will restore the people's confidence in the people's government and our party. That confidence is indispensable for the realization of our aims."

The Central Committee convened again Oct. 21 to debate Gomulka's speech, then voted in a new Politburo. The members of the new Politburo were Gomulka (first secretary, with 75 of 75 possible votes), Ochab, Cyrankiewicz, Foreign Min. Adam Rapacki, Planning Commission Chairman Stefan Jedrychowski, Col. Loga-Sowinski, Jerzy Morawski (all with 72 or 73 out of 75 possible votes), Roman Zambrowski and Aleksander Zawadski, with 56 votes each.

Excluded from the new Politburo were Marshal Rokossovski, (with only 26 of the 50 votes needed for election), Natolin faction adherents Nowak and Jozwiak-Witold, Vice Premier Roman Nowak, Vice Pres. Franciszek Mazur and Wladyslaw Dworakowski. News of the new Politburo's election was greeted by student and worker demonstrations in Warsaw and other major Polish cities Oct. 22. The demonstrations had begun among Warsaw Polytechnic students, 5,000 of whom cheered Gomulka's name at a rally Oct. 19, then spread to other groups and cities across Poland Oct. 19-22, often taking on an anti-Soviet character.

The new Polish regime acted Oct. 23 to reduce Soviet influence on the armed forces by naming Gen. Marjan Spychalski as chief of the army's Political Education Department. He replaced Lt. Gen. Kazimierz Witaszewski, an aide to Rokossovski and reported adherent of the pro-Soviet Natolin faction.

The Sejm convened Oct. 23 to debate the preparation of a new voting law to govern elections scheduled for Dec. 16. Debate was delayed, however, by demands for a review of the current political situation. Deputy Julian Hochfeld demanded that the Sejm stop being "the pseudo-parliamentary idiocy that it has been before."

Warsaw dispatches said Oct. 19-23 that the new government was taking steps against possible intervention by 3 Soviet divisions reported in Poland and Polish army units under the command of former Soviet officers. Polish sources said that workers in leading Warsaw factories, warned of the crisis, had been armed and massed in their plants as potential troops. It was reported that Security Police units, under Gen. Waclaw Komar, a Gomulka supporter, had been mobilized for 2 weeks before the Oct. 19 Communist Party Central Committee meeting.

Among incidents reported between Polish and Soviet forces Oct. 18-21:

● Soviet troops based in East Germany massed on the Polish frontier Oct. 19 and asked permission to cross into Sczeczin. When permission was refused, they attempted to cross anyway, were fired on by Polish units and withdrew.

● Soviet troops were reported to have crossed the Soviet-Polish frontier and to have reached Siedlce, 55 miles from Warsaw, Oct. 19. They reportedly began withdrawing toward their bases in the USSR Oct. 21.

● Other Soviet units, including an armored force estimated at 800 tanks, were said to be moving on Warsaw from Western Poland Oct. 19. It was reported that they were halted by Polish Security Police units near Sochaczew, 33 miles west of Warsaw, Oct. 19 and that they were withdrawn Oct. 21.

● An "incident" was reported between Polish forces and "a large concentration" of Soviet troops Oct. 19-20 near Sochabeztycz, 60 miles west of Warsaw.

● A Soviet tank unit moving on Warsaw before the Communist Party Central Committee meeting reportedly rammed a train Oct. 18.

Soviet forces in Poland, believed to be under Marshal Konev's command, began maneuvers Oct. 22 near Warsaw, Lodz and Lublin. It was reported that the new Politburo had been given assurances that the maneuvers would be ended quickly. Rokossovski reportedly had assured the Central Committee Oct. 21 of the Polish army's loyalty to the Warsaw government. Army, navy and air force units adopted resolutions of loyalty to the government at mass meetings Oct. 19-22. Civilian demonstrations for Rokossovski's ouster as Polish army chief were reported in Warsaw, Poznan, Wroclaw, Krakow and Sczeczin Oct. 22.

2 Soviet cruisers reported lying in the Zatoka Gdanska (Gulf of Danzig) since Oct. 19 asked and were refused permission to enter Gdansk's harbor Oct. 22. Polish sources said that Khrushchev, in phone conversations with Gomulka Oct. 23, had agreed to end all unusual Russian military activity in Poland by Oct. 24. Khrushchev was said to have pledged the withdrawal of the 2 Soviet cruisers off Gdansk and the removal of a Soviet army tank force encamped near Lodz (75 miles west southwest of Warsaw) to its base near Legnica in southwestern Poland. Russian destroyers sighted Sept. 22 off Puck (Putzig) and Swinoujscie (Swinemunde) were reported gone by Oct. 23.

Chinese Communist Party Chairman Mao Tse-tung Oct. 21 telegraphed congratulations to Gomulka on his election as party first secretary. Reports from Warsaw Oct. 15 said Chinese Foreign Min. Chou En-lai had backed the Polish campaign for independence in talks in September with the then First Secy. Ochab, who had been visiting the Chinese 8th Party Congress.

Polish Developments Strain Relations with Yugoslavia

A *N.Y. Times* dispatch from Warsaw Sept. 23 reported the existence of a Soviet Communist Party Central Committee letter that was said to have "reassessed" the role of the Yugoslav League of Communists. The *Times* quoted "well informed" Polish authorities as saying that the letter labeled the Yugoslav party as "leftist but not truly Marxist-Leninist."

The Polish informants said the letter was the outgrowth of a dispute in the Soviet Presidium over the continuation of de-Stalinization policies. (An "old Stalinist" majority in the Presidium, led by Molotov and Mikhail A. Suslov, the Soviet party's east European affairs expert, was said to have outvoted a minority bloc led by Khrushchev and Soviet Premier Nikolai Bulganin and demanded a further slowdown of the post-Stalin liberalization movement. Belgrade sources said Sept. 28 that Molotov and Suslov, joined by First Deputy Premiers Lazar M. Kaganovich, Mikhail G. Pervukhin and Georgi M. Malenkov, had attacked the Yugoslav influence on the Soviet Union's relations with other east European countries and had pointed out the Poznan riots as one result of the de-Stalinization campaign.)

On a mission believed to concern the deteriorating relattions with Yugoslavia, Khrushchev arrived in Belgrade Sept. 19 for a "private visit." He toured Zagreb and talked with Tito Sept. 22-26 on the island of Brioni. Tito and Khrushchev, accompanied by Tito's wife, Yugoslav Vice Pres. Aleksander Rankovic and Djuro Pucar-Stari, a Yugoslav party Politburo member and chairman of Bosnia-Hercegovina's Republican Assembly, then flew to Sevastopol on the Soviet Black Sea coast Sept. 27.

Belgrade informants Sept. 27 linked the abrupt Tito-Khrushchev flight to continued Yugoslav-Soviet differences, particularly in the sphere of party relations. The reported differences were blamed on (1) a slowdown in liberalization and independence promised the members of the Soviet bloc in the Yugoslav-Soviet declaration of June 20, (2) Soviet anger at harsh Yugoslav treatment of ex-Stalinists returning to Yugoslavia from the Soviet bloc and (3) a letter sent by the Soviet Communist Party Central Committee to east European leaders warning against acceptance of the Yugoslavs as true Communists.

Yugoslav Foreign Ministry spokesman Branko Draskovic confirmed Sept. 29 that Tito had taken up "open questions" of "state and party relations" in the Brioni talks with Khrushchev. Draskovic said that the Yugoslav-Soviet differences were "ideological." He acknowledged that Yugoslav leaders knew of the Soviet Communist Party letter, but he said that "we don't know its contents." Draskovic defended Yugoslavia's right to "its own opinions" and denied that the USSR would wring concessions from Tito.

Talks between Tito and Khrushchev at Yalta were joined Sept. 30 by Soviet Premier Bulganin and Hungarian Premier Erno Gero, successor to Matyas Rakosi, ex-leader of the anti-Tito campaign. The Yalta talks remained secret but were reported to concern the Soviet Communist Party letter and continued tensions between Yugoslavia and Hungary. Yugoslav sources in London said Oct. 2 that Khrushchev had urged Tito to join in a new Cominform-type association of east European Communist parties.

Belgrade sources said Sept. 28 that Tito had left for the USSR after receiving warnings from U.S. State Secy. John Foster Dulles that any Yugoslav move closer to the USSR would endanger U.S. aid for Yugoslavia. The U.S. foreign aid bill passed July 9 had stipulated that Pres. Eisenhower must decide by Oct. 16 whether continued aid to Yugoslavia was in the interest of the U.S. $1 billion in military aid held up pending Eisenhower's decision was reported Sept. 30 to include 300 jet fighter planes.

(The U.S. State Department confirmed Sept. 29 that Dulles had written Tito Sept. 19 but denied any threat of termination of the Yugoslav aid program. The State Department said that the message had been in reply to Yugoslav inquiries of Sept. 14 about the International Cooperation Administration's refusal in August to supply Yugoslavia with wheat to relieve severe shortages.)

Dulles said Oct. 2 that the President had asked that the aid bill be studied to see if the decision could be delayed further. Dulles said at a news conference that he believed Tito's "unexpected" and "dramatic" flight to the Crimea was evidence that the USSR had "set in motion forces which they do not dare completely to repress, but on the other hand are not willing to welcome and encourage." Dulles said there was no indication that Tito had shifted from his previous policy of continued Yugoslav independence and greater freedom for the Soviet satellites.

Tito returned to Belgrade Oct. 5 from 9 days of talks in the USSR. He told the Yugoslav press agency Tanjug Oct. 5 that his talks with Soviet leaders had been "strictly private" and centered on "matters of mutual interest." The Belgrade and Zagreb newspaper *Borba,* organ of the Yugoslav League of Communists, conceded Oct. 7 that Tito and Khruschev had discussed Yugoslav-Soviet differences "of an ideological character." *Borba* said the 2 leaders had reviewed disagreements on the "elements of socialism and on the degree of permanent Socialist development in the world."

Judging from what ensued, Tito seemed to have made his points with the Soviet leaders. Tito met Oct. 7 with Bulgarian Communist Party Secy. Gen. Todor Zhivkov in Belgrade. Zhivkov, visiting Yugoslavia since Sept. 22, said Oct. 7 that it was "natural that Yugoslavia and other countries should follow different paths to socialism." An agreement, signed Oct. 7 after 2 days of talks between Yugoslav Vice Pres. Rankovic and Bulgarian Deputy Premier Georgi Chankov, restored Yugoslav-Bulgarian party relations, broken off in 1948. The news agency Yugopress Oct. 9 described the accord as only a "preface" to a "long and gradual" effort to end "distrust and doubt."

Yugoslav Vice Pres. Svetozar Vukmanovic-Tempo met Oct. 6-7 with a delegation of Italian Communists led by Deputy Secy. Gen. Luigi Longo of the Italian Communist Party. The group had arrived Oct. 6 for what Longo termed a study of "the experiences of the Yugoslav party in building socialism." Rome reports said Sept. 30 that the Italian party had moved to back Tito in his discussions with Soviet leaders and was studying the dissolution of the Trieste Communist Party, headed by Stalinist Vittorio Vidali. (Secy. Gen. Palmiro Togliatti urged a 3-day Italian party congress ending Sept. 29 to seek "an Italian, national way toward socialism.")

The Moscow CP organ *Pravda* Oct. 7 printed a speech by Istvan Kovacs, a Hungarian Socialist Workers' (Communist) Party secretary, lauding "further decisive improvements" in Yugoslav-Hungarian relations. Kovacs said the Soviet bloc at last could expect "sincere, close and friendly" ties with

Yugoslavia. *Pravda* Oct. 9 published a speech by East German Premier Otto Grotewohl on the "new relations" between Yugoslavia and East Germany. *Pravda* Oct. 3 had hailed USSR-Yugoslav ties as "built on the firm foundation of the community of Socialist goals."

The Yugoslav Foreign Ministry said Oct. 17 that it "appreciated" Pres. Eisenhower's decision to continue U.S. aid although not sending any heavy military equipment to Yugoslavia until the "situation can be more accurately appraised." The Foreign Ministry, however, rejected Eisenhower's contention that a threat exists "to the independence of Yugoslavia on the part of the Soviet Union." Eisenhower's report Oct. 15 to the U.S. Congress, it said, was "not in conformity with the principle of independent and equal cooperation."

'National Communism' in Action

In what appeared to be an affirmation of "national communism," Polish officials revealed a new leniency toward political prisoners. Polish Prosecutor Gen. Marian Rybicki Oct. 23 reportedly ordered reviews of all sentences imposed on Poznan rioters not accused of either robbery or murder during the June 28-30 uprising. Rybicki, in a report to the Sejm's Justice Committee Oct. 14, had disclosed that 19 Polish army, navy and air force officers executed in 1952 as spies had been posthumously cleared. Rybicki said the executed men had been condemned by "unpermitted methods" in connection with the trial of Brig. Gen. Stanislaw Tatar, World War II Polish Home Army operations chief. Tatar was freed in Apr. 1956. Justice Min. Sofia Wasilkowska said in the report Oct. 14 that more than 35,000 persons, including nearly 6,000 political prisoners, had been freed under amnesty provisions disclosed earlier in 1956. Pres. Eisenhower said Oct. 20, during his campaign for reelection to a 2d term as President, that "all friends of the Polish people recognize and sympathize with their traditional yearning for liberty and independence." He added that "our hearts go out" to all the "captive peoples" of eastern Europe. Eisenhower then said at a jubilee meeting of the United Brotherhood of Carpenters & Joiners Oct. 22 that the U.S. was ready to give aid to Poland and other "freedom-loving" east

European states if they "need and want it and can profitably use it." The President saw such aid as part of an American "mission as the champion of human freedom." The Warsaw Communist Party newspaper *Trybuna Ludu* Oct. 22 charged Eisenhower with "interference in our internal affairs." The newspaper rejected the idea that "changes here mean a new turn in our foreign policy." It asserted that Poland would continue "unity and friendship with the Soviet Union, based on the ideological unity of our parties."

State Secy. Dulles told CBS-TV's "Face the Nation" questioners Oct. 22 that he did not "think we would send our armed forces to East Germany or Poland" to counter possible Russian military moves against the new Polish regime. Intervention in the current political crisis, Dulles said, would be "the last thing the Polish people want." Dulles doubted that the USSR would intervene with "mass military means." He said the U. S. would be ready to aid Poland economically.

Polish officials disclosed Oct. 28 that Marshal K. Rokossovski had returned to the USSR "on leave." A special commission had found evidence that he and pro-Soviet aides had tried to organize a military coup against Gomulka. Many other Soviet military officers and secret police advisers were reported returning to Russia Oct. 29.

Gomulka and Premier Cyrankiewicz assured Poles Oct. 24 that Soviet troops maneuvering in Poland would withdraw to their bases (largely in Poland). Gomulka approved the stationing of Russian troops in Poland as long as NATO bases were retained in West Germany. The 2 to 3 Soviet divisions normally in Poland were said to have been augmented by 3 or 4 shifted from East Germany during the crisis Oct. 19-22. Warsaw Radio reported Oct. 24 that of 154 Poles indicted or convicted for the June 28 Poznan riots, all except 3 youths convicted of killing a secret police corporal had been released.

Stefan Cardinal Wyszynski, 55, Roman Catholic primate of Poland, was released Oct. 28 and resumed the primacy in Warsaw. Gomulka announced Oct. 30 a "complete agreement" with the Roman Catholic hierarchy to restore all seized church property but to bar the formation by the church of any political party or youth movement.

The Polish government Nov. 13 announced Marshal Konstantin K. Rokossovski's resignation as vice premier and defense minister. The Defense Ministry was assigned to Gen. Marjan Sypchalski, a political purge victim in 1950 who served 5 years in prison.

A massing of strong Soviet forces on the Polish-Soviet frontier was reported in Warsaw Nov. 7. Gomulka said in a statement to the Polish people Nov. 4 that they must exhibit "iron discipline" to avoid Hungary's "terrible fate." Cardinal Wyszynski, in his first sermon since his release, indicated Nov. 4 his support of the current regime. He said that Poles must work for "the good of our country" and that "confidence is growing that the appreciation of the meaning of religious peace in our country is deepening."

A Polish delegation won concessions on independence, Soviet military activities in Poland, war debts, a repatriation of Poles from the USSR and economic aid during talks in Moscow Nov. 15-18. Gomulka, Cyrankiewicz, Pres. Aleksander L. Zawadski and Stefan Jedrychowski, State Economic Planning Commission chairman, headed the Polish delegation. Khrushchev, Bulganin, Mikoyan and Voroshilov took part in negotiations for the USSR.

Concessions won by Poland:

● The 2 sides agreed that Soviet forces would continue to be maintained "temporarily" in Poland because of the threat of German aggression against its Oder-Neisse frontier. However, Poland was assured that Soviet troops would not interfere in Poland's "internal affairs" and would abide by Polish laws. The Soviet Union would seek Poland's consent beforehand on the number of Soviet troops to be stationed in Poland, their movements through the country and their activities outside their military bases.

● The USSR cancelled Poland's 2.4 billion-ruble debt for credits received against Polish coal deliveries to the USSR since World War II. The Soviet Union granted Poland credit to buy 1,400,000 tons of grain in 1957 and 700 million rubles worth of other commodities.

● The USSR agreed to aid in the repatriation of Poles "having families in Poland" and those stranded in the USSR since 1945. The Soviet Union promised action soon by the Supreme Soviet

on the "early release and repatriation ... of persons in cap-
tivity" in the USSR.

The communique said that Polish-Soviet relations would be
conducted "on the basis of Lenin's principles of equality among
nations" and that the 2 countries reaffirmed their "similarity of
views" on "basic international questions." Gomulka received a
hero's welcome when he returned to Warsaw Nov. 19 for having won what Poles regarded as a veto over Soviet troop movements in the country.

The Polish Trade Unions Central Council Nov. 18 named
new leaders loyal to Gomulka, with Col. Ignacy Loga-Sowinski
replacing Wiktor Klosiewicz as chairman. The council declared
the trade-union movement "independent" of the Communist
party and state. According to the council's announcement, the
party's only role should be to supply members to serve as union
officers.

The Polish government and the Roman Catholic Church
reached tentative agreement Dec. 7 on church-state relations. A
communique issued by a Joint Commission on Church-State
Problems said that Poland's church leaders had "expressed support" for all government policies aimed at the extension of
Polish democracy. In return the government pledged to lift all
barriers to "full freedom of religious life" in Poland. The
government agreed to curtail its veto over Polish church
appointments and to permit religious instruction in the public
schools on request. The government had permitted the
independent Catholic weekly *Tygodnik Powszechny,* suspended
in 1953, to resume publication Nov. 26. Primate Stefan Cardinal Wyszynski was reported to have voiced support of the
church-state agreement Dec. 7.

Another Polish-Soviet accord signed in Warsaw Dec. 17
defined the status of Soviet armed forces based in Poland under
the Warsaw Pact. The agreement made public Dec. 18 by the
Soviet Tass news agency, stated that the "temporary" presence
of Soviet troops in Poland "can in no way affect the sovereignty of the Polish state and cannot lead to their interference
in the internal affairs of" Poland. The pact specified that
Soviet troops could move outside their designated bases only
with prior approval of the Polish government. The accord was
signed by Soviet Defense Min. Georgi K. Zhukov, Soviet
Foreign Min. Dmitri T. Shepilov, Polish Defense Min. Marjan

Spychalski and Foreign Min. Adam Rapacki. The strength and location of Soviet forces and their entry into and exit from Poland was to be subject to future accord. Soviet troops, technicians and dependents would be subject to Polish law. Soviet military construction would require Polish consent. Payment for military facilities would be by special agreement.

The conclusion of the military accord followed increasing anti-Soviet unrest in Poland. Poznan workers climaxed 3 days of anti-Russian demonstrations Dec. 12 by adopting resolutions demanding the withdrawal of Soviet forces from Hungary and their replacement with mixed Warsaw Pact troops or UN forces. Poznan workers abandoned strike threats Dec. 13 after the government promised that their demands would be forwarded to UN Secy. Gen. Dag Hammarskjold. Poles rioting in Szczecin Dec. 10-11 attacked police and wrecked the Soviet consulate before being dispersed. 88 arrests were reported. Demonstrations of sympathy for Hungary's anti-Soviet movement were reported in Wroclaw (Breslau) Dec. 12, Legnica Dec. 13 and Lublin, Kutno and Kalisz Dec. 15.

HUNGARIAN UPRISING

Anti-Communist Riots & Revolt

The pace of liberalization in Hungary quickened markedly after the state funerals and reinterment ceremonies Oct. 6 for former Foreign Min. Laszlo Rajk, Party Central Committeemen Gyoergy Palffy and Tibor Szonyi and the party organizer Andras Szalai, all executed as traitors in 1949. Ex-Premier Imre Nagy's readmission to the Hungarian Workers' (Communist) Party was confirmed by mid-October.

Hungarian writers and students indicated, however, that they wanted more visible changes. Students Oct. 18 demanded that the projected political trial of ex-Defense Min. Mihaly Farkas, arrested Oct. 12, be an open one; they and some trade union journalists blamed ousted Premier Matyas Rakosi for Farkas' alleged crimes.

3,000 students in Budapest quit the Hungarian Communist Youth Union Oct. 20 and formed an independent group. A delegation of students from the Budapesti Muessaki Egyetem (Technical University of Budapest) Oct. 20 called on the

government and left a list of demands, threatening to demonstrate unless the government yielded. The demands included a
free press, abolition of the death penalty, the freedom to travel
abroad for all Hungarians, an end to restrictions on the import
of Western literature, the abolition of compulsory attendance
at courses in Marxism-Leninism and a public trial for Col. Gen.
Farkas. Students Oct. 21 formed their own youth organization
in the southeast Hungarian city of Szeged, where a science
school and a medical college were located.

At an open meeting in Gyor in northwest Hungary Oct.
22, Gyula Hay, a Kossuth Literary Prize winner, presided over
the first "free public and outspoken debate" in the country since
1948. Hay called for the withdrawal of Soviet troops from the
country and an end to interference in Hungarians' freedom of
religion.

News of the mass meetings and demonstrations of
Hungarian students Oct. 20-21 spread quickly among the
population. Mobs estimated at 100,000 gathered in downtown
Budapest Oct. 23 and near the Budapest Radio Building to
demand the ouster of the party's First Secy. Erno Gero, the
formation of a new government by ex-Premier Imre Nagy, the
withdrawal of Soviet troops from Hungary and the trial of the
Stalinist ex-First Secy. Rakosi. Police who fired into the crowd
were reported to have killed one person and wounded others.
500 soldiers and officers of the Hungarian army had been seen
in orderly anti-Soviet demonstrations earlier Oct. 23.

Budapest Radio reported Oct. 22 that an "independent"
"internal and foreign policy" and Nagy's restoration had been
demanded at the student mass meetings. A "stormy ovation"
was given a student speaker who said "Poland has set an
example." Demonstrations were begun Oct. 21 by students
from Budapest Technical College and the Szeged and Pecs
universities.

Gero, in a speech broadcast during the demonstrations Oct.
23, warned against attempts to harm Soviet relations and
charged that some mob leaders sought to restore capitalism. He
pledged to defend socialism. Gero had returned earlier Oct. 23
from Yugoslavia, where he and Yugoslav Vice Pres.
Aleksander Rankovic Oct. 22 had signed a joint communique
calling for closer political and economic cooperation between
their countries. (Hungary Oct. 20 had ended all restrictions on

travel by foreign diplomats except in border areas barred to Hungarian citizens.)

Mass unrest flared into armed revolt in Hungary Oct. 23-30. Severe fighting began in Budapest Oct. 23 after swelling mobs obtained light firearms, reportedly from sympathetic Hungarian soldiers and the Danubia arms factory. Actual violence was said to have begun as security police arrested a delegation of students when they presented a 16-point manifesto for broadcast over the Budapest radio.

The Hungarian government, headed by Premier Andras Hegedus, asked Soviet armed forces to intervene Oct. 23. A Russian armored division moved 80 tanks and some artillery into the city early Oct. 24. Meanwhile communications between Budapest and the outside world were cut, a curfew imposed and the rebels told by radio to surrender by nightfall Oct. 23 under an amnesty offer. Soviet jets reportedly swept Budapest Oct. 23 to track rebel strongpoints. But travelers from Budapest reported that gunfighting continued and that several government buildings were afire in the city. An estimated 150-200 persons were killed in the initial fighting in Budapest.

Nagy Becomes Premier

The Hungarian Workers' (Communist) Party Central Committee, at a meeting Oct. 23-24, readmitted ex-Premier Imre Nagy to the Central Committee and the Politburo and named him premier to replace Andras Hegedus. Nagy, 59, veteran Communist who had previously been chosen premier July 4, 1953, had opposed the policies of the Stalinist ex-First Secy. Rakosi and had been replaced by Hegedus as premier Apr. 14, 1955. Nagy had advocated the restoration of land to farmers, the liberalization of the economy, limited private enterprise and the decentralization of heavy industry. The Central Committee Oct. 24 retained Erno Gero as party first secretary but reorganized the Politburo to include Janos Kadar, 44, deposed as interior minister and as a party leader in 1950-1 for Titoism and held for 2 years without trial under charges of treason and nationalist deviationism. Other members of the revised Politburo: Antal Apro, Sandor Gaspar, Gyula Kallai, Karoly Kiss, Jozsef Koboly, Gyorgy Marosan, Zoltan Szanto, Hegedus and Nagy.

Nagy went on Budapest Radio Oct. 24 to pledge his government to extend democratization, raise living standards and develop an independent Hungarian communism. Kadar said in an Oct. 24 broadcast that the rebels must "capitulate or we will crush them."

Budapest rebel resistance faltered Oct. 24-25 but was renewed Oct. 25 after Soviet tanks and Hungarian security police fired on unarmed crowds in front of the Hungarian Parliament Building and killed an estimated 170 persons. Eyewitnesses said that Soviet tank crews had mistaken security police fire for an attack on their unit and had shot blindly into the crowd. Surviving demonstrators reformed in Szabadsag (Liberty) Square and defied Hungarian troops by shouting for Gero's ouster. 2,000 Hungarians gathered before the U.S. embassy and cried: "The workers are being murdered! We want help!"

Kadar replaced Erno Gero as Hungarian party first secretary Oct. 25. Kadar said in a speech broadcast Oct. 25 that "the leadership of the party is determined to face ... all the burning problems" revealed in the revolt "by deepening of democratization in the life of the party." He promised that talks would be begun with the USSR in "complete equality" for the withdrawal of Soviet troops. Premier Nagy said Oct. 25 that the Russian forces would be "recalled [from Hungary] immediately after the reestablishment of peace." Nagy linked the revolt to "exasperation" with the regime and pledged "a well-founded program of reform."

Rebel leaflets, signed by "the Provisional Revolutionary Hungarian Government" and "National Defense Committee" (leaders unidentified) appeared in Budapest Oct. 25. The leaflets demanded: (1) "A provisional national government." (2) The "recision of martial law." (3) "Denunciation of the Warsaw [Pact] agreement" and the withdrawal of Soviet troops. (4) An "immediate political amnesty." (5) Hungarian socialism on a really democratic basis." (6) Disarmament of the political police. (7) Continued "demonstrations until victory." (8) Recognition of "citizens Imre Nagy and Janos Kadar" as "members of the Revolutionary Hungarian Government."

Fighting continued in Budapest Oct. 27 and spread throughout Hungary, with rebels reported attacking or in control of Gyor, Szeged, Pecs, Miskolc, Szolnok, Sopron, Vac and Hatvan. Soviet troops were said to have evacuated Gyor but fired on crowds in Moson Magyarovar, near the Austrian frontier, killing an estimated 70 persons and wounding 200. Rebel radio broadcasts from major Hungarian cities were monitored Oct. 27, and reports cited mass desertions of Hungarian troops to the rebel side. Soviet troops and Hungarian security police, however, were reported still fighting. Casualties were estimated in the thousands.

Premier Nagy Oct. 27 announced the formation of a "National Front" cabinet, including 2 leaders of the suppressed Smallholders' Party: ex-Premier Zoltan Tildy, also a former president, named state minister without portfolio; and ex-Justice Min. Bela Kovacs, named minister of agriculture.

Others in the new cabinet: Vice Premier and Public Works Min. Antal Apro; Vice Premier Jozsef Bognar; Vice Premier Ferenc Erdei; Foreign Min. Imre Horvath; Interior Min. Ferenc Muennich; Defense Min. Karoly Janda, an army general; Foreign Trade Min. Ferenc Bognar; Commerce Min. Janos Yausz; Education Min. Gyorgy Lukacs; Finance Min. Istvan Kossa; Justice Min. Erik Molnar; Food Min. Rezsoe Nyers; Chemical Industry Min. Gergely Szabo; Machine Industry Min. Janos Csergo; Postal and Telecommunications Min. Lajos Bebrits; Light Industry Min. Mrs. Jozsefa Nagy.

Rebellion among civilians—often joined by Hungarian troops and sometimes befriended by Russians—continued to spread in northern and western Hungary Oct. 27-28. More sporadic fighting was reported from Budapest, which was said to have been ringed by Soviet tanks. Budapest Radio told rebels Oct. 28: "You have won. We must realize that a huge democratic movement has developed which included the whole Hungarian nation. Your demands will be fulfilled." The radio said 3,500 wounded had been hospitalized in Budapest and that 250 of these had died. The Hungarian Red Cross appealed for supplies for 10,000-50,000 wounded.

The Hungarian party Central Committee Oct. 28 delegated its powers for the duration of the crisis to a 6-man group: Kadar, Nagy and the Politburo-and-cabinet members Apro, Kiss, Muennich and Szanto. Nagy Oct. 28 announced a general amnesty offer to all rebels, the dissolution of the security police in favor of a new corps, and plans for Soviet withdrawal from Budapest as soon as the new police force was created.

Nagy announced Oct. 30 that, "in the interests of furthering democracy in the country, the one-party system will be abolished." Nagy reportedly restored legality to the Smallholder, Peasant and Social Democratic parties. He promised to hold free elections, proclaim Hungarian neutrality and insist on the departure of Soviet troops. He said that his government "begs for [rebel] support."

Party First Secy. Kadar and Vice Premier Erdei, ex-Peasant Party leader, broadcast announcements Oct. 30 that the collective farm system would be abolished and enforced produce deliveries to the state ended. Kadar urged all party members to cooperate with Hungary's "fighters for freedom."

Soviet Retreat & Intervention

The Soviet Army—said to have been bolstered from 2 divisions in Hungary to 7 by reinforcement from Rumania and the USSR—began mass evacuation of its troops from Budapest Oct. 30 amid conflicting reports that other Soviet forces were both entering and leaving Hungary through the Subcarpathian border city of Zahony; some were coming from the Ukraine, others going to the Ukraine. Rebels stormed the Budapest security police headquarters, and the 10,000-man security force offered to surrender if granted amnesty. The Hungarian air force charged Oct. 30 that Soviet units still in Budapest had violated cease-fire agreements; it threatened to attack the Soviet units if they were not gone within 12 hours.

The Soviet government announced Oct. 30 that it was "ready to examine" the "question of the Soviet troops stationed on the territory of" Hungary, Poland and Rumania under the Warsaw Treaty. Moscow conceded that there had been "violations and mistakes" in "relations between Socialist states," particularly "in the economic and military spheres." The Soviet leadership expressed "deep regret that the Hungarian uprising had "led to bloodshed" even though forces of "black reaction" had joined in it. The declaration conceded that the "further presence of Soviet troops in Hungary can serve as a cause for an even greater deterioration"; it said Soviet army units would withdraw from Budapest "as soon as this is recognized by the

Hungarian government to be necessary." For 4 days the Soviet government yielded to Hungarian pressure to withdraw from the country. Soviet army units moved out of Budapest to other Hungarian bases Oct. 31, leaving the city under the control of civilian rebels and Hungarian army units. The Hungarian government Oct. 31 sent Moscow a note asking that the Russians fix a time and place for negotiations on their leaving Hungary.

Within a week, however, the situation had been drastically reversed. The Soviet armed forces launched a powerful nationwide attack in Hungary Nov. 4. Reports from Vienna, unconfirmed by the Russians, said Nov. 4 that Soviet Defense Min. Marshal Georgi K. Zhukov was in Budapest at that time. Before the attack, the Soviet army had deployed throughout Hungary an estimated 200,000 men (10 times the normal Soviet force in Hungary) and about 5,500 tanks (3,300 of 20 tons, 1,100 each of 30-ton and 15-ton size, according to a *N.Y. Herald Tribune* report by Barrett McGurn Nov. 12). About 1,000 tanks were brought into Budapest and its outskirts to patrol streets and demolish centers of rebel resistance. The Russians had taken control of Budapest airport and ringed it with tanks to prevent the Hungarian air force from going into action against Soviet forces. Many Hungarians and foreign observers reported that the Russians sometimes violated rules of war by moving men and equipment into position under white truce flags, then taking down the flags when the units were deployed for action.

While pretending to be giving ground in their negotiations with Hungarian Defense Min. Pal Maleter (successor to Gen. Janda) for their withdrawal from the country, the Russians, without any warning, mounted their attack at 4 a.m. Nov. 4 with tank and artillery barrages in the suburbs of Budapest. They spread through Hungary's capital and seized control of it within 2 hours. No effective resistance could be organized by the Hungarian army, whose leadership was displaced, with Maj. Gens. Maleter and Istvan Kovacs, chief of staff, away on their negotiating mission to Soviet army headquarters on Csepel Island 5 miles outside Budapest.

(In testimony before the House Un-American Activities Committee Sept. 10, 1959, Gen. Bela Kiraly, Budapest garrison commander during the revolt, said the temporary armistice agreement between Budapest rebels and Soviet forces had been negotiated by Anastas I. Mikoyan and Mikhail A. Suslov of the Soviet Communist Party Central Committee. Kiraly said Soviet troops had broken the agreement and had crushed the revolt after a Hungarian peace delegation sent to sign the pact had been arrested by Col. Gen. Ivan A. Serov, then-Soviet security chief, on direct orders of Khrushchev.

Khrushchev disclosed Dec. 2, 1959, that some Kremlin leaders had opposed the use of Soviet armed forces to crush the revolt. Speaking at a rally at the Ganz-Mawag engineering works in Budapest, Khrushchev said that "some Soviet comrades expressed anxiety that any aid [against the revolt] would be misconstrued.")

Hungarians learned shortly that Janos Kadar, first secretary of the new Hungarian Socialist Workers' (Communist) Party before his disappearance in Budapest Nov. 3-4, had gone over to the Soviet side, as had several members of Nagy's cabinet. Radio Moscow announced at midday Nov. 4 that a "Hungarian revolutionary workers' and peasants' government" had "appealed to the Soviet command [in Budapest] for help in suppressing the mutineers shielded by the Nagy government." The Moscow-proclaimed government, situated in Szolnok at the junction of the Tisza and Zagyva rivers in east-central Hungary, consisted of Kadar as premier and 7 other men: Deputy Premier Ferenc Muennich, also armed forces-and-public security minister; State Minister-without-Portfolio Gyorgy Marosan; Foreign Min. Imre Horvath; Finance Min. Istvan Kossa; Heavy Industry Min. Antal Apro; Agriculture Min. Imre Dego, and Trade Min. Sandor Ronai. According to the Moscow announcement, ministries not filled for the time being were open to "other parties and nonpartisan persons loyal to our people's democracy and ready to defend ... our Socialist conquests."

Premier Nagy, whose overthrow in favor of Kadar's pro-Soviet cabinet was thus announced, was reported detained when he went to the Soviet embassy to protest the attack. He previously had broadcast news of the attack and had appealed to Maleter and Kovacs (currently prisoners of the Soviets) to return to their defense posts. Ministers-without-Portfolio Zoltan Tildy, Istvan Szabo and Istvan Bibo were the only members able to get to the Parliament Building for an urgent cabinet meeting called by Nagy to consider the new crisis. Tildy, Smallholders' Party leader, negotiated an agreement for Soviet troops to occupy the building after civilians left it.

Bibo went thence to the U.S. embassy, where he dictated a statement saying: Hungary "has not been following an anti-Soviet policy.... It wants to live in a community of free eastern European countries organizing their lives with freedom [and] justice and [to live in] a society without exploitation. I reject the slander that fascism or anti-Semitism stained our glorious revolution. The entire Hungarian nation took part in the fight ... against the oppressive foreign army and the gangs of its henchmen." Bibo told Hungarians "to use all weapons of passive resistance against the occupying army and the puppet government it will set up. I am in no position to order an armed resistance." Bibo then returned to the Parliament Building to remain there as a symbol of the Nagy regime, which he regarded as Hungary's legitimate government.

As Hungarians individually or in groups and mostly youths, began to resist the Russians with small arms fire and homemade "Molotov cocktail" gasoline grenades, the Soviet troops resorted to obliteration tactics. Tanks and artillery heavily shelled buildings, street barricades and other points of resistance, and Russian soldiers armed with tommyguns hunted down rebels. An estimated 20,000-25,000 Hungarians and several thousand Soviet soldiers were reported killed in Budapest fighting Nov. 4-8. Witnesses charged that the Russians blasted buildings and raked streets with gunfire without regard for women, children and other non-combatants and hanged rebels from lampposts—partly in retaliation for reported hangings of Hungarian security policemen hunted down by rebels in the 2 preceding weeks. (Rumors spread that the Soviet bombardment of Killian Barracks, a strongpoint of Hungarian army resistance formerly commanded by Maleter had resulted in the destruction of a nearby children's clinic, most of whose patients were killed. However, a pooled report from U.S. correspondents in Budapest, Nov. 12 said that the clinic, although hit by thousands of bullets and shells, had not been wrecked and that no children had been injured there.)

Rebels ignored a 24-hour surrender ultimatum issued Nov. 5 by Maj. Gen. K. Grebennik, Soviet commander in Budapest, and continued to fight until overcome by force in all but a few isolated districts Nov. 8. Significant armed resistance in the Budapest area continued Nov. 13 only on Csepel, an industrial island in the Danube. Hundreds of public and private buildings, including South Station in Buda, were reported destroyed Nov. 4-8; thousands of structures, including the Czechoslovak, British, French and Egyptian Legations, were damaged; city transit facilities were heavily damaged. Destruction in the city was rated worse than in World War II.

Communist and rebel reports indicated that the Soviet take-over had met with resistance in other parts of the country, including Pecs, Dunapentele, Hegyeshalom, Szeged, Szolnok, Gyor, Kecskemet, Kalocsa and Mohacs. Revolutionaries were said to have dynamited the Becsek Hills uranium mines.

Hungarian Pres. Istvan Dobi served notice Nov. 10 that rebels suspected of murder, arson or looting would be liable to summary execution within 24 hours after their capture. The deportation to Siberia of captured rebel youths was reported under way Nov. 13.

Western newsmen and diplomats, held in Budapest during the fighting Nov. 4-8, often were under fire in going about the city on professional or rescue missions. Austrian Min.-to-Hungary Walther Peisipp, 50, cut off from his legation for several days, made many trips into fighting zones to deliver medicine and food to hospitals and needy civilians. Photographer Jean-Pierre Pedrazzini, 29, of the Paris magazine *Match,* died Nov. 7 of wounds received in a Soviet tank attack. The Soviets let a convoy of U.S. diplomatic families go to Vienna Nov. 5, and a group of U.S. and other Western newsmen was allowed to follow Nov. 10.

UN Action

The UN Security Council, in an extraordinary session in New York Oct. 28, voted 9-1 (Russia opposed, Yugoslavia abstaining) to place on its agenda, at U.S.-British-French request, "the situation created by the action of foreign military forces in Hungary." Soviet delegate Arkady A. Sobolev charged that the inclusion of the item would "incite the armed uprising of a reactionary underground against the legitimate Hungarian government"—for which purpose, he said, the U.S. had appropriated $25 million. He said the revolution was a domestic matter outside UN jurisdiction. Yugoslav delegate Joza Brilej explained that his government opposed "the presence of foreign troops" but thought the issue was being used for "political purposes." (Hungarian Rep.-to-UN Peter Kos, who sided with Sobolev in a statement to the council, was dismissed by Premier Nagy's government Oct. 30.)

The UN General Assembly in New York Nov. 9 approved resolutions against the Soviet attack on Hungary and interference with the delivery of relief to the Hungarians. Measures passed:

● A resolution sponsored by Cuba, Ireland, Italy, Pakistan and Peru demanding that the Soviet Union withdraw its forces from Hungary "without any further delay" and "cease immediately actions against the Hungarian population which are in violation of ... international law, justice and morality." Vote: 48-11 (Soviet bloc, India, Yugoslavia opposed; 16 abstentions, mostly by Arab, African and Asian states except Nationalist China and the Philippines).

● A U.S.-sponsored resolution calling on the USSR to stop interfering with the transport and distribution of Hungarian relief supplies. Vote: 53-9 (Soviet bloc opposed, 13 abstentions). The Assembly rejected efforts by India, Ceylon and Indonesia to amend the measure so as to soften a passage noting the flight of refugees from Hungary due to "harsh and repressive action of the Soviet armed forces."

● An Austrian-sponsored resolution asking that all UN-member countries "participate to the greatest extent possible" in providing humanitarian relief to Hungary; passed without a negative vote but with the Soviet bloc (except Hungary) abstaining.

UN Secy. Gen. Dag Hammarskjold Nov. 8 sent the pro-Soviet Hungarian government a request that it admit UN observers as provided for in a resolution passed Nov. 4 by the General Assembly. Hammarskjold then revealed Nov. 11 that he had asked the Soviet government Nov. 10 for its "assistance" in persuading Hungary to admit UN observers to "travel freely" and "report their findings." Hammarskjold also asked that the Soviets in Hungary cooperate with the observers.

The Soviet-supported Kadar government informed Hammarskjold Nov. 12 that it considered the sending of UN observers to Hungary "not warranted" because "Soviet troops

are in Hungary at the request of the Hungarian government."
However, Hammarskjold said he would not abandon his efforts
to get Hungary to admit observers. Hammarskjold then
announced Nov. 13 that he had made an offer to Hungarian
Foreign Min. Horvath to go to Budapest to arrange for the
distribution of relief supplies through UN agencies.

After Hammarskjold had appealed Nov. 14 for the
Hungarian government to reconsider its refusal to admit UN
observers, the government suggested Nov. 15 a conference on
relief problems between Hammarskjold and Hungarian
representatives in Rome during the UN secretary general's current trip to the Egyptian war zone. Hammarskjold said Nov.
16 that he would meet instead with Hungarian UN delegates in
New York if he could not go to Budapest to establish "personal
contact" with Hungarian officials "directly concerned with the
matter."

(British Prime Min. Sir Anthony Eden said Nov. 20 that
Britain was "glad to have UN observers" in the Suez area to
"limit the effects of the conflict" and that "the world would
welcome similar action by the Soviet government in
Hungary.")

The UN General Assembly passed by a vote of 55-to-10
Nov. 21 Cuba's resolution (a) asking for a halt in deportations
and the return of those deported and (b) holding that the USSR
and the Soviet-supported Hungarian regime were "associated"
with the crime of genocide. The resolution was opposed by the
9-vote Soviet bloc and Yugoslavia. 14 nations abstained
(Afghanistan, Egypt, Finland, India, Indonesia, Jordan,
Lebanon, Libya, Morocco, Saudi Arabia, Sudan, Syria,
Tunisia, Yemen).

An Indian-Ceylonese-Indonesian resolution for the admis-
sion of UN observers carried by 57-8 in the General Assembly
Nov. 21. It was opposed by all Soviet-bloc countries except
Poland, which abstained along with Chile, Nationalist China,
Cuba, Dominican Republic, Egypt, Ethiopia, Jordan, Panama,
Paraguay, Saudi Arabia, Syria and Yemen. Nations voting for
the resolution after having abstained on a similar U.S.-
sponsored measure adopted Nov. 4: Afghanistan, Burma,
Ceylon, Finland, India, Indonesia, Iraq, Nepal.

(A resolution calling on governmental and nongovernmental agencies to give Hungarian refugees emergency aid and help in resettlement was passed by the General Assembly Nov. 21 by 69-2 vote with Hungary and Rumania opposed, other Soviet-bloc nations and Sudan abstaining.)

The UN General Assembly Dec. 4 passed, 54-10, a resolution demanding that the Hungarian government be given a "final chance" to admit UN observers by Dec. 7. Shortly before the vote was taken, Hammarskjold told the Assembly he had asked Hungarian Foreign Min. Imre Horvath, heading Hungary's UN delegation in New York, for permission to visit Budapest Dec. 16-18, after a preparatory visit to the city by UN Undersecy. Philippe de Seynes. Hammarskjold said Horvath had relayed the suggestion to Budapest. The 14-nation resolution was sponsored by Argentina, Australia, Belgium, Cuba, Denmark, El Salvador, Ireland, Italy, Netherlands, Norway, Pakistan, Sweden, Thailand and the U.S. The 9 Soviet-bloc nations and Yugoslavia voted against it. There were 14 abstainers: Afghanistan, Burma, Ceylon, Egypt, Finland, India, Indonesia, Jordan, Morocco, Saudi Arabia, Sudan, Syria, Tunisia, Yemen.

During debate on the measure Dec. 3-4, several delegates suggested that the UN resort to sanctions against Hungary if UN observers were not admitted. India favored the sending of observers but held that Hammarskjold could arrange this during his projected trip to Budapest. (Indian Prime Min. Jawaharlal Nehru told the Indian parliament in New Delhi Dec. 3 that the 14-nation resolution was designed to "humiliate" the Hungarian government. He said he was not convinced that Soviet forces were deporting Hungarians but that Hungary cast suspicion on itself by barring UN observers.)

Horvath led the Hungarian delegation out of the Assembly Dec. 11 after Horvath had protested that Hungary had been "rudely and disgracefully offended" by delegates denouncing the suppression of the Hungarian revolution. Horvath said that Hungary would not participate in the Assembly's work as long as debate on the Hungarian crisis "does not proceed in the spirit of the [UN] Charter."

Hungary Dec. 5 had rejected Hammarskjold's plan to visit Budapest Dec. 16-18. A Budapest broadcast said that his proposed survey of the Hungarian situation would be "unsuitable" at that time. Hammarskjold told the General Assembly Dec. 8 that he had requested permission for UN observers to enter Hungary, Czechoslovakia, Yugoslavia, Rumania and Austria but that only Austria had granted permission.

A U.S. draft resolution presented in the General Assembly Dec. 10 called for condemnation of the USSR for the destruction of Hungary's "political independence." The U.S. resolution, indorsed Dec. 9 by 15 delegations, called for the withdrawal of Soviet armed forces from Hungary and the restoration of an independent Hungarian state. (The U.S. Dec. 7 had proposed informally a resolution calling for the suspension of Hungary's delegation to the Assembly and condemnation of both Hungary and the USSR for the suppression of the revolt.)

A 2d resolution submitted in the Assembly Dec. 10 urged that Hammarskjold travel to Moscow "without delay" to discuss solution of the Hungarian crisis with the Soviet government. The resolution, submitted by India, Burma, Ceylon and Indonesia, "deplored" Soviet refusals to withdraw troops from Hungary. It noted that the suppression of the revolt had brought "violence and bloodshed." It urged the "cessation of existing foreign intervention" in Hungary.

The General Assembly voted by 55-8 (13 abstentions) Dec. 12 to pass a U.S. resolution, co-sponsored by 19 other nations, condemning the Soviet Union's "violation of the [UN] Charter ... in depriving Hungary of its liberty and independence and the Hungarian people of their fundamental rights." The resolution called on the USSR to make "immediate arrangements" for the withdrawal of its armed forces from Hungary under UN supervision. It asked Hammarskjold to "take any initiative" necessary toward ending the Hungarian crisis. The resolution, regarded as the first such direct condemnation measure to be voted by the General Assembly, was supported by all Western and Latin nations and by Lebanon, Iraq, Burma and Ceylon, the latter 2 co-sponsors with India and Indonesia of a compromise Asian resolution withdrawn earlier Dec. 12. India and Indonesia abstained, together with Yugoslavia, Egypt, Jordan, Syria, Saudi Arabia, Yemen, Cambodia, Afghanistan, Finland, Morocco and Sudan. The U. S. resolution was opposed by the Soviet and satellite bloc, which was reduced to 8 votes by the Hungarian delegation's walkout.

Soviet Deputy Foreign Min. Vasily V. Kuznetsov asked the General Assembly Dec. 12 to consider a complaint against U.S. "intervention" in "the domestic affairs of the peoples' democracies and its subversive activity against those states." The Assembly voted by 58-2 (8 abstentions) Dec. 14 to include the Soviet complaint on its agenda. The complaint had been approved for consideration of the Assembly's Steering Committee Dec. 13 after U.S. Deputy Rep.-to-UN James J. Wadsworth supported its inclusion "to have the full truth made known."

Hungarian Foreign Min. Horvath, in a note to Hammarskjold Dec. 12, confirmed earlier reports that, according to his government, Hammarskjold's planned Dec. 16 visit to Hungary would not be considered "appropriate." Horvath, who left New York for Hungary Dec. 14, said that Hungary would reopen talks on a Hammarskjold visit later. Indian Amb.-to-USSR Kumara P. S. Menon met with Soviet Foreign Min. Dmitri T. Shepilov Dec. 12 to urge Hammarskjold's admission to Hungary.

The U.S. State Department Dec. 17 challenged the USSR to open Hungary to UN observers in order to determine whether the rebellion had been spontaneous or planned from abroad. The statement followed Soviet rejection Dec. 17 of an American complaint (lodged Dec. 6) against the deployment of Soviet tanks around the U.S. legation in Budapest.

The special UN investigating committee on conditions in Hungary suspended work Dec. 26 after members Alberto Lleras of Colombia, Oscar Gundersen of Norway and Arthur Lall of India decided that further meetings would be useless.

Other Worldwide Repercussions

Pres. Eisenhower, in a statement issued Oct. 25, called the Hungarian uprising "a renewed expression of the intense desire for freedom long held by the Hungarian people." He said Soviet troops, which under the peace treaty should have been withdrawn, sought "to continue an occupation of Hungary by the forces of an alien government for its own purposes." Eisenhower said at his news conference Nov. 14: "The U.S. doesn't now, and never has, advocated open rebellion by an undefended populace against force over which they could not possibly prevail. We ... have always urged that the spirit of freedom be kept alive; that people do not lose hope. But we have never ... urged or argued for any kind of armed revolt which could bring about disaster to our friends."

State Secy. Dulles, discussing the Hungarian and Polish anti-Soviet uprisings, had told the Dallas Council on World Affairs Oct. 27 that "the captive peoples" could "draw upon our [U.S.] abundance to tide themselves over the period of economic adjustment ... as they rededicate their productive efforts to the services of their own people rather than the service of exploiting masters." He said such aid would not be conditioned "upon the adoption by these countries of any particular form of society." Dulles also indorsed the "freedom of choice" of "newly independent nations [that] prefer not to adhere to collective security pacts." Both Dulles and Defense Secy. Erwin Wilson Oct. 28 denied Soviet charges that U.S. funds and agents had fomented the Hungarian revolt.

(Officials of Radio Free Europe's station in Munich, which some Hungarians said had led them to expect military help in a revolt, contended Nov. 19 that the station had broadcast only "straight news, with nothing slanted or twisted," and that Hungarians may have read into Radio Free Europe broadcasts promises not actually made.)

Anti-Soviet student demonstrations began in Paris Nov. 5. Communist jeering of speeches in praise of Hungarian rebels caused such disorder in the Chamber of Deputies that it had to be cleared Nov. 6. Communist Party Headquarters and the French Communist Party newspaper *L'Humanite*'s offices were sacked by 3,000 demonstrators in Paris Nov. 7. 8,000 Communists, of whom 130 were arrested for disorder or carrying arms, staged counterdemonstrations in the city Nov. 8, while pro-Hungarian rioters invaded Communist Party offices in Marseilles, Rennes, Strasbourg, Alencon, Roanne, Nancy and Lyons.

In West Berlin, crowds estimated at 75,000-100,000 demonstrated in support of Hungarian rebels Nov. 5 at Brandenburg Gate, just inside the city and opposite the East Berlin boundary. (East German secret police were said to have seized the Hungarian embassy in East Berlin Nov. 4 and to have arrested the revolutionary committee of staff members that had taken it over during the Hungarian uprising. Several Hungarian trade officials were revealed Nov. 7 to have fled from East Germany to West Berlin.)

In New York, emigre Hungarians and American supporters, who maintained anti-Soviet pickets near UN Headquarters, demonstrated outside the Soviet UN delegation when a reception for other UN delegates was given there Nov. 7—the 39th anniversary of the Soviet revolution. The reception was boycotted by the U.S. and numerous other Western delegations, as were anniversary celebrations in Moscow. A Madison Square Garden rally held Nov. 9 in protest against the "massacre" in Hungary was addressed by Gov. Averell Harriman of New York, Sen. Clifford P. Case (R., N.J.) and Leo Cherne, Rescue Committee chairman and a leader in Hungarian relief efforts. (The New York *Daily Worker* Nov. 5 criticized the Soviet Union's use of force against Hungary as an action that "retards the development of socialism," "damages the relations between Socialist states" and "weakens the influence of the Soviet Union." The *Worker* Nov. 12 then published a letter from the U.S. Communist Party First Secy. Eugene Dennis taking issue with the paper's criticism of the Soviet Union.)

The Hungarian attack was the target of anti-Soviet demonstrations: in Copenhagen Nov. 6 (a homemade bomb was thrown at the Soviet embassy but failed to explode); in Vienna, Buenos Aires, Montevideo and industrial cities of northern Italy Nov. 8; in Calcutta Nov. 11, where Socialists denounced Indian Prime Min. Jawaharlal Nehru for his failure to rebuke the Soviets for their action in Hungary. Denmark observed a nationwide 5 minutes of silence in honor of Hungarian rebels Nov. 8.

Pope Pius XII appealed in a broadcast to Western and Communist countries Nov. 10 for free nations to work for Hungary's liberation "by all permissible means." Nationalist Chinese Pres. Chiang Kai-shek said Nov. 12 (the birthday anniversary of Sun Yat Sen) that "the Soviet empire ... has been badly shaken [and] is actually on the brink of total collapse." He called on free Chinese to take a vow to "liberate our brethren on the Chinese mainland."

Jean-Paul Sartre, who quit the French-Soviet Friendship Society Nov. 9, announced that he would have no further relations with the French Communist Party and denounced the Soviet action in Hungary "with no reservations." The Rev. Dr.

Hewlett Johnson, the so-called "Red Dean of Canterbury" said in London Nov. 12 that he was "no more able to condone" the Soviet attack on Hungary "than our [Britain's] attack on Egypt," although he held that Soviet intervention was "invited by the Hungarian government" (of Janos Kadar) whereas the Egyptian government opposed Britain's move against the Suez Canal. The Norwegian Communist Party Nov. 12 issued a statement of "worry and concern" over events in Hungary and said that "each nation should decide its own future."

2 prominent British Communists who announced their resignations from the British Communist Party Nov. 13 because of the Soviet attack on Hungary were John Horner, general secretary of the Fire Brigades Union, and Alex Moffat, a National Union of Mineworkers leader in Scotland. 7 other influential members resigned Nov. 14. British Communist Party Secy. John Gollan fled into a police station for protection Nov. 14 when he was chased by a crowd of students in Cowes, Isle of Wight after he tried to speak on events in Hungary and Poland.

Harry Binder and Norman Penner of Toronto resigned Nov. 15 from the Canadian Labor Progressive (Communist) Party because of party leader Tim Buck's defense of Stalinism and of Soviet actions in Hungary and Poland. Italian Communist Party leader Palmiro Togliatti Nov. 18 defended Soviet action in Hungary as a "necessity." The AFL-CIO Transport Workers Union's international executive board announced in New York Nov. 16 that the TWU would refuse to handle air cargo bound to or from the USSR and its allies because of the Soviet Union's "inhuman treatment" of Hungary and "warlike interference in Israel."

The prime ministers of India, Burma, Indonesia and Ceylon ended a 3-day meeting in New Delhi by issuing a communique Nov. 14 expressing "regret" that Soviet troops "were reintroduced into Hungary" after Moscow had indicated that they would leave. The statement urged that Soviet forces "be withdrawn from Hungary speedily" and that Hungarians "be left free to decide their own future and the form of government they will have without intervention from any quarter." The statement also expressed "strong disapproval and distress at the aggression and intervention by the great powers against weaker countries" in the Middle East.

Indian Prime Min. Jawaharlal Nehru further criticized Soviet actions in Hungary when he told the Indian parliament in New Delhi Nov. 19 that "the Soviet army is there against the wishes of the Hungarian people" and "no other explanation is adequate." He pointed out that "in the course of 10 years, the Hungarian people could not be converted to Soviet ideas." He held that continuing anti-Soviet strikes and demonstrations after the Soviet army had crushed armed rebels were "more significant than armed revolt ... organized by some groups here and there." (In further debate over foreign policy Nov. 20, Nehru rejected Socialist demands that his government withdraw recognition of the pro-Soviet Kadar government and Communist demands that India quit the Commonwealth because of the British-French attack on Egypt. He defended the recent action of Indian Delegate-to-UN V. K. Krishna Menon in refusing to vote for a UN resolution condemning the USSR's attack on Hungary. Nehru said eastern Europe feared new aggression by a rearmed Germany. He referred to his scheduled December conferences with Communist Chinese Premier Chou En-lai in New Delhi and Pres. Eisenhower in Washington as indicative of India's opportunity to "become a link between peoples who do not have such links.")

Delegates of all UN factions except the Soviet bloc indicated their support in the UN General Assembly Nov. 19-20 for a Cuban-sponsored resolution calling on the Soviet Union to end the deportation of rebellious youths from Hungary and to return those already deported. Soviet Foreign Min. Dmitri T. Shepilov told the Assembly Nov. 19 that reports of such deportations were "a monstrous fabrication aimed at poisoning the international atmosphere." U.S. Amb.-to-UN Henry Cabot Lodge Jr. replied that a broadcast by the pro-Soviet Budapest radio had referred to the deportations and that reliable informants had reported 16,000 deported from Budapest alone Nov. 14.

Premiers Viliam Siroky of Czechoslovakia and Kadar of Hungary issued a statement Nov. 16 after a 2-day conference of Czechoslovak and Hungarian leaders in Budapest. The statement expressed agreement that: (a) Neither the UN nor individual countries should interfere in Hungary's internal affairs; (b) the Hungarian revolution was launched "on the basis of an exact military plan" devised by capitalist imperialists, although many persons who were not "counterrevolutionaries" joined in the revolt; (c) the Hungarian government (led by Kadar) acted "in the exercise of its sovereignty and by virtue of international law" when it called for Soviet help to prevent the restoration of capitalism in Hungary.

Resistance & Repression Continue

A general strike in Budapest and many other localities was adopted by Hungarians as a weapon of resistance to the pro-Soviet regime after fighting ended. The strike was reported still in effect Nov. 13 despite pleas by Communist officials for the resumption of work. Kadar Nov. 11 broadcast a pledge to exact "no revenge" against nationalist rebels who would accept his regime. He promised to negotiate for the withdrawal of Soviet troops after order was restored, to abolish the security police and to perpetuate many rebel-inspired symbols of Hungarian nationalism, such as restoration of the Kossuth coat of arms to the national flag, discontinuance of compulsory Russian language courses in schools and adoption of Hungarian-style instead of Soviet-style army uniforms. Hungarian trade union leader Sandor Gaspar appealed by radio Nov. 13 for an end to the general strike on the promise of no reprisals, government recognition of "workers' councils" formed by revolutionaries and workers sharing in "new profits of factories" as decided by the councils.

The Kadar government Nov. 9 "gladly and thankfully" announced its acceptance of an International Red Cross offer to send convoys of relief supplies to Hungary from Vienna. The Red Cross reported that it was receiving 500 tons of supplies a day from Europe and the U.S. Hungarian officials reported a threat of famine in Budapest and blamed it on rebel looting of available food supplies. Food dealers were ordered to open their stores Nov. 8, and pawn shops were ordered to return some pawned clothing without payment.

With the populace persisting in its passive resistance to his regime, Kadar met Nov. 11 with deposed Premier Nagy in an effort to win Nagy's support for the new government— represented in propaganda broadcasts as offering Hungary a nationalistic version of communism and blaming Hungary's troubles on "fascists and reactionaries" who had won control of the revolution. Nagy was reported to have received political asylum in the Yugoslav embassy in Budapest after his meeting with Kadar and to have given no decision on Kadar's offer of a minister-without-portfolio post in the cabinet. Soviet troops barred Western newsmen who tried to enter the Yugoslav embassy Nov. 12 to interview Nagy.

A delegation of Soviet leaders, known to include Deputy Premiers Anastas I. Mikoyan and Mikhail A. Suslov and rumored to include Communist Party First Secy. Nikita S. Khrushchev, arrived in Budapest Nov. 12 to try to help Kadar's group win more political support.

Soviet troops and tanks subdued rebel resistance on Csepel Island 5 miles south of Budapest Nov. 14, thus ending the fighting. However, the general strike continued. The Budapest Central Council of Workers voted Nov. 15 to continue the strike until the Communists agreed to restore Nagy as premier and until the USSR agreed to withdraw its forces from the country.

Kadar, in a radio broadcast Nov. 15, argued against a neutralist foreign policy for Hungary on the ground that it would be misused by "imperialists and counterrevolutionaries." He said that elections involving more than one party could be tolerated only if the Communist system would survive, and he conceded that the Socialist Workers' (Communist) Party could expect "thorough defeat" in an open multiparty election at present.

Hungarian refugees said in Vienna Nov. 16 that rebels had raided a Budapest railroad station and rescued 1,000 youths from a deportation train. Strikes by railroad workers and the dynamiting of rail lines were said to have been enployed to halt the movement of deportation trains toward the Hungarian-Soviet border.

After an all-night conference with Kadar, leaders of the Budapest Central Council of Workers announced Nov. 16 that he had convinced them that the country could not survive the hardships of a prolonged general strike in winter, and they appealed for a return to work. But Budapest trade unions generally reaffirmed their determination to continue the strike until their demands for Nagy's restoration and Soviet evacuation were met. Some unions ousted Central Council of Workers delegates who had joined in the back-to-work appeal.

Western observers in Budapest reported Nov. 20 that 70%-80% of the city's workers remained idle despite the government's threat to cut off food supplies to strikers. (The government's estimate of those still on strike was 55%-60%.) Some workers who reported to their places of employment were said to have begun sitdown strikes. The Budapest radio estimated Nov. 20 that Hungarian coal mines were producing only 10,000 tons a day (the norm was 70,000) and that only $\frac{1}{3}$ of the country's normal electric output of 900,000 kilowatt hours a day was being produced.

Yugoslav, Western and Hungarian sources reported Nov. 23 that Nagy and 51 colleagues had been arrested that day by Soviet security police in Budapest and deported to Rumania. The Soviet forces were said to have betrayed a written pledge of freedom and safety given to Nagy by the Kadar government when he emerged Nov. 22 from 19 days in sanctuary at the Yugoslav embassy in Budapest. In reports coming through Vienna it was said that Gen. Ivan A. Serov, Soviet security police chief, had arrived in Budapest Nov. 18 and ordered Nagy's exile.

The Hungarian government contended Nov. 23 that Nagy had "sought permission" to go to "another Socialist country" and had been admitted to Rumania according to his own wishes. The Yugoslav government, in notes of protest to the USSR and Hungary Nov. 24, said Nagy had refused while at the Yugoslav embassy to agree to go to Rumania and had expressed a desire to go to Yugoslavia if he must leave Hungary. Yugoslavia asked that the Soviet Union let Nagy return freely to Budapest or take asylum in Yugoslavia.

Kadar, in a radio speech Nov. 26, conceded that Nagy had been "exiled" and denounced him as having permitted the killing of "scores of Communists" during the "murderous counterrevolution." Kadar said that Nagy, in effect, had condoned the killings by failing to resign as premier when the revolution was taken over by "terrorist" factions "under the sway of such reactionaries as" Jozsef Cardinal Mindszenty, Istvan Szabo and Prince Pal Eszterhazy (a wealthy anti-Communist aristocrat later reported to be in Austria). Nagy was deposed Nov. 4, Kadar said, after he had "called for resistance against the Soviet troops who had been called in for help against terrorist murderers."

Aid to Refugees

Throughout the world, manifestations of sympathy mounted for the population of Hungary. Many Hungarians suffered death or deportation to the east; probably more of them, however, fled to the west. According to a report by the UN High Commission for Refugees Nov. 2, 1957, more than 195,000 Hungarian residents crossed the borders into Austria or Yugoslavia during or soon after the fighting. Besides these 2 states, countries in western Europe, North and South America and even in the Middle East offered themselves as havens to the refugees.

The U.S. held great attraction for many of the refugees and took an early initiative to welcome them. Pres. Eisenhower announced Nov. 8 that he had directed the U.S. Refugee Relief Administration to rush processes for admitting to the U.S. up to 5,000 of the then estimated 14,000 to 16,000 refugees from the "brutal purge of liberty" carried out by "imperial communism" in Hungary. He urged that American citizens and organizations volunteer quickly to assure the incoming refugees employment, housing or financial aid in conformity with U.S. law and in keeping with traditional American hospitality toward the politically displaced and dispossessed.

Congress was stirred into action. Rep. Francis E. Walter (D., Pa.), coauthor of the McCarran-Walter Immigration Act (highly restrictive of immigration from that quarter of Europe) and House Immigration Subcommittee chairman, announced in Washington Nov. 16 that he had drafted legislation to let 5,000 Hungarian refugees live in the U.S. "permanently or until heroic Hungary is free again." He said he would go to Vienna to "help cut red tape" in the admission of Hungarian refugees to the U.S.

Walter witnessed the shooting of a Hungarian escapee by Soviet police Nov. 21 when he visited the frontier swamp area near Andau, Austrian Burgenland—a principal escape point. Back in the U.S., he proposed in Washington Nov. 24 that the U.S. admit as many Hungarian refugees as welfare and church agencies could establish in homes and jobs.

The first refugees were already arriving in the U.S. 7 planeloads of Hungarians, 486 persons in all, touched down between Nov. 21 and Nov. 24—6 at McGuire Air Force Base near Trenton, N.J. and the 7th in Milwaukee, Wis. A camp for arriving refugees went into operation Nov. 21 at Camp Kilmer, N. J. Many charitable, religious and welfare organizations responded to U.S. government appeals to help care for and establish the refugees in the U.S. Eisenhower received 12 refugees at the White House Nov. 26. The President announced Dec. 1 that the U.S. quota for the admission of refugees would be increased to 21,500 from the original 5,000, with 6,500 to be admitted under the Refugee Relief Act and 15,000 as "parolees" in the U.S. temporarily.

Eisenhower Nov. 29 had appointed Tracy S. Voorhees, 66, a New York attorney, Defense Department consultant and ex-Army undersecretary, as coordinator of the U.S. relief and resettlement program for Hungarian refugees. Voorhees Dec. 5 named Gen. J. Lawton Collins to aid him in his assignment and William Hallam Tuck, ex-general director of the International Refugee Organization, to serve as Voorhees' representative in Austria. The White House Dec. 12 announced the formation of a President's Committee for Hungarian Refugee Relief. Voorhees was named chairman, Collins and Tuck co-chairmen.

Another White House statement Dec. 12 announced that Vice Pres. Richard M. Nixon, acting as Eisenhower's personal representative, would investigate the refugee problem in Austria and determine what U.S. action was needed to aid the Hungarian refugees and ease the burden on Austria. Nixon was accompanied to Austria Nov. 18 by Deputy U.S. Atty. Gen. William P. Rogers, who was studying legal barriers to U.S. acceptance of more refugees, and International Cooperation Administrator John B. Hollister.

Nixon said Dec. 24 on returning to Washington from a 7-day tour of Hungarian refugee camps in Austria and West Germany that he carried "specific recommendations" for increased U.S. refugee assistance. (He also said that the Hungarian rebellion had proved communism a "gigantic failure" and that Hungary's rebels had given communism "a mortal blow from which it cannot recover.") Nixon appealed in a nationwide radio-TV broadcast Dec. 25 for increased U.S. private donations to Hungarian relief.

The Vice President had said on arriving in Vienna Nov. 19 that although the U.S. had done much for Hungary's refugees, "much more remains to be done." He said that the U.S. would study "changes in existing [immigration] law" and assist Austria in helping meet the problem. Nixon visited Austrian Pres. Theodor Koerner and Chancellor Julius Raab Dec. 20, then toured refugee camps near Traiskirchen, Lower Austria, and Andau near the Hungarian border. He visited a border-crossing point Dec. 21, toured camps in the Austrian autonomous province of Salzburg Dec. 22 and left via Munich, Bavaria for the U.S. Dec. 23.

Eisenhower Dec. 26 ordered U.S. officials in Austria to continue the "tentative" processing of Hungarian refugees. His action was taken as an indication that the U.S. government intended to raise its quota on the admission of Hungarian escapees from the already determined level of 21,500. The President acted after Nixon had reported to him Dec. 26. Nixon indicated after his meeting with Eisenhower that the U.S. refugee quota might be further increased to benefit other east European refugees as well. (U.S. Atty. Gen. Herbert Brownell Jr. Dec. 19 authorized the entry into the U.S. of 40 east European athletes who had defected during the 14th Olympic Games in Melbourne, Australia and had asked the U.S. for asylum.)

Maj. Gen. Bela Kiraly, deputy commander-in-chief of the Hungarian army in Budapest and the rebels there under the Imre Nagy regime, was revealed to have reached the U.S. Dec. 30. Kiraly, reportedly aided by some Yugoslavs, had been said Dec. 12 to have been reorganizing the revolt. It was reported Dec. 30 that Kiraly had fled to Austria after Soviet forces took Budapest. (Kiraly told the *N.Y. Times* that Nagy was of the opinion that he could bargain with the Soviets—a view Kiraly did not share. He also said that the Soviet Union had 12 to 14 divisions in Hungary.)

Rep. Walter said Dec. 30 that he was "thoroughly convinced" that many Hungarian refugees entering the U.S. had been Communist Party members in Hungary. He urged that all Hungarian escapees be admitted to the U.S. as "parolees" and later be "fully investigated." Vice Pres. Nixon, touring the Hungarian refugee reception center at Camp

Kilmer, N.J. Dec. 27, said that he knew of no subversives concealed among entering Hungarian escapees.

(Lucy Santo, wife of a former Transportation Workers' Union official, John Santo, who had been deported to Hungary in 1949 for Communist activities, returned to the U.S. Dec. 16 with her 2 children. Santo, a former Hungarian government meat industry official who had fled to Austria with his family, remained in Vienna pending a decision on his application for reentry into the U.S. Stetson Kennedy, an American newsman who had gone to live in Hungary with his family in 1954, reportedly escaped to Yugoslavia Dec. 12 and requested permission to return to the U.S.)

Other Western countries also welcomed fleeing Hungarians. Canada Nov. 6 and Britain Nov. 8 had announced efforts to speed their admission of Hungarian refugees, and Canada widened its quota again Dec. 19. The British and French governments Nov. 24 announced plans to admit an unlimited number of Hungarian refugees. The Argentine government announced Nov. 26 that 7,500 Argentine families had offered to adopt orphaned refugee children. Israeli asylum was accepted by 900 of the 14,000 Jewish escapees from Hungary Dec. 21.

The situation was at first quite fluid. Secy. Gen. Dag Hammarskjold submitted to the UN General Assembly in New York Nov. 20 a report (prepared by Philippe de Seynes, UN undersecretary for economic and social affairs) that nearly 40,000 refugees had left Hungary since the rebellion began Oct. 23 and that the flight of refugees continued at the rate of 2,000 a day. According to the report, most escapees had gone to Austria, others to Yugoslavia and Switzerland.

The number of Hungarian refugees entering Austria was reported Nov. 27 to be declining because of increased Soviet army efforts to block escapees across the western border. Frequent killings of escapees were reported from the frontier. Nevertheless, the refugee exodus into Austria continued, with 137,000 escapees reported to have passed through reception centers by Dec. 18 despite the increasing severity of Hungarian and Soviet border patrols. Austrian sources estimated Dec. 18 that 65,000 Hungarians had left for asylum offered by other nations—7,000 of them for the U.S. The Intergovernmental Committee   European Migration, an international organization founded in 1951 (it had 30 member countries and 7 observer countries in 1968), reported Dec. 25 that 151,218 Hungarian escapees had registered at Austrian centers since Oct. 23, and that 82,312 Hungarians had left Austria by Dec. 25 for asylum offered in other free lands. 2 more Soviet soldiers deserted to Austria Dec. 25; they raised to 6 the number who had sought asylum as refugees from Hungary since the revolt began.

Austrian Chancellor Raab said Dec. 23 that, in spite of Soviet threats, "we [Austrians] will continue to do our duty" toward the Hungarian refugees. Raab had denied Dec. 19 that Austria's welcome to the escapees "even slightly amounts to a violation of [the] neutrality" that Austria was bound to guard perpetually by its governmental declaration of May 15, 1955 (after Foreign Min. Leopold Figl had signed a peace treaty with the U.S., the Soviet Union, Britain and France). Raab told the *N.Y. Herald Tribine* that Austrian government expenditures for refugee accommodation would total $7.5 million and private and local government donations $4.5 million by Jan. 1, 1957.

Radio Moscow Dec. 25 broadcast a denunciation of Austria for aiding the Hungarian refugee movement. Its author(s) charged that Austrian Socialists had "played no small part in organizing the counterrevolutionary uprising in Hungary" and that Western agents were screening refugee camps "to recruit cheap labor." (It had been charged in a report by the Soviet news agency Tass Dec. 22 that the U.S. had "staged" the Hungarian revolt in a move to restore the Austro-Hungarian monarchy and place the Archduke Otto of Hapsburg, the royal pretender, on the throne. The Soviet government daily *Izvestia* had reported Dec. 22 that the historic crown of St. Stephen of Hungary had been moved from the U.S. to West Germany in preparation for the coup.)

The cost of housing, feeding, clothing and transporting the Hungarian escapees was from the outset expected to be great. From the White House it was reported Nov. 20 that the U.S. government and voluntary agencies had raised ¼ of the $20 million worth of emergency aid pledged to Hungary by Eisenhower Nov. 2. (The President appealed Nov. 20 to colleges and universities throughout the free world to make scholarships available to refugee Hungarian students.)

The UN appealed to 87 countries Nov. 29 to give the international organization $10 million in additional funds for the relief of Hungarian refugees. The American Red Cross Dec. 3 launched a drive to raise a special relief fund of $5 million for the refugees. The (U.S.) National Council of Churches appealed Dec. 4 for $2 million in contributions to relieve Hungarian and Middle Eastern refugees through Church World Service. The Canadian House of Commons appropriated $1 million for Hungarian relief Nov. 29.

The UN General Assembly Dec. 10 approved by acclamation the nomination of the Swiss UN observer, Dr. Auguste R. Lindt, as UN high commissioner for refugees. Lindt replaced Deputy Commissioner James M. Read, acting high commissioner since the death of C. J. van Heuven Goedhart. The UN Children's Fund voted Dec. 11 to allocate $900,000 for Hungarian children's relief. Under an agreement revealed Dec. 5, all UN relief for Hungary was to be distributed through the International Committee for the Red Cross.

Eisenhower Dec. 14 made $4 million available to the UN fund for the aid of Hungarian refugees in Austria. He had made a $1 million U.S. contribution to the fund Nov. 13 as an immediate incentive for refugee work and as an example for other Western countries to follow.

5 U.S. relief organizations—CARE, Church World Service, Catholic Relief Services, United Jewish Appeal and the American Red Cross—reported Dec. 21 that private U.S. donations for Hungarian aid were lagging below announced goals. (Red Cross spokesmen said that only $2,564,757 of the $5 million it sought had been collected. CARE reported $608,000 subscribed toward its goal of $2 million.) The Rockefeller Foundation Dec. 28 disclosed a 2d contribution of $600,000 to aid young Hungarian refugees remaining in Austria.

The office of the UN High Commission for Refugees demanded Dec. 8 that Yugoslavia explain the planned repatriation of 141 Hungarian refugees. Yugoslavia had reported Dec. 7 that 859 Hungarians had requested asylum since Oct. 23 and that 141 of these had "freely elected" to return home under a repatriation agreement signed Nov. 29. The 141 were repatriated—51 Dec. 7 and 90 Dec. 9—to Hungary amid reports that Hungarian officials had been permitted to screen escapees and apply pressure for their return home.

Hungarian Events Revive Soviet-Yugoslav Friction

Yugoslav Pres. Tito, in a speech in Pula, Croatia Nov. 11, said that the Soviet authorities and Erno Gero's Stalinist faction in Hungary had made a "fatal mistake" when they first employed Soviet troops against Hungarian demonstrators in late October. He said another "error" occurred when Hungarian Communists relied on a 2d Soviet intervention to save them instead of acting immediately—as they acted eventually after the 2d Soviet intervention—to revise their government and policies. Tito said the deposed regime of Imre Nagy had invited the 2d Soviet attack by not preventing "anarchy and the killing of Communists by reactionary elements." He declared himself "always ... against the intervention and use of a foreign military force," but he added: "if [Soviet intervention] saves socialism in Hungary ... we will be able to say, although we are against the intervention, that Soviet intervention is necessary."

Tito also said that the Soviet leadership was split into Stalinist and anti-Stalinist factions. He said he had warned the Soviet leaders that they might expect what actually developed in Hungary if repression were attempted there: a surge of rebellious spirit "only interested in being nationally independent," with no regard for whether "the bourgeoisie and a reactionary system would be restored in the country." He predicted that, as a result of the "bloodshed" and "terrible sacrifices" in Hungary, "a little light will reach the eyes of the comrades in the Soviet Union, even those Stalinist elements, and ... they will see that it is no longer possible to work in this way." Tito called for defense of the Kadar regime in Hungary, which he said was "honest" but weakened by Soviet intervention.

The Soviet Communist party newspaper *Pravda* said Nov. 19 that Tito echoed "reactionary propaganda" in blaming the Hungarian disaster on Stalinists and had betrayed his tendency to "interfere in the affairs of other Communist parties."

Ex-Vice Pres. Milovan Djilas of Yugoslavia, in an article published Nov. 14 in the American anti-Communist liberal weekly *The New Leader,* criticized both the Soviet and Yugoslav leadership. He said: The USSR had shown that it would "resist the breakup of the empire" and employ "national communism" only as "a means and a mask for its imperialist, expansive policies"; Yugoslavia revealed itself "ready to yield" its "principles of equality and noninterference in internal affairs" rather than support the Hungarian revolution when Communists lost control of it. Djilas predicted that Polish Party First Secy. Wladyslaw Gomulka would work for Polish independence rather than for maintenance of "national Communist" domination of the country. (Yugoslav authorities disclosed Nov. 19 that Djilas had been arrested in Belgrade, presumably for violating his probationary release from an 18-month jail sentence for deviationism.)

Tito was urged by *Pravda* Nov. 23 to halt his attacks on the "Socialist system of other countries" and to join the Soviet Union in ending differences by a "comradely exchange of opinion." *Pravda* asserted that the receipt of U.S. aid had put Yugoslavia in a special position. It disputed Tito's efforts to make Yugoslavia the model for all Soviet-bloc states. *Pravda* rejected criticism of the USSR on the grounds of "Stalinism" and asserted that a "new look" had come to Soviet-satellite relations since the 20th Communist Party Congress in February. The Yugoslav League of Communists' newspaper *Borba,* in a reply to *Pravda* Nov. 26, warned that the USSR must choose between a "return to Stalinism or the establishment of democratic relations of equality among Socialist countries." *Borba* blamed the USSR for the Hungarian revolt for insisting on absolute control over Soviet-bloc states.

Soviet Pres. Klimenti Ye. Voroshilov, in a personal message to Tito on Yugoslavia's National Day Nov. 29, urged closer Yugoslav-Soviet friendship and agreement.

Pravda, in an article Dec. 23 directed at Poles and Yugoslavs, denounced east European leaders who placed "nationalism" above the Soviet bloc's "solid front." The paper attacked "imaginary national communism" as contrary to Marxist doctrine. *Pravda* admitted Stalin's "serious errors" but asserted that the "fight against so-called Stalinism" was being used by Soviet enemies. It warned that Communists owed primary loyalty to the USSR and other states "on the Socialist path."

Soviet Communist Party First Secy. Khrushchev, in a year-end interview Dec. 31 for the Czechoslovak Communist Party newspaper *Rude pravo,* said that "so-called national communism" was in "opposition" to valid Soviet practice and harmed "the whole family of Socialist nations." Khrushchev warned that "enemies of the working class" used "the most treacherous actions [to] cause discord inside the Communist movement, to impair the unity of the Communist and workers' parties." Khrushchev said that Western attempts to start a war or support anti-Communist forces in eastern Europe would "meet with a proper rebuff."

Tito had confirmed to the Yugoslav League of Communists' newspaper *Borba* Dec. 29 that differences existed between Yugoslavia and the USSR but asserted that he wanted "no noisy polemics" and was "against the sharpening of tension" between the 2 countries. Tito said that ideological disagreements between the Yugoslav and Soviet Communist parties should not harm relations between the 2 states. He expressed satisfaction at Chinese Communist publication of his views on the Hungarian revolt, and he dismissed Chinese criticism as "not too important."

The Chinese Communist Party Central Committee Dec. 28 had attacked Tito and Yugoslav leaders for their criticisms of "righteous action taken by the Soviet Union" against Hungary's rebels. In a statement broadcast by Peking radio, the Central Committee charged that Tito, in his Nov. 11 speech on Hungary, had "attacked almost all the Socialist countries and many of the Communist parties." A *Jenminh Jih Pao* editorial reprinted by *Pravda* Dec. 30 warned that Tito's statement on Hungary was "extremely harmful." (In a Peking broadcast Nov. 21 the Communist Chinese government had warned the USSR to avoid "great-nation chauvinism" in its relations with other Communist states.)

Yugoslav Vice Pres. Edvard Kardelj, speaking in the Yugoslav Federal Assembly Dec. 7, had labeled the Hungarian revolt "a working-class rebellion against a socially intolerable system in which there was no democracy." Kardelj said that the USSR had erred in its "intervention" in Hungary. He urged that Hungary follow the Yugoslav factory council system and institute "direct democracy." *Pravda* Dec. 18 charged that Kardelj's analysis had aided attempts to "split the international Communist movement." (But a Soviet trade union delegation report appearing in *Pravda* Nov. 29 had viewed the Yugoslav factory council system "with interest.")

In Poland, the Gomulka government Dec. 31 affirmed its agreement with Yugoslav views "that various countries may achieve socialism in various ways." A communique issued on talks begun Dec. 19 between Polish leaders and a Yugoslav cabinet delegation announced that the 2 groups had agreed "on the necessity of bilateral cooperation between the parties." The statement indicated that the 2 groups were in accord on opposition to Soviet interference in the internal affairs of Communist states. *Trybuna Wolnosci,* official weekly of the Polish United Workers' (Communist) Party Central Committee, had disclosed Nov. 25 an offer by Tito of Yugoslav cooperation in Poland's struggle against Stalinism. The paper had indicated that Poland had accepted the offer and that the PUWP indorsed Tito's analysis of the Hungarian revolt.

Greek Premier Constantine Karamanlis and Foreign Min. Evangelos Averoff conferred with Tito in Belgrade Dec. 5-8 on the possibility of reviving activities of the Greek-Turk-Yugoslav alliance (dormant for months because of Greek-Turk differences over Cyprus). Tito was said to have supported Greece's position on the Cyprus dispute.

Apart from the Polish leaders, Yugoslavia found no friends among those in power in the Soviet bloc. Albanian Defense Min. Beqir Balluku, in a Tirana broadcast Dec. 8, called Tito "a traitor in the hands of the imperialists." Yugoslav newspapers charged Albania Nov. 28 with mass arrests of Yugoslav sympathizers. The Czechoslovak Communist Party Central Committee was disclosed Dec. 8 to have passed a resolution condemning Tito for having "damaged" the international Communist movement. Walter Ulbricht, East German deputy premier and Socialist Unity (Communist) Party first secretary, said Dec. 30 that "the Hungarian events" had shown the need for Communist unity. Ulbricht said he hoped the Yugoslavs "will draw their conclusions" from the Hungarian example. State Security Min. Ernst Wollweber warned Dec. 21 that "so-called free discussion" led to "antidemocratic and anti-Socialist ideologies" and would not be permitted in East Germany.

(Milovan Djilas received a 3-year prison sentence in a court in Belgrade Dec. 12 for "slandering" Yugoslavia, "misleading world opinion" about the country and seeking to "provoke interference by foreign powers in Yugoslav affairs." Jakov Levi, *Borba* correspondent in the U.S., disclosed Nov. 28 in New York that he had resigned and applied for asylum in the U.S. in protest against Djilas' arrest.)

Protest Strike Movement

The National Council of Workers issued a new 3-day general strike declaration (only the food industry excepted) in Budapest Nov. 21 after Hungarian police and Soviet troops had prevented the council from meeting in the Budapest Sports Hall. The council previously had yielded to Kadar's pleas and urged Hungarians to resume work. The Workers' Council in Budapest decided Nov. 25 to ask the membership to return to their jobs for 24 hours as a demonstration to the government that the council spoke for workers. Many strikers reported for work Nov. 26, and the council requested Nov. 27 that the back-to-work movement be continued "in the interest of the people." The council that day, however, reaffirmed its opposition to Kadar's regime. Production was reported at low ebb in Budapest on account of a shortage of electric power and raw materials and popular opposition to the Soviet occupation.

Reports via Vienna Nov. 27 said the Kadar regime was increasing its arrests of persons branded "criminals and counter-revolutionaries." But in a concession to Hungarian nationalism, the Kadar regime announced Dec. 1 that university students would no longer be compelled to take courses in Soviet Communist Party history.

Spokesmen for the Budapest Workers Council had indicated Nov. 30 that they had made no progress in negotiations with Kadar for the return of ousted Premier Imre Nagy. The Kadar government Dec. 1 pleaded for protection of livestock and equipment on collective farms, which it said were being depleted by rebel forays, and reinstated penalties for quitting collective farms.

Pres. Istvan Dobi Dec. 2 broadcast a plea for the people to end strikes, which, he said, would mean "anarchy" if continued.

Reports reaching Vienna that the pro-Soviet Hungarian Communists held little control except in Budapest were partially confirmed Dec. 3 by Istvan Szirmai, press chief of the Kadar government. He told correspondents in Budapest that rebel bands were still active in the countryside outside Budapest and that Hungarian coal production was still only $\frac{1}{3}$ of normal. Hungarian workers had not responded generally to back-to-work pleas. Guerrillas were said to be most active in the northern province of Miskolc, the southern uranium-mining area near Pecs, the university town of Sarospatak (reported in the hands of student revolutionaries) in Borsod-Abauj-Zemplen County, northeastern Hungary, and the Bakony Forest and Lake Balaton region in Zala County, where Maj. Gen. Bela Kiraly—2nd in command to Maj. Gen. Pal Maleter in the October uprising in Budapest—was still reported to be leading rebel forces.

The continuing rebellious spirit of Hungarians was signified by a demonstration by women and children Dec. 4 in Heroes Square, Budapest. About 5,000 women and girls bearing flowers and wearing symbols of mourning, supported by at least 10,000 other demonstrators, went to the square to put flowers on the tomb of the Hungarian Unknown Soldier. Soviet troops were jeered and jostled when they sought to intervene. They agreed after a conference with Hungarian Defense Min. Ferenc Muennich to let 5,000 women take flowers to the tomb. Soviet troops, aroused by the crowd's verbal abuse, fired a volley over the demonstrators and wounded one woman. (The Hungarian Reformed Church, largest Protestant church in the country, had announced Nov. 30 that it had formed a new church administration without the "outside political influence" heretofore prevalent.)

The Hungarian rebellion apparently entered a decisive phase Dec. 5-11 when events led to a government effort to crush the workers' councils by declaring them dissolved and instituting martial law. Hungarians defied the Kadar regime by launching another general strike.

Hungarian police supported by Soviet tanks dispersed anti-government demonstrators in central Budapest 4 times Dec. 5. The marchers, largely women, gathered at the U.S., British and

French embassies to shout anti-Kadar slogans and demand the restoration of ex-Premier Nagy. A Hungarian writers' proclamation appearing in Budapest Dec. 5 warned that "suppressing the Hungarian revolution with bloodshed" was an "historical mistake." The Hungarian Federation of Writers Dec. 6 protested the arrests Dec. 5 of writers Lajos Tamasi, Gyula Obersovszky and Zoltan Milnar. The government ignored a 2-day deadline for a reply to the proclamation. A Workers' Council delegation including authors Peter Veres and Aron Tomassy met with Kadar Dec. 7 and protested the arrests.

Sporadic street fighting and work stoppages in Budapest were reported Dec. 6-7. 4 persons were killed Dec. 6 when flag-carrying rebels clashed with parading Kadar supporters during a "silent hour" protest against repression of the revolt. Soviet tank forces reportedly intervened Dec. 6-7 to clear streets and arrest demonstrators, some of whom were protesting a Soviet roundup of Budapest students Dec. 6. An estimated half of Csepel Island's 38,000 iron and steel workers struck Dec. 7. The Budapest Central Workers' Council warned Dec. 7 that the Kadar government had begun an "organized hunt" for council leaders and that these government tactics could precipitate "a general strike, bloodshed and a new national tragedy."

Scores of Hungarians were reported killed as fighting flared Dec. 8 in industrial and farming centers throughout the country. 80 persons were said to have been killed by police in Salgotarjan, 53 miles northeast of Budapest, during demonstrations against the arrest of regional peasant and workers' council leaders. Fighting was reported in Bekescsaba, 53 miles northeast of Szeged; in Tatabanya, 30 miles west of Budapest, and in Pecs, 106 miles south-southwest of Budapest; the Soviet commander in Pecs was reported killed. 1,500 rebels were said to be resisting Soviet troops in the Mecsek Mountains near Pecs Dec. 8.

The Budapest Central Workers' Council Dec. 9 ordered a 48-hour general strike to begin at midnight Dec. 10, and an 8-day general strike followed. The council charged that the Kadar regime had refused to halt arrests of rebel leaders and was incapable of ending the Hungarian crisis. The council had delayed its strike call Dec. 8 after the government had released 96 imprisoned council leaders. Kadar and State Min. Gyorgy

Marosan were reported to have warned the council Dec. 8 that all but direct government supporters were classified as "counterrevolutionaries."

The Kadar government reacted to the general strike call by decreeing dissolution of all regional workers' councils Dec. 9 and imposing martial law throughout Hungary. The decrees, signed by Pres. Dobi, provided for rebel trials by military courts beginning Dec. 11 and summary execution of persons possessing weapons after that date. The government said the action was taken because of increased provincial unrest. It ruled that even arms issued to pro-Kadar militia must be turned in. The government charged that workers' councils had tried to "build a new state power."

Hungarian workers began striking Dec. 10 after the Budapest Central Workers' Council refused to withdraw its general strike call. Budapest news dispatches to the West (interrupted Dec. 9 but resumed briefly Dec. 10) reported the city surrounded by Soviet-manned roadblocks. Street-by-street searches for hidden arms were being made by Soviet and Hungarian government forces. Budapest and all other Hungarian industrial centers except Salgotarjan and Zalaegerszeg, 52 miles west-southwest of Veszprem, were reported paralyzed by the strike Dec. 11. Rebel bands were said to be holding out Dec. 11 against Soviet troops in Harmashatarhegy, high in the North Buda Mountains; in Borsod-Abauj-Zemplen County, and in the Bakony forests outside of Veszprem.

(The U.S. State Department protested Dec. 10 against the rupture of communications with the U.S. legation in Budapest. Contact was reported restored between Budapest and Washington Dec. 11.)

The Budapest radio appealed to workers Dec. 10 to "stop committing suicide" and give up the strike, which, the radio said, "does not exist" except in "provocations from Western broadcasters." Budapest dispatches Dec. 10 reported a revival of rumors (previously discounted) that Soviet First Deputy Premier Georgi M. Malenkov had visited Budapest Dec. 6-7 and would return to the city Dec. 11 to advise Kadar on suppressing the general strike.

Hungarian workers prolonged their general strike Dec. 12-16 amid government arrests of workers' council leaders throughout the country.

Sporadic street fighting was reported Dec. 12 in Budapest, in Hungary's 2d industrial center, its northern suburbs and Miskolc 90 miles northeast of Budapest, as the strike paralyzed Hungary's economy. The Hungarian Socialist Workers' (Communist) Party's newspaper *Nepszabadsag* of Budapest said Dec. 12 that the "workers' movement has never seen such a strike." It complained that efforts to resume work had been halted by "terrorists" and "toughs."

The Budapest radio said Dec. 12 that all persons found guilty by newly organized military courts would be executed automatically. The radio said Dec. 15 that Janos Soltesz, first rebel to be tried by a summary court, had been hanged. The execution of Lajos Nagy, 2d rebel sentenced, was delayed Dec. 15 pending an appeal. The radio reported 3 more rebels condemned Dec. 17 but said that none had been executed. Budapest rebel informants Dec. 17 listed 178 persons executed in Budapest and 80 more in the provinces.

The Kadar government Dec. 12 had disclosed the arrest of Sandor Racz, Budapest Central Workers' Council chairman. Racz and an aide, Sandor Bari, were said to have been arrested Dec. 11 when they accepted government invitations to open new negotiations on ending anti-government unrest. The Kadar regime reported that Racz and Bari had been arrested for organizing provocative strikes and urging workers' councils to overthrow the government. Racz reportedly told an Italian newsman before his arrest that the Kadar regime "will never succeed in crushing the will of the workers."

The general strike was extended for 24 hours Dec. 13 by the Budapest Central Workers' Council in protest against the arrests of Racz and Bari. The council ordered transport, communications and power tieups under a plan for "creeping paralysis" until Racz and Bari were released. A council statement asserted Dec. 13 that Kadar's government "has received its last blow and its hours are numbered. The same fate awaits any ... who are trying to save the situation by setting up a puppet coalition."

(Associated Press dispatches from Budapest Dec. 13 relayed rumors that the Kadar government's collapse was imminent and that power had been concentrated in the hands of Col. Gen. Ivan A. Serov, Soviet MVD chief. Rumors also were circulated that Soviet First Deputy Premier Malenkov had returned to Hungary Dec. 13.)

The Kadar government Dec. 14 banned all demonstrations and meetings on pain of terms of 6 months to 5 years of imprisonment. Budapest radio appealed to strikers to return to work Dec. 14. It warned that the collapse of the Hungarian economy was imminent. Of 184 large plants in the Budapest area, only 16 were reported in partial production Dec. 14. Mass arrests of workers' council leaders were reported Dec. 14 in Budapest, in Szolnok, at the junction of the Tisza and Zagyra rivers in east-central Hungary, in Gyor, in Kecskemet, 50 miles southeast of Budapest, and in Nagykoros, 10 miles away. Nearer Budapest, Csepel Island iron and steel workers voted Dec. 15 to ignore the government's dissolution of the Workers Councils.

Various reports told of fighting between rebels and Soviet troops in the provinces Dec. 14-15. Rebels were said to have taken the suburbs of Miskolc Dec. 15 and to be in complete control of Pecs, an ancient city 106 miles south-southwest of Budapest, and Tatabanya, 30 miles west of Budapest. Soviet deserters were reported in action with rebel bands in the Pecs and northeastern Hungary's Buekk Mountain areas Dec. 15. Budapest radio said Dec. 15 that Soviet troops had burned a theater filled with rebel prisoners in Miskolc Dec. 13.

The strike was finally called off Dec. 17 as the government apparently moved toward granting limited concessions to rebel and workers' council demands.

Kadar Consolidates Regime

The Central Workers' Council ordered the general strike ended Dec. 17 after workers had been reported returning to work and rebel activity ceasing throughout Hungary Dec. 16-17. Workers were reported limited to cleanup tasks in most plants due to severe shortages of electricity and raw materials. The Kadar government Dec. 17 appealed for volunteers to work coal mines in the Gyor area, but Workers Councils opposed the move as "unsafe." Budapest rumors Dec. 16-17 concerned Kadar government moves to seek a "Polish" solution for Hungary and open talks with exiled members of the Imre Nagy government.

Budapest dispatches indicated Dec. 18 that the Kadar government was preparing to meet some rebel and workers' council demands. Budapest radio said that Hungarian trade unions had denounced their 1949 collective bargaining agreements Dec. 17 and had voted to work for new wage scales with workers' council cooperation. The government Dec. 18 accepted workers' council protests and withdrew its appeal for volunteers to work in mines where pits, pitprops and housing were reported damaged. The formation of a League of Revolutionary Hungarian Youth, to be independent of the Communist Party and government, was announced over the Budapest radio.

The newspaper *Nepszabadsag* reported Dec. 18 that more than 200 "counterrevolutionary terrorists" and 150 "escaped convicts" had been arrested and a new political police force formed to replace the Hungarian Security Police (*allamvedelmi hatosag* or AVH). Armed rebellion was reported at an end in Hungary Dec. 19-25.

Premier Kadar said Dec. 19 that his government was in a position to repress "provocations" without calling for help from Soviet troops in Hungary. Kadar said that there had been no armed clashes in Hungary for several days. He attributed government strength to the formation of "new revolutionary troops" and new police leadership.

The Kadar government moved Dec. 19 to spur lagging Hungarian production by decreeing a 10% wage raise for industrial workers and miners and announcing the creation of a new Hungarian Commission for Economic Planning with 6 members drawn from the Budapest Central Workers' Council. The announcements followed reports that most Hungarian heavy industries had been cut back from a 6-day to a 3-day work week. Sandor Gaspar, Trade Union Federation general secretary, appealed over Budapest radio Dec. 19 for "urgent measures," including cuts in "expenditure for government administration and defense," to aid Hungary's economy.

The Kadar regime Dec. 20 decreed up to 6 months detention without trial for disturbance of public order or "endangering of production". Budapest radio Dec. 20 announced the formation of an Information Bureau to "control the press" and have charge of entry permits and activities of foreign newsmen. The radio reported that Hungarian State Atty. Geza Szenasi had indicated that a joint Soviet-Hungarian High Command would try Soviet commanders who had interfered in local Hungarian affairs. The government Dec. 20 announced the execution of 2 more rebels for possessing arms and for "terrorism." 3 rebels had sentences commuted to life Dec. 20, and 2 were condemned to death Dec. 21. The Hungarian Trade Union Federation newspaper *Nepakarat* charged Dec. 19 that many workers had been arrested and "held in various prisons without trial." Budapest dispatches Dec. 21 reported rumors that Central Workers Council member Sandor Bari had been freed. Other reports Dec. 23 said that Council Chairman Sandor Racz had begun a hunger strike in prison.

The government Dec. 21 announced a new agricultural marketing system that would free farmers to sell to the state, cooperatives or consumers but retain government control of food wholesaling. Hungarian police began a drive Nov. 21 on the Budapest black market, where eggs were reported selling for 45¢ each.

The Kadar government, in apparently contradictory moves Dec. 23, ordered that Dec. 23 and 24 be full work days but closed the Csepel Island iron-and-steel complex outside Budapest until Jan. 2, with Csepel workers to be given half pay. Hungarian production was reported near a standstill Dec. 23 because of coal shortages despite the government's announcement that coal imports were en route from the USSR, Poland, East Germany and Czechoslovakia. *Nepszabadsag,* Budapest organ of the Socialist Workers (Communist) Party, warned Dec. 23 that the rebellion had destroyed 25% of Hungary's power sources. The paper estimated that 200,000 Hungarians would remain jobless in 1957.

The Kadar government Dec. 23 ordered the 9 p.m. curfew lifted to permit the celebration of Christmas in Hungary. Budapest churches were reported crowded Dec. 24-25. Budapest radio played *Silent Night* Dec. 24, reportedly for the first time in 10 years.

The government decreed Dec. 29 that "all workers who cannot be fully employed because of the present shortage of coal and energy" be dismissed by Jan. 1, 1957. The mass dismissal affected thousands of industrial workers and 32,000 civil servants displaced by mergers of the Mining and Chemical Industry ministries (into the Heavy Industry Ministry) and the Culture and Education ministries Dec. 30, and the abolition of the Crop Collection, Town & Village Management, State Farm and State Control ministries. The government announced Dec. 31 that discharged state employes would be given credit and licenses necessary to set up small businesses. It was reported Dec. 31 that 40,000-50,000 craft licenses would be issued and the punitive income tax on craftsmen abolished. The Budapest City Council Dec. 31 announced the issuance of trade licenses to "revive private initiative, which has long been neglected." Finance Min. Istvan Kossa minimized the seriousness of unemployment in Hungary Dec. 29 in view of the "great need of workers" in coal mines and farming.

Budapest observers reported signs of Soviet troop withdrawals from Hungary Dec. 28-31. It was estimated that 25% of the 12 to 20 Soviet divisions had returned to bases in the USSR and other eastern European countries. Soviet tanks were withdrawn from Budapest's Danube River bridges Dec. 27, and guards on Hungarian government buildings were reduced in number Dec. 31.

The government announced Dec. 30 that the USSR had lent Hungary $50 million to buy goods in the West to help rebuild Hungary's shattered economy. *Nepszabadsag* indicated Dec. 30 that other provisions of the Soviet loan had exceeded $50 million. Budapest radio said Dec. 30 that loan negotiations were under way with Rumania, East Germany, Czechoslovakia, Bulgaria and "several capitalist countries." It reported that Communist China had been asked for a "large loan" and that talks would begin soon with Poland and Yugoslavia.

The USSR had granted Hungary a 100 million-ruble ($25 million) emergency credit Oct. 4 in an unsuccessful attempt to ease the Hungarian economic crisis. Of the total, 60 million rubles were to have been spent in the USSR for coke, cotton, synthetic rubber and lead, and 40 million rubles were in the form of a cash loan. (Poland made a $25 million loan of goods available to Hungary Nov. 25.)

Budapest radio conceded Dec. 30 that loans had been sought in an effort to spur crippled production, especially in mining. It said that many engineers and supervisors had fled to the West during the recent fighting. Budapest newspapers reported Dec. 30 that 42,618 miners (half of Hungary's mine force) had reported for work Dec. 28 and had mined 25,855 tons of coal, less than 30% of Hungary's daily requirements.

Indian Prime Min. Jawaharlal Nehru estimated in the Indian Parliament Dec. 13 that 25,000 Hungarians and 7,000 Soviet soldiers had been killed in fighting in Budapest since Oct. 23, according to Indian diplomatic reports. Nehru characterized the Hungarian rebellion as "national" and "widespread." His was the first authoritative estimate of Hungarian casualties to be made public. Scandinavian newsmen reaching Vienna from Budapest Nov. 10 had estimated Hungarian casualties as 20,000 killed. Diplomatic reports from Budapest Nov. 8 had given estimates of 6,500 killed in fighting in the city to that date. But Budapest radio said Dec. 30 that "only between 1,800 and 2,000" Hungarians had been killed in Budapest street fighting during the revolt. It disputed Nehru's estimate of Hungarian casualties.

1957

After the upheavals of 1956, the Soviet bloc regained stability slowly. In Hungary, the counterrevolutionary terror of the renewed Soviet occupation continued despite rapidly diminishing resistance. The severe reprisals, which included summary trials and deportations, were Khrushchev's response to the critics of "de-Stalinization" among his colleagues. The strong verbal hostility of the outside world irritated rather than impressed the Kadar regime and its Soviet sponsors and thus encouraged their intransigence. Worldwide sympathy for the Hungarian revolution had the most tangible effect in the assistance offered to the masses of refugees who had fled the country for the West after the Soviet intervention. Thousands of highly-motivated Hungarians were subsequently integrated into Western societies.

Regardless of the reversal in Hungary, Poland at first preserved most of the freedoms attained in 1956. The Hungarian tragedy enhanced solidarity between the Polish people and their leaders. But in the absence of institutional guarantees for their exercise, the liberties won were of limited duration. Beginning with the prohibition of the outspoken magazine Po prostu (Plain Talk) and the suppression of the subsequent student demonstrations in October, the government gradually repressed dissent. At the same time, it tried to maintain relative freedom of action in foreign affairs, manipulating the support from both the Yugoslav and the Chinese Communist parties. Poland advocated nuclear disengagement in central Europe—a proposal which, if implemented, could have diminished the Soviet tutelage.

Information reaching the West on the suppression of renewed dissent in East Germany—this time of a largely intellectual character—indicated that Stalinism apparently was still alive and in power in at least one other country of the Soviet bloc.

The upsetting consequences of "national communism" continued to strain the Moscow-Belgrade relationship. Each partner tried to exploit the uneasy friendship in order to strengthen its own diplomatic position while preventing the other side from doing so. On the one hand, the Soviet Union hampered economic assistance to Yugoslavia. On the other hand, the Tito regime, by punishing Djilas for his anti-Stalinist book The New Class, *tried to avoid insulting the Soviet leaders. But Belgrade resisted Moscow's efforts to reintegrate Yugoslavia into the Soviet bloc. In November, the Yugoslavs abstained from signing the Moscow declaration on Communist unity.*

OPPOSITION IN HUNGARY SUPPRESSED

Crackdown on Revolutionaries

The Kadar government, supported by Soviet forces in Hungary and guided by Soviet secret police experts, continued during early 1957 to attempt to eliminate all traces of resistance. Further executions took place, and the first major public trial of rebels opened just after mid-February. Passive resistance continued, however—as did the Soviet-inspired measures designed to suppress it.

The International Commission of Jurists estimated June 20 that the Kadar regime had executed 2,000 to 5,000 persons since it began the repression of the 1956 revolt. But Acting Premier Ferenc Muennich asserted in an interview with *N.Y. Times* correspondent Harrison E. Salisbury that no writers and few of the political leaders active in the 1956 movements had been executed. He said that executions had totaled only a "few scores"—at most, 100 persons.

Among executions revealed by the Kadar government was that of Gaza Szivos, 25, put to death for the possession of firearms; his execution had been announced Jan. 6. The executions of ex-Chairman Jozsef Dudas of the All-Hungary Revolutionary Council and of his aide, Janos Szabo, as leaders of the uprising were announced Jan. 19. The government announced Feb. 2 that Ersebet Manyi, 20, and Mihaly Farkas, a Hungarian army officer, had been hanged for organizing and leading riots. 3 rebel leaders—medical student Ilona Toth, 25, Miklos Gyongyosi and Ferenc Gonczi—were sentenced to death Apr. 8, and their sentences were confirmed June 20 by a Supreme Court people's council. (At her trial, which had opened in Budapest Feb. 18, Miss Toth had testified that she had attacked Soviet tanks and had killed a Hungarian security policeman.)

7 rebels, including members of a unit led by Dudas, were condemned to death by a Budapest court May 7, and 2 of them were shot May 7. 3 Hungarians were sentenced to death (and 4 others to long prison terms) by a Budapest court June 8 for the killing of the village council chief of Kakucs, a community 25 miles southeast of Budapest, during the revolt. A Supreme Court people's council June 20 imposed death sentences on the journalist Gyula Obersovsky and the playwright Jozsef Gali, who originally had been sentenced to prison for producing an antigovernment newspaper.

Testimony given before the U.S. Senate Internal Security Subcommittee included reports that 46,000 Hungarian youths of both sexes had been sent to 6 Soviet concentration camps and that 1,600 survivors of the Csepel Island seige in Budapest had been deported to Communist China, it was disclosed June 5 by Sen. Roman L. Hruska (R., Neb.), the subcommittee chairman.

The government had confirmed Jan. 25 that 8 of Hungary's leading writers and journalists (Domoskolos Varga, Tibor Kardos, Balazs Lengyel, Gyula Hay, Zoltan Zelk, Pal Loescei, Sandor Novovaczky, Gabor Folly) had been arrested Jan. 20 on "suspicion of having carried out counter-revolutionary activities." (The government had suspended the Federation of Hungarian Writers and National Association of Hungarian Journalists Jan. 20.) The Supreme Court Nov. 13

imposed jail sentences of 6 years on Hay, 56, and of 3 years on Zelk, 52. It simultaneously sentenced 2 more leading Communist writers who also had been convicted of complicity in the 1956 revolt: Tibor Dery, 63, got a 9-year term and Tibor Kardos an 18-month sentence.

It was reported unofficially in Budapest May 29 that Istvan Bibo, a Peasant Party leader and minister-without-portfolio in the Nagy government during the revolution, had been arrested. The arrest of Laszlo Kardos of the Peasant Party, ex-director of the Union of Colleges, for revolutionary activity was reported unofficially June 3. Ex-Hungarian Pres. Zoltan Tildy, Smallholders' Party leader and a member of the 1956 Nagy government, was reported to have been freed June 16 following his arrest May 24 for questioning in connection with the expected trial of ex-Premier Imre Nagy. The Hungarian Socialist Workers' (Communist) Party newspaper *Nepszabadsag* disclosed June 16 the earlier arrest of the Rev. Egon Turcsanyi, secretary to Jozsef Cardinal Mindszenty.

The West German newspaper *Bildzeitung* Jan. 5 had quoted ex-Premier Nagy as predicting the fall of the Kadar government because Kadar "rules against the will of the people." Nagy, in an interview said to have been granted to a Yugoslav reporter at the Yugoslav embassy in Budapest 6 weeks earlier, foresaw "the end of communism in its present form." Nagy said that "at first" he thought he "could speak openly with the Russians," but it had been "proved an error." "The Hungarian revolution went far beyond its aims and has therefore failed," he declared.

The Kadar regime charged Jan. 6 that the "treason of the Imre Nagy government had paved the way for a counterrevolution" aimed at "erecting a feudal and capitalist state and turning Hungary into a scene of fire."

Warsaw dispatches reported June 25 that Nagy had been returned to Budapest from Rumania to stand trial for his role in the 1956 revolt.

(The Kadar government had announced Apr. 25 that Lt. Gen. Mihaly Farkas, ex-defense minister and Stalinist Security Police [AVH] chief reputed to have tortured Kadar during his imprisonment under the Matyas Rakosi regime, had been sentenced to 16 years' imprisonment for "serious violations of law." A U.S. House Committee on Un-American Activities report Mar. 20 had said that Sandor Kiss, secretary general of the exiled Hungarian Revolutionary Council, had related that Kadar once was "arrested, his teeth were knocked out and he was finally castrated" while an AVH prisoner. A spokesman for the UN General Assembly's special committee investigating the Hungarian revolution denied in New York June 4 a report that the group had taken evidence that Kadar was tortured and castrated by Soviet agents to force him to abandon support of the revolution.)

The government had promised Jan. 6 that it would "conduct talks with the various factions of public life" on the "participation in the government" and "consolidation of progressive forces of the nation." But Associated Press dispatches reported Jan. 6 that leaders of the Smallholders, National Peasant and Social Democratic parties had met in Budapest and agreed not to enter into separate negotiations with the Kadar government. The *N.Y. Times* Jan. 2 had reported negotiations under way between the government and non-Communist parties on demands for: (a) an end to martial law, summary courts and deportations; (b) legal rights for prisoners and dissolution of the political police; (c) access to press and radio for government coalition parties; (d) the entry of the Social Democrats into the cabinet; (e) continuance of the Workers and Peasants Councils formed in 1956; and (f) a Soviet statement on withdrawal of troops from Hungary.

The Kadar regime warned workers Jan. 6 that "irresponsible practices" must "be stopped." This apparently was an allusion to sporadic work stoppages. 75% of the coal miners at Tatabanya had refused to enter the pits Jan. 4 because of the arrest of 12 Tatabanya miners Jan. 1. Industry Min. Antal Apro received a Tatabanya miners' delegation Jan. 5 but rejected the miners' demands that Workers Council members be freed from production work. The National Trades Union Council Jan. 8 postponed indefinitely promised union elections.

Budapest area Workers Councils, led by Csepel Island Council heads, resigned Jan. 9 in protest against the government's refusal to grant them a voice in Hungarian factory operations. A proclamation issued by dissident council leaders after a meeting Jan. 10 with Sandor Gaspar, Trade Union Federation general secretary, recognized the councils as "part of the community of workers" but condemned the resignations as "provocative." Soviet troops and Hungarian militia patrolled the Csepel area Jan. 10-12 and killed at least 2 of 5,000 workers who demonstrated against the government Jan. 12. (Radio Budapest announced Nov. 19 that the Workers Councils had been abolished and would be replaced by factory councils controlled by government-run trade unions.)

The government Jan. 12 ordered the formation of summary civilian courts empowered to pass "normal" sentences of death for strikes and other forms of labor unrest, including loitering near factories, interfering with work and unauthorized entrance into plants. The decree, in which it was conceded that some sentences might be limited to long prison terms, applied to all factories employing 100 or more workers.

The government had halted a scheduled meeting of the independent MEFESZ student organization by arresting 8 of its leaders Jan. 11.

Bela Kovacs resigned as secretary general of the Smallholders Party Jan. 14 in protest against repressive policies of the Kadar government. The Petofi (formerly National Peasant) Party announced its dissolution Jan. 12 in a similar protest.

Kadar charged at a meeting of Hungarian Socialist Workers' (Communist) Party activists Feb. 4 that a new revolt was being planned for March. He said villages and schools were principal centers of rebel activity. He warned that his regime would "proceed pitilessly against all who attack the People's Democracy." Education Min. Albert Konya, announcing Feb. 3 that the University of Budapest would be reopened Feb. 4, had said that arms had been found in searches of students' homes. He warned that "the government will take draconian measures against them."

Chain letters urging Hungarians to join in silent demonstrations of protest Mar. 15 (anniversary of the 1848 Hungarian revolt against Habsburg rule) were reported circulating in Budapest Feb. 11.

Budapest dispatches reported June 8 that speeches by Kadar and State Min. Gyorgy Marosan indicated a mounting struggle for power within the Communist Party between "rightist" followers of Stalinist ex-Premier Rakosi and "leftist" proponents of liberalized government policies. Kadar, speaking at a Budapest rally for visiting Bulgarian Premier Anton Yugov, warned June 8 that his government could not "afford to be sentimental" about the fate of Hungarians who clung to "the bourgeois conception of freedom" or those "who cannot cure themselves of old mistakes." Marosan, speaking at a Communist Party meeting on Csepel Island June 8, denied that the government had been forced to suppress "a neo-Stalinist putsch." He warned, however, that "some who used to sit in higher places" were "discontented with the lower function."

Kadar, speaking in Kisujszallas, Szolnok County, on Hungarian Constitution Day, declared Aug. 20 that some Hungarians had complained that his regime was "not cruel enough," presumably in dealing with its opponents. Archbishop Joszef Grosz, acting Roman Catholic primate of Hungary, in a statement broadcast Sept. 10 by Budapest radio, denied that he or any of his bishops had been arrested or hampered in their movements. (A Vatican decree, published Sept. 6 by the Sacred Congregation of the Council, forbade Hungarian Catholic clergymen to serve in the Hungarian Parliament or in other political posts on pain of excommunication.)

Pres. Istvan Dobi announced Nov. 3 the abolition of summary courts.

Disposition of Refugees

The flow of Hungarian escapees into Austria continued into 1957 despite police searches of Hungarian trains in the border area and shootings of several refugees.

The Yugoslav Foreign Ministry reported Jan. 4 that 2,236 Hungarians had entered Yugoslavia since the revolt began. Yugoslavia listed 132 returnees to Hungary, 29 emigrants to asylum in France and Italy.

Pres. Eisenhower Jan. 1 had ordered an unspecified number of additional Hungarian refugees admitted to the U.S. "until such time as Congress acts" on new refugee legislation. Eisenhower acted following the release Jan. 1 of a formal report by Vice Pres. Nixon on his tour of Austrian and West German refugee camps. A 2d U.S. refugee airlift began from West Germany Jan. 8 under plans to admit 6,814 Hungarian "parolees" above the announced 21,500 U.S. quota.

The International Rescue Committee (IRC) Jan. 1 disclosed the appointment of John Alexander-Sinclair, ex-aide to the UN High Commission for Refugees, to replace Joseph L. Buttinger as chief of the IRC's Hungarian refugee program.

30 Hungarian border guards pursued 20 fleeing refugees into Austrian territory near Nikitsch, 11 miles south southeast of Sopron, Jan. 20. They were said to have forced some of the escapees to return to Hungarian soil. The Hungarian government demanded in a complaint to the UN Jan. 19 that refugee children be returned from Western countries to their parents in Hungary and that oth~r refugees be encouraged to return under an amnesty offer good until Mar. 31. The complaint charged that some refugees in the West had been grilled about military matters, forced to work in British mines against their will and mistreated in other ways.

A UN General Assembly investigating committee met with prominent escapees in New York Jan. 28-29 to hear testimony on Soviet intervention in Hungary. Anna Kethly, state minister in the deposed Nagy government, appealed to the committee Jan. 28 for UN action to free Hungary from Soviet rule, for financial aid for a restored Nagy government and for the expulsion of the Kadar regime's UN delegation. Maj. Gen. Bela Kiraly, ex-rebel commander for Budapest, told the committee Jan. 29 that the USSR had armed Hungary to serve as an advance Soviet base "in the event of an attack on Western Europe." Joseph Kovago, mayor of Budapest (1945-7 and 1956), reproached the UN Jan. 29 for mere "factfinding" action on Hungary.

Hungarian Foreign Ministry officials conceded Feb. 16 that 196,000 Hungarians had fled the country since Oct. 23, 1956: 180,000 to Austria, 16,000 to Yugoslavia. They claimed that 16,000 refugees had returned from Austria and nearly 1,000 from Yugoslavia. A Hungarian government repatriation mission attempted to interview refugees in Austrian camps Feb. 2 but was stoned and succeeded in talking to only 2 of the 1,500 escapees brought before it by Feb. 6.

Austrian Interior Min. Oskar Helmer Jan. 29 demanded European and U.S. aid to help support the 70,000 Hungarians remaining in Austria. He said at a UN Refugee Fund Executive Committee meeting in Geneva that Austria was "tired" of having to "beg and haggle" for refugee funds and visas for the escapees. Austrian notes sent Jan. 15 to the UN High Commission for Refugees and Intergovernmental Committee on European Migration had warned that Austrian relief funds were depleted. The notes appealed for speedy evacuation of Hungarians from Austrian camps, citing their growing "unrest" and anti-Semitism.

Chairman Francis E. Walter of the U.S. House Immigration & Naturalization Subcommittee had opened hearings Jan. 25 on refugee entry "irregularities." Walter said Jan. 25 that he was convinced that 6,200 refugees had been issued U.S. visas illegally under the Refugee & Relief Act. Immigration Commissioner Joseph M. Swing told the subcommittee Jan. 25 that only 3 of the 23,000 refugees then admitted had been found to be subversives. Walter said on NBC-TV's "American Forum" Feb. 10 that many of the first Hungarian refugees admitted to the U.S. had been "Communists fleeing from the ire of their fellow countrymen."

Auguste R. Lindt, UN High Commissioner for Refugees, urged Mar. 24 that the U.S. and other non-European countries help resettle 16,168 Hungarian refugees receiving asylum in Yugoslavia. He reported that only 869 escapees had been evacuated from Yugoslavia to the West. Lindt and UN Secy. Gen. Dag Hammarskjold, in a joint appeal to 88 nations Mar. 1 (made public Mar. 12), had called for a final solution of the Hungarian refugee problem during 1957.

The U.S. Mar. 21 made available $4 million to the Intergovernmental Committee for European Migration for the resettlement of Hungarian refugees from Yugoslavia in countries other than the U.S. The U.S. Immigration & Naturalization Service was said to have barred Hungarian refugee entrants from Yugoslavia Feb. 23 on White House orders.

U.S. officials in Vienna said Apr. 5 that the current U.S. immigration program for Hungarian refugees would be ended within 2 weeks unless Congress acted on legislation extending the program. But State Department officials in Washington said Apr. 6 that the program would be slowed but not ended. Robert S. McCollum, head of State Department refugee affairs, said Apr. 8 that he would urge the White House to begin a new 3-month Hungarian refugee program. Sen. Joseph R. McCarthy (R., Wis.) said Apr. 8 that he would sponsor a bill to allow the entry of an additional 75,000 Hungarians to the U.S.

Eisenhower May 14 dissolved his Presidential Committee for Hungarian Refugee Relief but said that the U.S. would "continue to meet its full share of ... responsibility ... to help these people." The committee, in a final report issued May 14, said that 32,075 refugees had been resettled in the U.S. by May 1. It reported that 13,120 refugees had been brought to the U.S. by the Military Air Transport Service, 9,664 by chartered planes of the Intergovernmental Committee on European Migration and 8,945 by the Military Sea Transport Service. The U.S. refugee reception center at Camp Kilmer, N.J. was closed May 7. The State Department had said Apr. 13, however, that the U.S. would continue to accept limited numbers of refugees as parolees.

The U.S. May 14 made available to Austria $10 million worth of surplus farm products for the benefit of the estimated 35,000 Hungarians remaining in Austria. The League of Red Cross Societies had reported May 7 that 59 nations had contributed more than $30 million in emergency relief for Hungarian refugee programs.

The Austrian Interior Ministry disclosed May 2 that 5,901 Hungarian refugees had chosen voluntary repatriation to Hungary—4,464 from Austrian refugee camps and 1,437 from countries in which they had been resettled.

2,000 refugees at Camp Siezenheim, near Salzburg, rioted May 7 and began a hunger strike in protest against restrictions on emigration to the U.S. and other Western countries. The fast ended after Mrs. Eleanor Roosevelt visited the camp May 10 and promised to "inform the American people about your situation."

Atty. Gen. Herbert Brownell announced May 15 liberalized parole requirements for the admission of Hungarian refugees to the U.S. UN High Commissioner for Refugees Lindt disclosed May 15 that Canada, Belgium, West Germany and France had offered to admit 8,000 of the Hungarian refugees remaining in Yugoslavia.

The U.S. Immigration Service disclosed May 29 that Samuel Gombos, 37, had been sent back to Austria as a Communist military intelligence agent. He was the 9th Hungarian refugee officially reported to have been admitted to the U.S., then deported as a Communist. (A U.S. Information Service official said May 27 in Richmond, Va., however, that about 40 Hungarians had been returned to Austria for concealing past Communist affiliation.)

Mrs. Maria Maleter, 33, divorced wife of Maj. Gen. Pal Maleter, petitioned UN Secy. Gen. Hammarskjold Sept. 10 to intercede with Soviet and Hungarian authorities on behalf of the imprisoned rebel leader. She had fled Budapest to Vienna and had been admitted to Canada with her 3 children. She charged that Maleter had been "treacherously arrested" by Col. Gen. Ivan A. Serov, Soviet MVD chief, Nov. 3, 1956 while negotiating a rebel-Soviet truce at Tokol, Soviet Army Headquarters on Csepel Island just south of Budapest.

The League of Red Cross Societies reported in Vienna Sept. 28 that Red Cross contributions for Hungarian refugees in Austria had totaled $14.6 million and 19,191 tons of supplies since the revolt. The American Red Cross reported Oct. 22 that it had provided $5,463,795 in aid for the refugees.

Miklos Szabo, Hungarian Smallholders deputy and founding member of the Revolutionary Council who fled to Austria in 1956, disappeared from Vienna Sept. 8 and was presumed to have returned to Hungary. Letters received from Szabo Sept. 11 said that he had planned to go back after realizing "that the Western powers have betrayed and sold us." (Chief Counsel Robert Morris of the Senate Internal Security Subcommittee charged Oct. 22 that Szabo was a "secret Communist agent who posed as a Hungarian refugee leader" in order to compile the names of refugees who testified before the UN Special Committee on Hungary.)

Paul Benko, 29, 1948 Hungarian chess champion, arrived in the U.S. Oct. 17 after defecting from a Hungarian chess team while playing in Iceland.

The office of the UN High Commission for Refugees announced Nov. 2 that of 195,000 Hungarians who fled to Austria during and after the 1956 revolt, 165,000 had emigrated to 34 other countries (10,500 remained in Austrian refugee camps), 10,000 had been repatriated voluntarily to Hungary, and all but 4,800 of 20,000 who fled to Yugoslavia had been resettled in other countries.

UN Action Frustrated

UN efforts to fix responsibility for the Hungarian bloodletting reached a crescendo in 1957. A majority of the member states in the General Assembly voted to condemn the Soviet Union anew for its suppression of the 1956 revolt. But the Kremlin dismissed the condemnation as a "propaganda bomb," and the Kadar regime refused to admit the UN's special representative on the ground that his mission was an "interference" in Hungarian internal affairs.

The General Assembly voted by 59-8 (10 abstentions) in New York Jan. 10 to establish a 5-nation investigating committee to gather information on "the situation created by the intervention" of Soviet armed forces "in the internal affairs of Hungary." The Special Committee on the Problem of Hungary (made up of delegates from Australia, Ceylon, Denmark, Tunisia and Uruguay) was empowered to seek its evidence either "in Hungary" or "elsewhere," presumably from Hungarians who had escaped to the West. The resolution, submitted to the Assembly Jan. 9 by the U.S. and 23 co-sponsors, was supported Jan. 10 by all states joining in the Dec. 12, 1956 UN condemnation of Soviet intervention in Hungary except Cuba, plus Morocco, Ceylon and Indonesia. Cuba opposed the new resolution on the ground that it would bury the Hungarian question in "dusty archives." The resolution had been written as an alternative to a threatened Cuban move to demand the expulsion of the Hungarian UN delegation.

The Kadar government Jan. 11 denounced the proposed UN investigation as "unprecedented, gross interference." It said that "no committee of any kind" had the right to probe Hungary's internal affairs. It protested the UN plan to interview "unauthorized and biased" Hungarian escapees and said that refugees who returned to Hungary would "not suffer harm or molestation."

The UN Special Committee on Hungary charged the USSR June 20 with armed repression of the 1956 uprising. The 5-member committee (Alsing Andersen of Denmark [chairman], Mongi Slim of Tunisia, Enrique Rodriguez Fabregat of Uruguay, R. S. S. Gunewardene of Ceylon and Keith C. O. Shann of Australia) detailed in a 150,000-word report its findings that Soviet armed forces had invaded Hungary to overthrow the legal government of Imre Nagy and impose a puppet regime led by Janos Kadar. Prepared under the Jan. 10 General Assembly resolution, the report was based on an investigation of evidence provided by 111 witnesses, the majority of them being Hungarian refugees.

The investigators sketched an hour-by-hour history of the revolt and ensuing intervention by Soviet forces, which it estimated at from 75,000 to 200,000 men with 2,500 tanks and armored cars and 1,000 supporting vehicles. They charged that simultaneously with the Oct. 30, 1956 withdrawal of Soviet forces from Budapest, new Soviet units were entering Hungary from Rumania and Czechoslovakia, so that "by the evening of 2 November, Hungary had to all intents and purposes been reinvaded." The signers of the report asserted that, following the suppression of the revolt, "thousands" of Hungarians had been deported to Rumania and the USSR.

The committee report, written by Shann, contained these conclusions for the General Assembly:

(1) The revolt "was a spontaneous national uprising, due to long-standing grievances," based on "the inferior status of Hungary with regard to the USSR," and a government system "in part maintained by the weapon of terror, wielded by the AVH [state security police] or political police."

(2) The uprising was led by Hungarians, "many of whom were Communists or former Communists," in hopes of installing "democratic socialism."

(3) Charges that the revolt had been fomented by exiles or Western "imperialists" had "failed to survive the committee's examination."

(4) Although the revolt began Oct. 23, Soviet troops were moving "as early as 20 October to make armed intervention in Hungary possible."

(5) The first shots of the rebellion were fired Oct. 23 by AVH members guarding the Budapest Radio Building.

(6) "Obscurity surrounds the invitation alleged to have been issued by the Hungarian government" for Soviet aid "in quelling the uprising by force."

(Items 7, 8, 9, 10) "The few days of freedom enjoyed by the Hungarian people," their acceptance of Nagy as a "symbolic figure," the hatred shown toward AVH members and the growth of the Workers Council movement, all "provided abundant evidence of the popular nature of the uprising."

(11, 12) Violations of the Hungarian people's "basic human rights," evident up to Oct. 23, 1956, were resumed Nov. 4 with the "2d Soviet intervention." There "has been no evidence of popular support for Mr. Kadar's government" since Nov. 4, 1956.

(13) Consideration of the Hungarian question by the UN, "requested by a legal [Nagy] government of Hungary," was legally proper "in the light of the extent of foreign intervention."

In a Moscow radio broadcast June 20, the UN report was ridiculed as a U.S. "propaganda bomb," "fabricated by false testimonies" and created by "dark machinations under the [UN] flag." The broadcast charged the inquiry committee with violating provisions against UN "interference in the internal affairs of member states." A Hungarian Foreign Ministry statement June 21 termed the UN report a "collection of lies" based on testimony by "political adventurers, common criminals and traitorous refugees."

24 nations co-sponsoring the Special Committee on Hungary met June 26 and appealed for renewed General Assembly debate on the subject. From a poll of UN member states it was indicated Aug. 12 that a majority desired to discuss the Special Committee's report. In response, Secy. Gen. Hammarskjold Aug. 19 called a special General Assembly session for Sept. 10.

Meeting informally with delegates of 60 non-Communist UN states, U.S. Amb.-to-UN Henry Cabot Lodge Jr. made public Sept. 3 a U.S. draft resolution renewing UN censure of the USSR for its repression of the Hungarian revolt. The resolution called for (a) approval of the report of the General Assembly's Special Committee on Hungary, (b) extension of the committee's work, (c) an end to "repressive measures against the Hungarian people" by the Soviet and Hungarian governments and (d) consideration of the Hungarian problem by the 12th (regular) General Assembly, scheduled to meet Sept. 17.

A 36-nation resolution, introduced Sept. 10 at the opening of a special UN General Assembly session, urged renewed UN condemnation of the Soviet Union for its suppression of the revolt. The resolution, a compromise version of the U.S. draft circulated Sept. 3, asked that Prince Wan Waithayakon of Thailand, General Assembly president, be appointed as a "special representative of the General Assembly on the Hungarian problem" to try to obtain Soviet and Hungarian compliance with previous General Assembly resolutions calling for the withdrawal of Soviet troops from Hungary, the entry of UN observers and the calling of free Hungarian general elections.

Lodge urged the General Assembly Sept. 10 to keep the Hungarian issue "in the forefront" of its discussions in the hope that the USSR would be forced to "respond to the judgments of public opinion." He assured the USSR Sept. 10 that "the [U.S.] has never thought that a free Hungary ... should have other than a neutral foreign policy, or that it should be brought into any military alliances with the West."

The special session, called to debate the report of the Special Committee on Hungary, was denounced Sept. 10 by Soviet delegate Arkady A. Sobolev and Hungarian Rep.-to-UN Peter Mod. Sobolev charged that the session had been arranged by U.S. "aggressive circles" in an attempt to convert the General Assembly into an instrument of "American foreign policy." Mod renewed charges that the Hungarian revolt had been aimed at restoration of the "Fascist Horthy regime." He challenged Hammarskjold to visit Hungary to "convince himself of the inaccuracy" of the Special Committee's report.

Kadar attacked the report Sept. 11. He said that the "American" resolution, as he termed it, demonstrated that "the imperialists" had not forgiven Hungary for repelling their assault in 1956. "The resolution," he said, "reproaches us with arresting people.... I ask what would happen to Americans who make armed plots against the state?"

Radio Budapest reported Sept. 8 that mass demonstrations had been held throughout Hungary in protest against charges contained in the report of the UN Special Committee on the Problem of Hungary, which was published in serial form by the Hungarian Socialist Workers' (Communist) Party newspaper *Nepszabadsag* beginning Aug. 27. Radio Budapest said that 50,000 persons had gathered in Miskolc to denounce the report for its "testimony bought with dollars from adventurers and traitors who fled to the West." Refugee sources in Vienna reported Sept. 8 that workers of the Csepel Island industrial complex just outside of Budapest had been forced to sign petitions denouncing the report, on the pretext that they were signing pay receipts.

(In a report circulated to UN General Assembly delegates Sept. 9, the exile Assembly of Captive European Nations charged that repressive conditions in Hungary surpassed "the worst days" of Stalinist rule under Matyas Rakosi. The report, intended to supplement the UN findings, was prepared with the aid of Adolf A. Berle Jr., ex-Assistant Secretary of State and Columbia University law professor, Mrs. Clare Booth Luce, ex-U.S. ambassador to Italy, Director Leo Cherne of the Research Institute of America and Dr. Reinhold Niebuhr, clergyman. In another report to the General Assembly, the International

Commission of Jurists charged Sept. 6 that Hungarian courts had become an active arm of the Kadar regime's repression and that Hungary was unworthy of UN membership.)

In a final meeting Sept. 14 of its special session on Hungary, the 11th UN General Assembly voted by 60-10 (9 Soviet bloc nations and Yugoslavia opposed) with 10 abstentions (9 Arab-Asian states and Finland) to condemn the USSR for its suppression of the revolt. The General Assembly resolution, presented by 37 nations, indorsed the report of the Special Committee on the Problem of Hungary, called on the Soviet and Hungarian governments to "desist from repressive measures against the Hungarian people" and named Prince Wan Waithayakon of Thailand as "special representative of the General Assembly" to take steps to achieve compliance with the UN resolution on Hungary.

The resolution was adopted after delegates of sponsoring states, led by U.S. Amb.-to-UN Lodge, refused to accept 3 amendments submitted Sept. 12 by Burmese Rep.-to-UN U Thant. The Burmese proposals, all defeated Sept. 14, were:

(1) To substitute "deplores" for "condemns" as the resolution's key word (rejected by 45-2 vote with 30 abstentions).

(2) To end the General Assembly's Special Committee on the Problem of Hungary (rejected by 43-3 vote with 32 abstentions).

(3) To soften to "main conclusion" the Special Committee's "conclusion" that "the events which took place in Hungary in October and November of 1956 constituted a spontaneous national uprising" (rejected by 40-4 vote with 32 abstentions).

As passed by the General Assembly, the resolution charged that:

(1) The USSR had "deprived Hungary of its liberty and the Hungarian people of the exercise of their fundamental human rights."

(2) "The present Hungarian regime has been imposed on the Hungarian people by the armed intervention of the [USSR]."

(3) "The [USSR] has carried out mass deportation of Hungarian citizens to the [USSR]."

(4) "The [USSR] has violated its obligations under the Geneva Convention of 1949."

(5) "The present authorities in Hungary have violated the human rights and freedoms guaranteed by the Treaty of Peace with Hungary."

Challenged by Enrique Fabregat of Uruguay on whether he had sided with the rebels during the revolt, Hungarian Rep.-to-UN Peter Mod said Sept. 13 that if the committee's work had been "more thorough," there would be no question of his [Mod's] status. Fabregat told the General Assembly Sept. 13

that Mod had been chairman of a rebel revolutionary committee in the Hungarian Foreign Ministry that called, Oct. 30, 1956, for Hungary's "liberation" and denounced the USSR's "unwarranted interference." Mod, 46, a World War II French Army veteran and resistance organizer, denied to newsmen Sept. 13 that he was the man Fabregat cited.

Hungarian Foreign Ministry spokesman Laszlo Gyaros told newsmen Sept. 14 that his government would not admit any person sent to Hungary "with the aim of interfering" in the nation's internal affairs. Gyaros said that the UN resolution naming Thai Prince Wan as General Assembly envoy on the Hungarian problem "seeks to send Prince Wan to our country with precisely such an assignment." Gyaros said, however, that Hungary was prepared to welcome either Wan or UN Secy. Gen. Hammarskjold "as private persons at a proper time suitable both to the Hungarian government and the individual concerned."

UNEASY LIBERALIZATION IN POLAND

General Election

The failure of Hungary's rebellion against Soviet domination left the stubborn defiance in Poland very much in the international spotlight as 1957 progressed. United Workers' (Communist) Party First Secy. Wladyslaw Gomulka, who continued to enjoy at least the tacit backing of the Roman Catholic Church in Poland, sought support from Yugoslavia and Communist China for his "national Communist" policies.

The Gomulka regime won overwhelming indorsement in a single-list election held Jan. 20. State Election Commission tallies released Jan. 22 showed that of 17,499,000 eligible voters, 16,833,316 (94.14%) had participated, and of these, 16,563,314 (98.4%) had cast ballots for the Communist-backed National Front slate. Western newsmen covering the Polish elections reported no signs of voter coercion at polling stations.

Polish citizens, voting with partial freedom for the first time since the last pre-World War II election in 1935, received the right to cross out in secret the unwanted candidates' names listed among 723 in the running for 459 vacancies in the new Sejm (parliament). Of the approved candidates' names appearing on the prearranged single ballot, 370 to 400 were estimated to be Communist candidates' (listed on the top ⅔ of the ballot). 25% of the remaining names reportedly were of Peasants' Party members, 10% of Democratic Party candidates and the rest of independents. On ballots containing no crossouts, the vote went to as many top-listed names as were needed to fill vacancies. Fewer than 12% of the candidates were members of the old Sejm, in which the United Workers' Party held 273 seats, the Peasants' Party 90, Democrats 25 and independents 37.

Intensive Communist, government and National Front appeals in support of Gomulka preceded the election. These groups and forces urged voters to return untampered ballots and choose between "freedom, peace and prosperity" and "poverty, misery and war." The "Don't Cross Out" campaign and heavy electioneering was laid to government hopes of mass support for the preferred slate in order to (a) make Polish "negotiations from strength" possible with the USSR, (b) prove that "national communism" could command popular support and (c) forestall armed Soviet intervention aimed at "safeguarding" a repudiated Polish government.

The selection of candidates for the National Front list had begun Jan. 3 with political, cooperative, professional and mass organizations choosing from the ranks of the Communist, Peasant and Democratic parties only those committed to socialism in Poland. The government announced Jan. 12 that some candidates had been dropped for "lack of discipline." Edward Osobka-Morawski, the Socialist ex-premier, was banned from the list Jan. 17 for a "discordant" attitude toward the campaign. The Democratic Party's youth organization was dissolved Jan. 17 for "discordance" after the United Workers' Party Central Committee intervened in its activities. The youth group, largely Catholic and anti-Marxist, had been disavowed by the Democratic Party.

Gomulka told the voters in a radio address Jan. 19 that the "reactionaries'" propaganda to cross out the names of Communist candidates "is tantamount to calling for the liquidation of Socialist Poland." Gomulka asserted that "fraternal Polish-Soviet relations" were "the most vital interest of the Polish nation." He had said in a campaign speech Jan. 12

that the United Workers' Party would "never surrender power" for fear of a "tragic calamity for Poland."

Stefan Cardinal Wyszynski, Roman Catholic primate of Poland, refrained from public comment on the campaign Jan. 16-20, but Warsaw dispatches reported that he had made clear his support of the Gomulka regime. The Most Rev. Zygmunt Choromanski, Polish Episcopate secretary, ordered Jan. 16 that Sunday masses Jan. 20 be scheduled so that churchgoers could vote easily. He urged Catholics to "fulfill their duty of conscience by participating in the voting." Bishop Ignacy Swirski of Siedlce said Jan. 20 that it was "the duty of every Catholic to vote for the National Front list" and "give a vote of confidence to Gomulka." Many village priests were reported to have led congregations to the polls Jan. 20.

Jozef Cyrankiewicz was reelected premier Feb. 20 by the new Sejm, in which his United Workers' Party held 237 seats, the Peasants' Party 118, Democrats 39 and independents (including 12 Roman Catholics) 63. Cyrankiewicz Feb. 26 named a cabinet of 24 Communist and 8 Democratic, Peasant and nonpartisan allies. Zenon Nowak, "Stalinist" rival of Gomulka, was retained as a deputy premier.

Others in the new cabinet (United Workers' Party members unless otherwise designated):

Deputy Premiers — Piotor Jaroszewicz, Stefan Ignar (Peasant); *Planning Commission Chairman* — Stefan Jedrychowski; *Foreign Affairs* — Adam Rapacki; *Defense* — Marjan Spychalski; *Justice* — Marian Rybicki; *Internal Affairs* — Wladyslaw Wicha; *Finance* — Tadeusz Dietrich; *State Control* — Jan Gorecki; *Metallurgy & Engineering Industry* — Kiejstut Zemajtis; *Chemical* — Antoni Radlinski; *Coal Mining & Power* — Franciszek Waniolka; *Light Industry* — Julian Stawinski; *Small-Scale Industry & Handcrafts* — Zygmunt Moskwa (Democratic); *Agriculture* — Edward Ochab; *Agricultural Foodstuffs & Purchases* — Feliks Pisula (Peasant); *Forestry & Timber* — Jan Dab-Kociol (Peasant); *Railways, Road & Air Transport* — Ryszard Strzelecki; *Building & Building Materials* — Stefan Pietrusiewicz; *Shipping* — Stanislaw Darski (nonpartisan); *Domestic Trade* — Marjan Minor; *Foreign Trade* — Witold Trampczynski (nonpartisan); *Communications* — Jan Rabanowski (Democrat); *Education* — Wladyslaw Bienkowski;

Higher Education — Stefan Zolkiewski; *Public Utilities* — Stanislaw Sroka; *Health* — Rajnund Baranski (nonpartisan); *Labor & Social Welfare* — Stanislaw Zawadzki; *Art & Culture* — Karol Kurylek; *Minister Without Portfolio for Religious Affairs* — Jerzy Sztachelski.

Independence Reaffirmed

Chinese Communist Premier Chou En-lai, having arrived in Warsaw Jan. 11, toured Poland and held intermittent talks with Gomulka and other leaders Jan. 11-15. Speaking at meetings in Poland, Chou said: (Jan. 11) "The Polish nation may always count on the support of the Chinese nation." (Jan. 12) While "abnormal relations" could arise between Socialist states, their policies should avoid "fundamental conflicts." (Jan. 15) The Chinese Communist Party "supports your efforts."

Premier Cyrankiewicz said Jan. 14 that "talks with our Chinese friends reveal that they fully understand" Poland's "road" toward "reforming our life." "The coexistence of nations," he said, "should not be like the coexistence of fish living in one big pond or lake, the bigger fish devouring the smaller ones." "We are fighting against all forms of national oppression."

The Gomulka group consolidated its control over leadership during the 9th plenary session of the Polish United Workers' (Communist) Party Central Committee May 15-20 in Warsaw. After warning liberal "revisionists" May 15 to conform with party policy or leave the party, Gomulka attacked Stalinist elements and rejected Polish "servility" to the USSR. Gomulka May 19 nominated 2 of his strongest backers, Zenon Kliszko and Jerzy Morawski, as Central Committee secretaries. Kliszko replaced ex-Party First Secy. Edward Ochab, who was "relieved" of the Central Committee post May 19.

The Central Committee meeting, the first since the Oct. 1956 session that confirmed Gomulka in power, ended May 20 with a resolution affirming that a "Polish road to socialism" did not mean the abandonment of Communist internationalism. It rejected the "mechanical imitation" of the USSR during Stalin's regime and concluded that it had resulted in the "ossification of Marxist thought." The resolution said that the party would press its "fight on 2 fronts" against "dogmatism" and "revisionism."

In another sign of independence, Poland signed June 7 in Washington a $95 million loan agreement providing for initial Polish purchases of $48.9 million worth of U.S. machinery and surplus farm goods and pledging, pending Congressional authorization, the U.S. sale to Poland of an additional $46.1 million worth of farm surpluses. In return, Poland agreed "to take all possible measures" to insure that U.S. goods were not resold or transshipped to other states, presumably those of the Soviet bloc. The U.S. and Polish governments agreed to open negotiations on the release of pre-World War II Polish assets in the U.S. and U.S. claims resulting from postwar Polish nationalizations.

Gomulka had told factory workers in Poznan June 5 that hopes for massive U.S. aid had been "illusions" but that the "rather modest" U.S. credits would "to a certain degree alleviate our present economic difficulties." Gomulka, however, warned that, despite the U.S. loans, continued close ties with the USSR were "necessary for Poland to exist." He said: "We cannot always do what we like. In the present situation we are forced to abide by" the Warsaw Pact. He appealed to Poznan to honor victims of the 1956 riots "in a peaceful way with deep respect."

U.S. Vice Pres. Richard Nixon, addressing the Michigan State University commencement June 9, termed the Polish loan accord "a gamble worth taking" in the hope that Poland eventually would turn away from communism. Nixon rejected Senate Republican leader William F. Knowland's (Calif.) contention May 13 that the Polish loan program might be the beginning of a "Communist Marshall Plan." Nixon said that the accord announced "to the world that we are not writing off the Polish people or any of the other millions who are held behind the Iron Curtain."

The agreement in Washington caused wide comment. Informed Polish sources reported June 24 that Soviet Deputy Premier Anastas I. Mikoyan had been sent to Warsaw June 15 in an effort to end a dispute said to have been caused by Soviet Communist Party First Secy. Nikita S. Khrushchev's brusque rejection of economic claims by Gomulka during Polish-Soviet talks in Moscow May 24-27. Khrushchev reportedly had refused a Polish bill for 300 million rubles ($75 million) for postwar Polish transit facilities accorded the USSR. He was said to have warned Poland that it could not go on "milking" the USSR and to have suggested that its leaders look elsewhere, presumably to the U.S., for additional aid.

Toward autumn the new regime made another *demarche.* The Polish government announced Sept. 1 that Premier Cyrankiewicz and Gomulka would visit Yugoslavia shortly for talks with Pres. Tito. Warsaw's *Trybuna Ludu,* the United Workers' (Communist) Party daily, said Sept. 1 that the talks would bolster ties among all east European states "based on the real independence of all these countries." (Austrian government spokesmen disclosed Sept. 3 that Cyrankiewicz had made a secret 4-day visit to Vienna in late August.)

Gomulka, accompanied by Cyrankiewicz, Foreign Min. Adam Rapacki and Agriculture Min. Edward Ochab, arrived in Belgrade Sept. 10 and began their discussions with the Yugoslav leaders. In a joint declaration signed the 16, Tito and Gomulka affirmed their support of Soviet foreign policies and strong cooperation among all Soviet-bloc states. Tito had asserted Sept. 15 that he "would like to see Poland and Yugoslavia demonstrate that they are not adopting any form of national communism," although neither Poland nor Yugoslavia could "copy the experience of the Soviet Union in a stereotyped manner."

Widespread Unrest

Gomulka, speaking in Krakow Aug. 17, warned Polish workers against the activities of demagogues, who, he said, had incited Lodz tram workers into "wildcat strikes" Aug. 12-14. He denounced speculation, inflation and strikes as "cheating the workers." (The Polish government Aug. 16 expelled United Press correspondent Anthony J. Cavendish for his "tendentious" reporting of the Lodz strike.)

Kazimierz Szczepanski, Warsaw Central District United Workers' (Communist) Party first secretary, disclosed Aug. 21 that the district's entire executive corps, regarded as adherents of the pro-Soviet "Natolin group," had been forced to resign Aug. 4 for their refusal to support Gomulka.

The government Aug. 18 announced new regulations to enforce "labor discipline" through fines, demotion and dismissal for absenteeism and illegal strikes. The government reported Aug. 18 that 1,500 miners had been dismissed for absenteeism.

70 of 800 Polish tourists aboard the liner *Batory* defected during a visit to Copenhagen Aug. 21-22; the Danish government granted political asylum to 64 of the Poles Sept. 3. The British government Aug. 17 had granted asylum to Mieczyslaw Reluga, 26, Polish commercial attache in London, and his son, Richard, 3, following their flight from the Polish embassy Aug. 13. Kazimierz Jaworski, demoted as industrial construction deputy minister when Gomulka rose to power, was reported Sept. 6 to have defected to the West while on a business trip to East Berlin.

Addressing workers in Warsaw Sept. 8, Gomulka called on the people to aid courts, police and control organs in maintaining order and social discipline.

The United Workers' Party Sept. 26 upheld workers' rights to strike but forbade its members to join in strikes. It demanded party trials for Communists refusing to aid antistrike efforts.

The government announced Sept. 4 that Marjan Minor, a member of the "Natolin group," had been demoted from domestic trade minister to deputy minister of light industry. Minor was replaced by Mieczyslaw Lesz, ex-State Planning Commission deputy chairman.

Several persons were reported injured and nearly 200 arrested when students and other civilians clashed with police and mobile guards in Warsaw Oct. 3-7. The rioting began Oct. 3 when police used tear gas and clubs to disperse an estimated 2,000 students demonstrating against government suppression of *Po Prostu (Plain Talk),* a student weekly prominent in the Oct. 1956 upheaval. Clashes continued Oct. 4 and 5. Observers reported that adults and apparent vandals joined the Oct. 5-7 riots.

The United Workers' Party Central Committee, in a communique, formally announced a ban on *Po Prostu* Oct. 5 despite student demands for a free press and an end to what was termed a "regime of fear." The students' declaration had been approved Oct. 4 at a mass meeting at the Warsaw

Polytechnic School. *Trybuna Ludu,* the United Workers' Party newspaper, said Oct. 5 that the student weekly had been banned for opposing party policy and for "falsely and mendaciously" representing "the economic and political situation in Poland." Gomulka, who was believed responsible for the ban, met with Warsaw newspaper editors Oct. 5 and made clear to them that he would enforce recent party decisions to end press criticism of the government.

Cardinal Wyszynski told Warsaw students Oct. 6 that he understood their "yearning for freedom of speech and thought" but that they "should respect what you [the students] have." Wyszynski, in a sermon marking the opening of the Polish academic year, asked students to "understand that our country is in a particularly difficult situation."

STUDENT UNREST IN EAST GERMANY

The Harich Trial

Renewed dissent in East Germany had taken the form of independent political discussion in the universities and, reportedly, within the Communist party itself. The Pankow regime stifled this development with a political trial early in 1957 and met ensuing student unrest with stringent measures.

Walter Ulbricht, first secretary of the East German Socialist Unity (Communist) Party (SED), reported to the party Central Committee Feb. 5 that students at Humboldt University in East Berlin had planned to overthrow the country's government Nov. 3, 1956 and that Dr. Wolfgang Harich, a professor of social sciences there, would be tried for conspiring against the regime. Ulbricht charged Harich with having headed a "counterrevolutionary group" that fell under the influence of the liberal Hungarian writers' Petofi Circle and, together with "some acquaintances from Warsaw," with having plotted to "break the ties linking the German Democratic Republic with the Soviet Union." Students from Humboldt University's medical school had wanted to "go out into the streets" and "pass [from talk] to action," but cooler-headed students "realized where the power really rested and renounced the idea," Ulbricht claimed.

Harich was arrested Nov. 29 on his return from a visit to Hamburg in the Federal Republic. Just before his arrest, according to West German sources, he had passed a memo on his political philosophy to Social Democrats in West Berlin, claiming support for his views from the famous dramatist Berthold Brecht, who had died in Berlin Aug. 14, 1956. The gist of the memo was:

● Harich, Brecht and other intellectuals and party figures had approached the East German party leadership early in 1956 and, later, the Soviet ambassador with proposals for reforming the SED from within by liberalizing the organization, expelling the Stalinists and adopting a modernized Marxist-Leninist ideology. Politically, the group urged the restoration of Parliament's supreme power, guarantees for complete freedom of thought, an end to secret trials and security police and the extension of genuine electoral choices to the voters. In economic matters, they advocated more rational production geared toward a broadbased increase in the popular living standard, the setting up of workers' councils after the Yugoslav example, the introduction of profitsharing and the abandonment of forced agricultural collectivization. The group looked forward to a reunification of East and West Germany and a merger of the SED and Social Democrats and called for "secret cooperation between oppositional comrades in the SED and Social Democrats in combatting Stalinism as a first step towards future cooperation."

● "Once the anti-Stalinist opposition has gained control of the SED from within, official contacts between the Social Democratic Party and the reformed SED should follow. From them the germs of future unity might develop, though neither party must swallow up the other. No Stalinists who have taken part in the crimes of the Ulbricht group must be admitted to the new [combined] workers' party, but only persons who have fought actively against the Stalinist degeneration of the SED."

Harich's trial opened Mar. 7 before the East German Supreme Court in Berlin. Accused with him were Bernhard Steinberger, Harich's colleague in publishing *Zeitschrift fuer die Philosophie,* and Manfred Hertwig, a Humboldt University lecturer. The 3 had been held incommunicado for 3 months between their arrest and the trial. All 3 pleaded guilty, according to *Neues Deutschland,* the SED daily. Harich received a sentence of 10 years at hard labor for treason; Steinberger got 4 years and Hertwig 2 years for conspiracy. (Prof. Gerhard Hasse of the Karl Marx Institute in Leipzig was sentenced Apr. 5 to 5 years at hard labor and his colleague Prof. Joachim Hofmann to 2 years at hard labor on similar charges.)

The sentences seemed a signal for intensified political discussion, particularly in academic circles. Matters came to a head before the end of the spring term. Students at Humboldt University early in May went out in support of Dean Guenther Schuetzler of the veterinary faculty who had fled to West Germany and whom East German spokesmen were terming a Western agent. 132 veterinary students subsequently were suspended for boycotting lectures, and several students were expelled.

Col. Emil Bormann, chief of the East German security police, admitted at a press conference at Humboldt University May 16 that students were protesting in East Berlin, Leipzig, Dresden, Jena, Babelsberg and Rostock. He announced that a number of students had been arrested and that a plot among Humboldt University students to stage a Hungarian-style uprising had been suppressed. He accused Western intelligence services of promoting discontent among the students.

State Secy. for Education Wilhelm Girnius May 16 announced the imposition of strict controls on travel by students to West Berlin and West Germany.

MOSCOW & BELGRADE

Between Polemics & Conciliation

Tito's continued independence irritated the Soviet leaders more and more; in their opinion, Yugoslav criticism sometimes assumed "blasphemous" proportions. Tito sought to forestall a renewal of the 8-year frost in Soviet-Yugoslav relations by meeting Khrushchev for 2 days of talks in Rumania early in August. The 2 countries' differences this time stemmed mainly from a bilateral economic policy disagreement.

Khrushchev had told guests at a Moscow reception Feb. 19 that "certain Socialist countries [presumably Yugoslavia] wanted the best of every transaction" but charged that they were victims of a "blockade" when others refused to deal with them.

Yugoslav Foreign Min. Koca Popovic accused the USSR Feb. 26 of leading a campaign to "isolate our country and discredit our policy." He told the Yugoslav Federal Assembly in Belgrade that the Soviet Union had turned on Yugoslavia because it had refused to accept Soviet hegemony. He charged that postwar Stalinism had done "more harm to the cause of socialism than all the imperialistic conspiracies put together." He confirmed that the Soviet Union had refused aid previously promised Yugoslavia for a $175 million hydroelectric project but had granted Yugoslavia $25 million in credits.

The Soviet Communist Party daily *Pravda* Mar. 11 denounced the Popovic statement as "monstrous and revolting blasphemy." The Yugoslav League of Communists' daily *Borba* replied that Yugoslavia wanted better relations with the USSR, but not at the price of "ideological capitulation." A joint Soviet-Albanian statement, signed in Moscow Apr. 18 by Khrushchev and Albanian Labor (Communist) Party First Secy. Enver Hoxha, expressed hope for better relations with Yugoslavia but said that "much depends in this matter on Yugoslavia." The declaration, signed after talks Apr. 17 among Soviet and Albanian leaders and Yugoslav Amb.-to-USSR Veljko Micunovic, criticized the Balkan Pact.

Tito said Apr. 18 in an address at a plenary session of the Yugoslav Union of Socialists: "It is essential in this dispute [with the USSR] that we adhere firmly to our course and are not drawn into any 'camp.'" "Ingrown Stalinist tendencies" had made Soviet leaders perpetuate "their old beliefs about the relations between Socialist states." "We must ... let them know that things cannot continue in this fashion" and that "Yugoslavia has no reason to change her attitude and policy."

Yugoslav Vice Pres. Aleksander Rankovic Apr. 18 accused the USSR of "doing everything to discredit the Yugoslav system." He said that Yugoslavia would continue to welcome de-Stalinization in eastern Europe. He lauded the "changes that have been brought about in Poland" and the "aspirations of the masses of Hungarians who were fighting for free Socialist development and for respect of national dignity."

3 U.S. jet aircraft, the first to be delivered to Yugoslavia under the renewed U.S. military aid program, arrived in Belgrade May 18. The Yugoslav government had warned May 17 that it was re-examining the U.S. aid resumption and expressed reservations at alleged U.S. statements that the aid would be at a slower rate than planned and would be contingent on a continued Yugoslav-Soviet rift. (Gen. Ivan Gosnjak, Yugoslav defense minister, arrived in Moscow June 7 on a 2-week visit for talks with Marshal Georgi K. Zhukov, Soviet defense minister.)

Tito charged June 25 that although "some Eastern countries" had paid "lip service" to better relations with Yugoslavia, they had issued "inside instructions to party members" denouncing Yugoslavia for revisionism and its cooperation with the West. Speaking at a national conference of workers' council delegates in Belgrade, Tito warned the USSR and its east European allies to "let everyone build socialism as he knows how." Tito, who in a 65th birthday interview May 21 had anticipated an end to the dispute with the USSR, said that his country did not want to force its social system on anyone else but would defend it against those "who are deaf and blind to the facts."

Khrushchev met in Moscow July 18 with Yugoslav Vice Presidents Edvard Kardelj and Aleksander Rankovic. They then met July 18 with Soviet Communist Party Presidium members and Enver Hoxha and Todor Zhivkov, leaders, respectively, of the Albanian and Bulgarian Communist parties. In Belgrade dispatches July 20 it was reported that talks had begun in Moscow on implementation of the USSR's 1956 pledge of $250 million in credits for Yugoslav industry. A compromise aid agreement signed in Moscow July 29 and made public July 30 renewed the Soviet pledges of $250 million in economic and technical aid for the construction of a hydroelectric and aluminum project in Montenegro and a 2d hydroelectric plant and fertilizer factory elsewhere in Yugoslavia. The accord, concluded by Hasan Brkic, Yugoslav Foreign Trade Committee chief, provided for the completion of the power stations in 1964, 3 years later than originally planned.

From both the USSR and Yugoslavia it was disclosed Aug. 3 that Khrushchev and Tito, meeting secretly in Rumania for 2 days, had reached agreement on "concrete forms of cooperation."

In a statement broadcast on Moscow radio Aug. 3 it was said that delegations led by Khrushchev and Tito had "discussed a number of questions concerning relations between the USSR and Yugoslavia" and had agreed "to work for a further all-round development of relations." In what observers termed a possible reference to a revival of the Cominform alliance of Soviet and east European Communist parties, the 2 sides "emphasized that particular importance attaches to the strengthening in every way of the unity and fraternal cooperation of the Communist and workers' parties ... of all the Socialist countries ... and progressive forces throughout the world." A similar Yugoslav government statement, issued Aug. 3 in Belgrade, contained the emphasized report that the Yugoslav and Soviet leaders had agreed that their relations would "develop on the basis of equality, mutual assistance and cooperation, the respect of sovereignty and noninterference in internal affairs."

Also attending the Rumanian talks: (For Yugoslavia) Rankovic, Kardelj, League of Communists Central Committeeman Veljko Vlahovic, Amb.-to-USSR Veljko Micunovic. (For the USSR) Deputy Premier Anastas I. Mikoyan, Communist Party Presidium member Otto V. Kuusinen, Communist Party foreign liaison chief Nikolai Ponomarev, Amb.-to-Yugoslavia Nikolai P. Firyubin.

The Communist daily *Borba,* in the first official Yugoslav comment on the Khrushchev-Tito meeting, indicated Aug. 6 that any concessions made to improve Soviet-Yugoslav relations had been granted by the USSR. *Borba* stressed that Khrushchev's recent ouster of a reportedly anti-Tito faction led by Molotov had been of "great importance and significance" for the effort to improve ties between the 2 nations. The party weekly *Komunist* contained an editorial in which it was conceded that "an abyss" still separated the Soviet and Yugoslav parties. The paper demanded Soviet action on pledges of party cooperation.

Tito, speaking at a Belgrade luncheon in honor of visiting North Vietnamese Pres. Ho Chi Minh, declared Aug. 5 that "complete equality" was the only basis on which "the Socialist countries and progressive movements" could develop effective "mutual collaboration." He asserted that "a policy of coexistence" was "the best means of securing our national existence" and that it would take the "common effort ... of all peoples and countries" to reach this goal. In a joint communique issued in Belgrade Aug. 9, Tito and Ho Chi Minh supported Yugoslav demands for independence from the USSR and coexistence with the West.

Djilas' 'New Class'

There had arisen meanwhile in the West a source of great embarrassment for Tito in his relations with the Kremlin. Ex-Yugoslav Vice Pres. Milovan Djilas, in excerpts from a forthcoming book, charged July 26 that the rulers of Communist societies, including those of Yugoslavia and the USSR, were a "new class of owners and exploiters" who ran their countries "on behalf of their own narrow caste's interest." The book, entitled *The New Class* and published by Frederick A. Praeger in New York, was smuggled in manuscript form out of Yugoslavia, where Djilas was in prison for his 1956 criticism of Tito's policies.

The Yugoslav Communist daily *Borba* denounced Djilas Aug. 10 as an "insane man" who had "betrayed his movement and his country." Belgrade sources Aug. 16 expressed concern lest the book harm Yugoslavia's nonaligned position between East and West.

The Soviet government newspaper *Izvestia* informed the Soviet people Aug. 18 of Djilas' new book and denounced it for "vile attacks" on the Soviet system. *Izvestia* stressed the use of the book by U.S.-led "reactionary circles."

Yugoslavia Abstains from Moscow Declaration

Soviet and foreign Communist leaders began talks in Moscow in mid-November on the coordination of their world policy. The talks, which followed preliminary meetings among national delegations in Moscow for the celebration of the 40th anniversary of the Bolshevik revolution, were said to center on proposals for the reestablishment of a Soviet-bloc organization to replace the Cominform (dissolved in 1956) and the pre-World War II Comintern (disbanded in 1943). The Moscow meetings took place Nov. 14-19.

The leaders attending the Kremlin talks included Khrushchev, Mao Tse-tung and Kardelj. Tito Oct. 29 had cancelled his projected visit to Moscow, ostensibly for health reasons. He was said Nov. 2 to have expressed concern at the ouster of Marshal Georgi K. Zhukov Oct. 26 as Soviet Defense minister. Zhukov had been dropped on his return to the USSR from visits to Yugoslavia and Albania.

In speeches before a special session of the Supreme Soviet in Moscow, Nov. 6, Mao of China and Gomulka of Poland reaffirmed the right of their countries to travel "separate roads to socialism." Kardelj told the Supreme Soviet Nov. 6 that Yugoslavia would continue to apply Soviet experience "not mechanically but creatively."

The Communist leaders, after ending their Moscow meetings, made public 2 policy statements Nov. 22:

● A declaration, signed by Communist party leaders from every Communist state except Yugoslavia, called for a new united front against "imperialism," "capitalism" and policies of "certain aggressive groups" in the U.S., which had become "the center of world reaction." The 12-nation Communist party declaration,* formulated in Kremlin talks Nov. 14-16, urged an alliance between the "3d of the population of the world—over 950 million people" living under communism and "700 million people [who] have shaken off the colonial yoke" since World War II.

● A peace manifesto, signed by Communist Party leaders from 64 nations, including Yugoslavia, indorsed Soviet foreign policies as necessary to peace and urged a cooperative struggle against the "capitalistic monopolies who have a vested interest in war." Asserting that Soviet advances had changed the East-West "balance of forces," the manifesto, drafted in talks Nov. 16-19, demanded action to end the arms race, nuclear weapons usage and tests, foreign military blocs and bases and tension in the Middle East.

---

*Signed by the Communist parties of Albania, Bulgaria, China, Czechoslovakia, East Germany, Hungary, North Korea, North Vietnam, Outer Mongolia, Poland, Rumania, USSR.

The 12-nation declaration restated the classic Marxist dogma on the achievement of communism but stressed that a Communist Party might assume power through either evolution or revolution. It warned against Stalinist "dogmatism" and rightist "revisionism" but emphasized the right of Communist nations to seek their own paths to socialism.

The declaration, although it did not reveal expected plans for the formation of a new organization to replace the Cominform and Comintern, said that the 12 participating Communist parties deemed it "expedient" to plan for additional Communist summit meetings. The *N.Y. Times* reported Dec. 2 from Warsaw that the Moscow talks had resulted in an agreement to publish a new Communist theoretic journal, despite the opposition of the Polish, Yugoslav and Italian parties.

(According to the July 15, 1958 issue of the *N.Y. Times:* Khrushchev warned Yugoslav leaders that "we will attack you" when the Yugoslavs refused to sign the Nov. 1957 Moscow declaration. Khrushchev reportedly asked Kardelj and Rankovic, "How long can you go on sitting on 2 chairs?")

Yugoslav Amb.-to-USSR Veljko Micunovic, attending a Lebanese National Day reception in Moscow, told newsmen Nov. 22 that Yugoslavia had not signed the 12-party declaration because "we did not agree with it." Kardelj and Rankovic returned to Belgrade from Moscow Nov. 22 but refused to explain their abstention from the declaration or to confirm reports of serious Yugoslav-Soviet differences over the declaration's anti-U.S. tone. A communique issued Dec. 7, at the end of a meeting on the island of Brioni of the Yugoslav League of Communists Central Committee, said that the 110-member committee had approved Yugoslavia's rejection of the Moscow declaration on the ground that it contained "incorrect" conclusions.

Tito reportedly reassured the U.S. Dec. 6 of Yugoslav intentions to remain independent of the USSR and to pursue an independent Yugoslav foreign policy. In a meeting on Brioni with U.S. Amb.-to-Yugoslavia James W. Riddleberger, Tito was said to have cited Yugoslav abstention from the Moscow declaration as proof of his country's independence.

1958

The campaign against "national communism" culminated in 1958. "Revisionists" were expelled from the party leadership in East Germany. In Poland, the government ignored the vigorous protests of the Roman Catholic Church against new restrictions on freedom of religion. The execution of Imre Nagy and other leaders of the 1956 uprising in Hungary marked the climax of the counterrevolutionary terror intended to discourage any potential followers of the Hungarian rebels.

In its desire to restore control over other countries of eastern Europe, the Soviet Union almost sacrificed the laboriously accomplished rapprochement with Yugoslavia. Moscow's and Belgrade's spokesmen again exchanged virulent polemics, and the Yugoslav defiance hardened.

CLIMAX OF CAMPAIGN AGAINST DISSENT

East German Critics Ousted

First Secy. Walter Ulbricht moved early in 1958 in his bid for domination over the East German Socialist Unity (Communist) Party (SED) and in his effort to remove all hopes of reunification with West Germany. It was disclosed Feb. 8 that the party had dismissed Karl Schirdewan and Ernst Friedrich Wollweber from its Central Committee and Fred Oelssner from the Politburo for "fractional activities" in opposition to Ulbricht. The 3, ousted by party action at a Central Committee meeting Feb. 3-6 in East Berlin, were charged with efforts to decentralize the economic system and relax political and intellectual controls.

Wollweber, 60, state security minister until Nov. 1, 1957, and Schirdewan, 51, party personnel chief, were accused of advocating German reunification "at any price," with Schirdewan demanding "a policy of safety valves" after the Polish model. Oelssner, 55, formerly chief party ideologist, was charged with conspiring with Schirdewan to oppose the collectivization of agriculture. The deposed leaders, who retained party membership, were replaced in the Central Committee and Politburo by Alfred Neumann, Paul Froelich, Erich Apel, Paul Werner and Erich Honecker. Apel was named to head the Politburo's economic commission.

In a speech before the Central Committee, published Feb. 25 in *Neues Deutschland,* Premier Otto Grotewohl reported that the dissidents led by Schirdewan and Fritz Selbmann had sought his support against Ulbricht. Central Committee members Albert Norden and Franz Dahlem, in addresses published Feb. 26, asserted that the alleged plotters planned to depose Ulbricht and replace him with Schirdewan. The speakers charged that Selbmann had attempted to discredit Ulbricht for spending the Hitler period in the USSR by noting that "some [Communist leaders] sat in concentration camps while others spoke over the radio." Selbmann was disclosed Feb. 24 to have been dropped as chairman of the State Commission for Industry and named as deputy chairman of the new Control Organ for Economic Planning Guidance.

Grotewohl, in a statement Apr. 20 for the SED's 12th anniversary, characterized as "fairy tales" reports of a cleavage between him and Ulbricht.

(64 persons were jailed for political offenses in East Germany during January, February and March, the West Berlin Free Jurists reported Apr. 15.)

Ulbricht said at the opening session of the 5th SED Congress in East Berlin July 10 that revisionism remained a major problem in East Germany and would be suppressed. He asserted that it would be opposed with "ideological persuasion" rather than "administrative [police] methods."

Selbmann confessed to the congress July 14 that he had known of an anti-Ulbricht revisionist faction in the party but had hidden his knowledge of it. Selbmann and 3 other leading East German Communists were dismissed from their Central Committee posts before the 5th Congress ended July 16. Those ousted with Selbmann were Oelssner, Amb.-to-Communist China Paul Wandel and Education Min. Fritz Lange.

Drive Against Opposition in Poland

A Polish United Workers' (Communist) Party communique Mar. 1 contained the disclosure that First Secy. Gomulka had defeated "Stalinist" challenges to his leadership during a 3-day Central Committee meeting in Warsaw Feb. 27-Mar. 1. It announced that Deputy Labor Min. Wiktor Klosiewicz, an opponent of Gomulka's efforts toward greater independence from the USSR, had been expelled from the Central Committee for "disrupting the unity of the party" with attacks on the regime's foreign policies and plans to reorganize the industrial labor force. Gomulka was backed by 69 of the 75 Central Committee members.

Factory workers' councils, established during the Oct. 1956 revolt, were brought under party control Apr. 14. Speaking at the opening session of the Polish Trades Union Congress in Warsaw, Gomulka said that the 5,600 councils would be merged with United Workers' Party, union and management committees in "workers' self-government conference[s]" to be formed in each factory. He affirmed that no new workers' councils were to be formed and that their functions would be assumed by the factory "conferences." Gomulka Apr. 14 also ordered a ban on industrial strikes (legally permissible since the Oct. 1956 upheaval). He condemned earlier Polish walkouts as "signs of anarchy appearing amid Socialist democratic freedoms." Chairman Ignacy Loga-Sowinski of the Trades Union Central Council said, however, that workers would be permitted brief work stoppages as a "warning" of legitimate grievances.

Church-state relations were entering a critical phase for the first time since the advent of the Gomulka regime. Politburo member Jerzy Morawski, a member of the committee that had negotiated for Catholic support of the Gomulka-backed government after the Oct. 1956 upheaval, warned May 23 that "certain religious circles" were trying to foment church-state strife and interfere in political activities "beyond the church's functions."

Bishop Zdzislaw Golinski of Czestochowa, in whose diocese an historic national shrine to the Madonna was located, asserted in a pastoral letter July 27 that state and secret policemen had invaded the Jasna Gora Pauline monastery housing the shrine July 21 and had confiscated all church archives and records. Spokesmen for Stefan Cardinal Wyszynski said July 28 that police had ransacked his office in Jasna Gora and beaten protesting priests and pilgrims.

Cardinal Wyszynski ordered Polish Catholics to begin 3 months of special prayers Aug. 11 in protest against increasing government attacks on the church. This order (ostensibly in protest against press disparagement of the Jasna Gora monastery and shrine) came after government and church leaders had met July 31-Aug. 2 and agreed on the distribution of aid from American Catholics to victims of floods in southern Poland and on the submission of Catholic publications to state censorship. The press renewed attacks on Wyszynski after the conference, the party daily *Trybuna Ludu* charging Aug. 12 that priests were engaging in political activity and had used force and threats to retake nationalized church property from peasant owners.

Catholic sources disclosed Aug. 26 that Wyszynski and Gomulka had met twice before summer in unsuccessful attempts to settle the growing church-state rift. The secret meetings reportedly centered on the church's alleged misuse of its renewed right to conduct Catholic religious education in Polish schools.

Meanwhile, the USSR took notice of a renewed flourishing of Polish cultural life. Soviet denunciations of prominent Polish writers and artists as pro-Western, anti-Marxist and revisionist were made in issues of *Zvezda* (the Moscow Writers Union monthly) reaching Warsaw Aug. 10.

Gomulka, speaking at the opening session of the Central Committee's 12th plenary meeting, warned Oct. 15 that revisionist politicians and intellectuals must cease opposition and undertake active support of party policies. Gomulka said that the party had expelled 206,737 members (15%) in 1958. (The party had reported June 3 that its membership had been reduced by more than 17%, from 1,266,754 to 1,052,809, during a "verification" campaign January-June 1958.)

Hungarian Revolt Leaders Executed

The Hungarian Justice Ministry announced June 17 that ex-Premier Imre Nagy and Maj. Gen. Pal Maleter had been tried, condemned and executed for their leadership of the 1956 revolt. A communique issued through the Hungarian MTI news agency said that Nagy and Maleter had been put to death for "a *putsch* attempt to overthrow the Hungarian People's Republic." No indication was given as to when the sentences, handed down by the People's Court Council of the Hungarian Supreme Court, had been passed and carried out.

The Justice Ministry disclosed that journalists Miklos Gimes and Jozsef Szilagyi had also been executed for their part in the alleged Nagy conspiracy. Other sentences announced: Sandor Kopacsi, life imprisonment; Ferenc Donath, 12 years at hard labor; Ferenc Janosi, 8 years; Zoltan Tildy, 6 years; Miklos Vasarhei, 5 years. Charges against Geza Losonczi, state minister in the Nagy cabinet, were dropped because he had died (from natural causes).

(In an Associated Press dispatch from Budapest it was reported June 20 that Maleter had been shot and Nagy and the 2 other civilian leaders hanged, probably early June 16. It also was said that Hungarian Chief Prosecutor Geza Szenasi had told newsmen that the trial had taken place in Budapest's Supreme Court building "this year—not too long ago" and had lasted 12 days. Szenasi said that defendants had been permitted to choose lawyers and request clemency.) The Justice Ministry charged in its June 17 communique that Nagy had founded "a small illegal group of his most intimate supporters [Losonczy, Donat, Gimes, Szilagyi] as early as the end of 1955 with the object of seizing power by force." "Zoltan Tildy and Pal Maleter became acquainted with" Nagy's aims "in Oct. 1956, agreed with them and actively joined the counterrevolutionary revolt." Nagy had turned the Petofi (literary) Circle into a "forum for the attacks against the party and the state" and had used it to provoke the Oct. 23, 1956 demonstrations that led to the revolt and Nagy's installation as premier.

The communique asserted that Nagy, Szilagyi and Maleter "denied their guilt but ... made partial confessions concerning the facts of their crimes." It charged that they had plotted the revolt in league with outlawed Hungarian bourgeois, rightist and fascist parties and "with active participation of imperialists," including officials of the U.S., British and Yugoslav legations, the emigre Hungarian National Council, U.S. intelligence services, Radio Free Europe and West German leaders. The West's aim, it said, was "the dismemberment of Hungary from the Socialist camp ... by a group that 'was called Communist.' " It also charged that Nagy and "his treacherous group" had sought to fulfill Western plans by attempting "to repudiate the defense organization of the country, the Warsaw agreement." "This attempt was crowned by Nagy's radio appeal of Nov. 4, 1956, in which he appealed for the open and armed intervention of the Western imperialists against the revolutionary worker-peasant government and the Soviet troops whose assistance was requested by it."

The Nagy government was accused of having abolished "legal organs of administration," replacing them with "so-called revolutionary committees" and "workers' councils" and institution of a "white terror." It was said to have (1) executed 234 persons, imprisoned 3,000 more and planned the execution of more than 10,000 people; (2) used Kopacsi's position as Budapest police chief to subvert security forces and distribute arms; (3) released Jozsef Cardinal Mindszenty, permitting him to proclaim "a program of capitalist restoration" in a Nov. 3, 1956 broadcast.

The U.S. State Department June 17 condemned the executions as a "shocking act of cruelty" that brought "to a tragic culmination the Soviet-Communist betrayal of the Hungarian people." The State Department asserted that the USSR "must bear fundamental responsibility for this latest crime against the Hungarian people and all humanity." U.S. State Secy. John Foster Dulles told newsmen June 17 that the Nagy-Maleter executions indicated "another step in the reversion toward the brutal terrorist methods which prevailed ... under Stalin" and were "so bitterly denounced" by Khrushchev before he began "copying" them. Dulles suggested that the executions had been intended as a warning to Yugoslav leaders.

The executions were denounced by Pres. Eisenhower June 18 as a shock to "the civilized world" and "clear evidence" that the USSR still used "terror and intimidation ... to bring about complete subservience" of its opponents.

The British Foreign Office had said June 17 that Nagy and Maleter deserved "the respect of all mankind" for their efforts to free Hungary.

Polish and Yugoslav officials June 17 expressed concern at the executions and linked them to the current Soviet-Yugoslav rift.

The UN Special Committee on the Problem of Hungary declared June 21 that the Nagy-Maleter executions had demonstrated "that the oppression of the Hungarian people has not abated and that the reign of terror which began when Russian forces moved into Hungary ... continues."

Hungarian allegations that Nagy had directed last-ditch resistance while under asylum in the Yugoslav Legation in Budapest were denounced June 23 by the Yugoslav government as "fabricated from the beginning to the end." A note delivered by Yugoslav Amb.-to-Hungary Jovo Kapicic asserted that in view of the secrecy of Nagy's trial and the falsity of charges of Yugoslav involvement, there was reason to doubt the "truthfulness of the rest of the indictment." Noting that the executions had been received in Yugoslavia "with deep bitterness," the Yugoslav government charged in the note that the trials and executions had been staged "to aggravate and justify" the current Soviet campaign against Yugoslavia.

The Czechoslovak Communist Party, ending a 4-day meeting in Prague June 21, indorsed the Nagy-Maleter executions and said that they had unmasked the menace of the Yugoslav-led revisionist campaign.

Gomulka said June 28 that the executions were an internal Hungarian affair and that "it was not for us to judge whose fault it is or the fairness of the punishment." Putting an end to reports of Polish Communist opposition to the executions, Gomulka termed them an "epilogue" to the 1956 "counterrevolution."

Chairman Alsing Anderson of the UN Special Committee on the Problem of Hungary reported July 11 that 105 persons were facing trial or retrial in Budapest for their parts in the revolt. U.S. State Department spokesman Lincoln White told newsmen July 10 that 100 cases had been tried in Budapest in June.

The Hungarian government July 10 denied persistent reports from Budapest that it had tried and executed Mrs. Julia Rajk, widow of executed Foreign Min. Laszlo Rajk, for her part in the 1956 uprising. (The return to Budapest of Mrs. Rajk from exile in Rumania since collapse of the Nagy regime was confirmed Nov. 5 by the Hungarian government.)

The UN special committee charged July 16 that the executions of Nagy and Maleter had been "striking, but, unhappily, not isolated, examples of the continued policy of repression in Hungary." The report said that the "continued presence of foreign [Soviet] armed forces in Hungary" was "likely to prevent the expression" of popular feelings against the executions.

Soviet Pres. Klimenti Ye. Voroshilov, visiting the Brussels Fair Aug. 13, commented that the Hungarian revolt had been "just foolishness," that Nagy had been "just a fool" and "not a real Communist." He conceded that Nagy's death sentence had been "too harsh."

Budapest officials confirmed Dec. 29 that Istvan Bibo, state minister in the Nagy government and last official to remain at government headquarters when Soviet tanks attacked Budapest Nov. 4, 1956, was serving a term of life imprisonment.

(In a British Broadcasting Co. dispatch from Vienna it was reported Jan. 30, 1960, that 150 Hungarian youths aged 18 had been executed in Dec. 1958 for taking part in the revolt. The youths reportedly had been held in a Budapest prison until old enough for legal execution. 54 other former rebels were said to have been executed in the 6 months prior to Jan. 1960. The report was denied Feb. 3, 1960 by the Hungarian Foreign Office.)

Refugees

Erich Mirbach, chief secretary to Pres. Wilhelm Pieck of the (East) German Democratic Republic, was reported Mar. 8 to have fled to West Berlin. West German officials reported Mar. 8 that nearly 9 million persons, 2,700,000 of them East Germans, had fled to West Germany from former German territories since the end of World War II.

Prof. Josef Haemel, 63, rector of the Friedrich Schiller University in Jena, fled to West Berlin with his family Aug. 22, 10 days before scheduled celebrations of the old university of Jena's 400th anniversary. Haemel was replaced Aug. 25 by Prof. Otto Schwarz, 58, a botanist and Jena rector in 1948-51.

Janusz Grochowski, ex-editor of the banned Polish student newspaper *Po prostu,* escaped to West Germany and told newsmen June 7 that 17 members of the paper's 22-man staff had been arrested.

Richard Eibel, 22, Polish seaman who deserted the freighter *Frederic Chopin* in New York July 24, was granted a temporary U.S. visa Aug. 8 to permit him to leave and reenter the U.S. as an immigrant.

2 armed Hungarian refugees, Sandor Nagy, 22, and Endre Papp, 21, invaded the Hungarian legation in Bern Aug. 16 and exchanged shots with several Hungarian diplomats before surrendering to Swiss police summoned by the envoy, Jozsef Marjai. Nagy was critically wounded in the raid, which was planned to seize legation documents.

Other Opposition

The Slovenian Republican government in Yugoslavia confirmed Jan. 27 in Zagreb that miners in the Trbovlje pits had conducted a 2-day "stay-down" strike in protest against the omission of promised Dec. 1957 wage bonuses. A Trbovlje striker who reportedly had fled to Austria told Vienna's *Die Presse* Jan. 25 that 4,200 miners had struck Jan. 15. It was the first strike to be acknowledged by the Yugoslav government since the end of World War II.

Yugoslav authorities early in 1958 presented for trial Dr. Aleksander Pavlovic and Bogdan Krekic, both prominent members of the Serbian Socialist Party before World War II, and Dr. Dragoslav Stranjakovic of the Serbian Orthodox theology faculty at Belgrade University. They were charged with—and quickly convicted of—conspiring to overthrow the federal government. The 3 had been arrested early in Dec. 1957. During World War II they had expressed support for the Chetnik movement of Gen. Draja Mihailovic, a royalist and wartime rival of Tito. In January the authorities arrested Dr.

Milan Zujovic, a law professor at Belgrade University, on a similar charge.

At the end of a 5-day trial Feb. 4, Pavlovic, Zujovic and Krekic were convicted. Pavlovic received a sentence of $8\frac{1}{2}$ years' imprisonment at hard labor, Krekic got 7 years and Zujovic 4 years. Stranjakovic, who testified at the trial, received a separate trial on the ground of poor health. After his trial, he was sentenced to 6 years at hard labor Mar. 3.

The arrests of 4 leading Gemeindebund (Jewish Community Association) officials in Czechoslovakia on charges of Zionism were reported in Vienna Sept. 26. Reported held were Ernest Meisel, Walter Stein, Ernst Loew and Tiberius Ney. The Rev. Karel Bartak, 33, a Catholic priest, was given 15 years at hard labor Oct. 1 for antistate activities.

A pastoral letter read by East German Catholic priests Oct. 19 condemned religious persecution in the country and disclosed that the church had appealed to Premier Otto Grotewohl for an end to "burdensome oppression" of Catholics.

In the autumn, the outside world learned more of the extent to which dissent had surfaced in Soviet cultural circles. Boris Leonidovich Pasternak, 68, poet and author living in Peredelkino, near Moscow, whose novel, *Doctor Zhivago,* critical of the Bolshevik revolution, was a best-seller in Western Europe and the U.S. although unpublished in the USSR, was named winner of the 1958 Nobel Prize for Literature by the Swedish Academy in Stockholm Oct. 23. He indicated his acceptance of the honor and its $41,420 cash award when first notified of it Oct. 23, although he told visitors at his home that it was "a lonely joy"—obviously because of the nonrecognition of his novel in the USSR. He then was attacked in the *Literaturnaya Gazeta* of Moscow Oct. 25 as the author of an "artistically squalid, malicious work replete with hatred of socialism," and the Soviet Communist Party daily *Pravda* Oct. 26 labeled him "malevolent ..., a through-and-through bourgeois reactionary [and] bourgeois intellectual." The Soviet publications denounced the Nobel award to Pasternak as politically motivated. He was expelled from the Soviet Writers Union Oct. 28. Pasternak wired the Swedish Academy Oct. 29 that "in view of the meaning given to this honor in the community to which I belong," he must convey his "voluntary refusal" to accept the prize. Academy officials said he would remain listed as 1958 prize winner even though he did not receive the cash award.

SOVIET-YUGOSLAV RIFT REVIVED

Polemics Renewed

A recurrence of Soviet-Yugoslav polemics developed just after mid-April, after the Yugoslav League of Communists circulated to other Communist parties in advance of its 7th Party Congress a program of party policy to be presented at the congress. The Soviet Communist Party seized on several points of the program as heretical and strongly criticized these views in an article in its theoretical journal *Kommunist.* Moscow Radio Apr. 19 beamed excerpts of the criticism in Serbo-Croatian to the Balkan country. Among these excerpts was the conclusion that the Yugoslav party had assumed an attitude of "petit-bourgeois nationalism" by abandoning the tenet of the party's "leading role" and prematurely considering the "withering away" of the state.

Tito called on the USSR Apr. 22 to "abandon" its "absurd" efforts to remold Yugoslavia into a docile member of the Soviet bloc. Tito, speaking at the opening session of the Yugoslav party's 7th Congress, held in Ljubljana, rejected the Soviet charges that Yugoslavia had left the Marxist path in its search for neutrality between East and West. He charged that "these comrades seem to think that internationalism is determined by adherence to the [Soviet] camp and not to the Socialist world in the broader sense." "It is difficult for us to understand such short-sightedness and tactlessness toward our country," Tito said. He asserted that "equal relations and a comradely attitude" between the Socialist states were infinitely better than the "old forms of operation" under Stalin. He blamed Stalinist interference for the Hungarian and Polish crises of 1956, which, he said, were a "heavy blow to Socialist forces in the world." He rejected Soviet contentions that Yugoslavia had made "any concessions" to the U.S. in return for U.S. aid.

Ambassadors of the USSR and all Soviet bloc nations except Poland* walked out of the Yugoslav Communist Congress Apr. 23 when Vice Pres. Aleksander Rankovic denounced Soviet leaders for their continued "pressure on Yugoslavia." He accused "certain very responsible people" of "sharpening the old rusty weapons of the Cominform" in an effort to "isolate" Yugoslavia. Rankovic warned that Yugoslavs did not have "flexible spines" and did not "sell out ... in 1948, even when there was a rattling of arms on the Yugoslav frontier."

The Yugoslav Communist daily *Borba* had disclosed Apr. 19 that the Communist parties of the USSR, China, Czechoslovakia, Poland,† Hungary, Bulgaria, Sweden, Italy and Britain had refused to send official party delegations to the Yugoslav Congress but that east European ambassadors would attend as observers. Albania, Rumania and East Germany refused to send any representation.

Kommunist had attacked the Yugoslav party Apr. 17 for the "anti-Marxist-Leninist" ideas contained in the draft program prepared for the Ljubljana congress. The article, signed by leading Soviet theoreticians P. Fedoseyev, I. Pomelov and V. Cheprakov, had also charged that Yugoslavia had spurred "chauvinism and nationalism" with an attack on Soviet practices, particularly bureaucracy, which distorted the "development of social life and theoretical thought" in the USSR.

The Yugoslav party's draft program was reissued Apr. 17 with modifications designed to temper Soviet criticism. However, it retained these views written into the original draft by a committee headed by Vice Pres. Edvard Kardelj:

● "The capitalist system in its classical form is ... becoming a thing of the past." Political developments had forced the state to assume control of the economy and monopolies and had produced "a swelling wave of state capitalist tendencies" that brought "contemporary capitalist society nearer to socialism."

---

* Polish Amb.-to-Yugoslavia Henryk Grochulski.

† The Polish United Workers' Party newspaper *Trybuna Ludu* Apr. 23 defended Poland's decision to send only an observer to the Yugoslav meeting but said that "this decision ought to have no influence on the further development of friendly relations between our party" and the Yugoslav League of Communists. Ignoring Soviet criticism of Yugoslav leadership, the editorial lauded the Yugoslavs' "fidelity to the cause of socialism" during "the full history of their party."

These developments were "obvious proof that mankind is ... moving into the era of socialism through a wide variety of different roads."

● The movement toward socialism had produced an entrenched bureaucracy that inevitably seeks to rule rather than serve society. These "contradictions" existed in Communist as well as capitalist-ruled nations. Socialist countries therefore must defeat their own "conservatism" by curbing state powers and moving toward "direct democracy." "Stalin ... did not fight the bureaucratic ... concentration of power in the state apparatus" but evolved a new "theory of the state, which does not wither away, but keeps growing stronger."

Mrs. Yekaterina A. Furtseva, Soviet Presidium member, told Western newsmen at a Warsaw reception Apr. 24 that there would be no repetition of the 1948 Soviet-Yugoslav break. She insisted that Soviet leaders "have been and will be friends of Yugoslavia—always."

Tito urged the USSR Apr. 26 to "solve our differences and disagreements in ... more comradely manner." However, in an address at the closing session of the party congress in Ljubljana, he reproached the USSR and the Soviet bloc for refusing to send party delegations to the congress. He warned that "expectation in any quarter that we shall renounce our principled stands" in domestic and foreign policy was "a loss of time and causes damage to all of us."

Yugoslav leaders were implicitly condemned in strong anti-revisionist statements by Gomulka in Budapest May 12 and in Bucharest May 15. Gomulka, considered a supporter of Yugoslavia, pledged the Polish United Workers' (Communist) Party to join with the Hungarian and Rumanian parties in a campaign against both "revisionism" and "dogmatism." The Budapest communique was signed by Hungarian Socialist Workers' (Communist) Party First Secy. Janos Kadar.

A Soviet Communist Party Central Committee ultimatum demanding a return to Soviet-bloc discipline was rejected in a reported Yugoslav League of Communists message drafted May 19-20 and delivered in Moscow a few days later. The Yugoslav reply was said to have reaffirmed the party's intention to remain independent and to have warned against any repetition of the 1948 break.

Tito's visit to Poland, scheduled to begin May 29, was cancelled by the Yugoslav government May 21.

Soviet Premier Nikita S. Khrushchev, in a message on Tito's 66th birthday, had expressed hopes May 25 that "existing misunderstandings" between Yugoslavia and the Soviet bloc "will be overcome."

Polish First Secy. Wladyslaw Gomulka ended his silence on the Yugoslav-Soviet rift June 28 with the charge that the "guilt" for current political differences within the Communist world "lies squarely on Yugoslavia's shoulders." He told government and party figures at a Polish Navy Day meeting in Gdansk that Yugoslav leaders' "mistaken revisionist theories" had separated "Yugoslavia from the commonwealth of Socialist states" and had "harmed the whole international workers' movement." Gomulka, whose criticism was markedly softer than other east European attacks, said that Yugoslavia was backed by the "whole international reaction."

(The *N.Y. Times* reported June 29 that Gomulka had been forced into his attack by a Soviet ultimatum, reportedly delivered in Warsaw by the Soviet Politburo member Yekaterina A. Furtseva on Khrushchev's behalf.)

The eruption of a Soviet-Yugoslav economic aid controversy May 27 was also believed to have had much to do with Gomulka's criticism. The Soviet example, it was thought, probably occasioned the harder line adopted by other Soviet-bloc countries, and the anti-Yugoslav campaign was intensified.

Delegates of Communist parties from 46 nations gathered in East Berlin July 10 to attend the 5th Congress of the East German Socialist Unity (Communist) Party. The meeting was considered to be part of the Soviet effort to unify east European opposition to Yugoslav revisionism.

Khrushchev, who had arrived in East Germany July 8, charged at the SED congress July 11 that Tito was a "renegade" who had attempted to dislocate and split the international Communist movement. Khrushchev repeated his description of Yugoslav communism as the "Trojan Horse" on which "Western imperialists" were "betting their last card" in efforts to undermine the USSR. He charged that "the Yugoslavs are aiding the class enemies of the workers and that is why the imperialists give them credits and ... value ... their so-called independence."

Economic Aid Controversy

The Soviet government informed Yugoslavia May 27 that it had postponed for 5 years the implementation of $285 million in Soviet credits pledged to Yugoslavia. The postponed Soviet credits included $110 million pledged in Jan. 1956 for mine, fertilizer plant and power-station development and $175 million promised in Aug. 1956 for construction, with East German equipment, of a Montenegrin hydroelectric and aluminum project. The 2 loans had been postponed shortly after the 1956 Hungarian revolt but had been restored in July 1957 as part of Soviet efforts to restore normal relations with Yugoslavia.

Yugoslavia, in notes to the USSR and East Germany June 3, denounced the postponement. In prior comment, Foreign Ministry spokesmen in Belgrade May 31 had rejected, as "completely arbitrary," Soviet contentions that the delay was necessitated by recent decisions to expand the USSR's chemical industries.

Khrushchev June 3 personally condemned Yugoslav Communist leaders as "revisionists" and defended the 1948 Cominform denunciation of them as "basically correct." In his first public statement on the renewed Yugoslav-Soviet rift, Khrushchev told the Bulgarian Communist Party Congress in Sofia that Yugoslav leaders had acted as "spies of the imperialist camp" against the Soviet bloc. Khrushchev described modern revisionism as a Trojan Horse designed "to corrupt workers and Socialist parties from the inside, to split the unity of the Socialist camp and bring disorder and confusion to Marxist-Leninist ideology."

Khrushchev derided Yugoslav and Western efforts to "find any shades of difference" in Soviet, east European or Communist Chinese attitudes toward revisionism. He indorsed recently expressed Chinese views that the 1948 offensive against Yugoslavia was correct and in "the interests of the revolutionary movement." He charged Yugoslavia with sheltering "predatory" leaders of the Hungarian revolt and said the USSR had made it clear that it would counter any future Yugoslav action "against any Socialist country."

The arrests of an estimated 100 pro-Soviet Yugoslav leaders who had sided with the Cominform in 1948 were confirmed June 13 by the Yugoslav Foreign Ministry.

Spokesman Jaska Petric disclosed that Col. Vlado Dapcevic, half-brother of Gen. Peko Dapcevic, transport and communications minister, had escaped to Albania May 31 with 10 other "Cominformist" leaders. Petric indicated that the escape had been aided by Soviet agents. Other Cominformists reported to be under arrest included Croatian ex-Vice Premier Dusko Brkic, ex-Amb.-to-Egypt Ferad Badnjevic, and former League of Communists Central Committeeman Bane Andrejev.

Tito denounced Khrushchev and Communist Chinese leaders June 15 for their attacks on Yugoslavia and hailed the U.S. for its aid in the struggle against hunger and Soviet domination. Addressing miners in Labin, Croatia, on the Istrian Peninsula, Tito charged that Khrushchev's description of Yugoslavia as the Trojan Horse of communism had "insulted not only the Yugoslav leadership but the Yugoslav people as a whole." Tito asserted that Khrushchev's speech to the Bulgarian Communist Party had "nothing in common with comradely criticism." He chided Khrushchev for having requested long-term U.S. credits immediately after his denunciation of Yugoslavia for accepting U.S. aid.

Tito agreed "that the Americans do not give us aid because they want to help us build socialism: In 1920-1, when the Americans aided hungry Russia, they did not do it for the cause of Socialism either." "They do not like Socialism," but, after 1949, "they gave us aid because there was a threat of famine and to strengthen our independence against Stalin." Tito rejected Khrushchev's contention that the U.S. had unloaded "tainted goods" on Yugoslavia. He said: "American wheat is not worse than Russian wheat. The difference is that we get wheat from America and we do not get it from the Soviet Union."

A Soviet note delivered to Yugoslavia June 28 and made public July 1 reaffirmed Moscow's intentions to delay $285 million in credits promised Yugoslavia but urged negotiations to secure Yugoslav approval for terms of the delay. The note denied as "groundless" Yugoslav contentions that the USSR had broken promises to Yugoslavia by delaying the credits. Yugoslav Vice Pres. Mijalko Todorovic told the Federal Assembly in Belgrade June 26 that Yugoslavia would seek loans "from the other side [West]" to replace the Soviet credits.

The U.S. State Department disclosed Aug. 19 that it was studying Yugoslav requests for $250 million in credits to finance development projects affected by the delay of the promised Soviet loans. Yugoslavia was said to be seeking $350 million in Western loans, principally from Britain and the U.S.' Development Loan Fund. Yugoslav Amb.-to-U.S. Leo Mates, leaving the U.S. to become aide to Tito, had told newsmen June 19 that his country had requested a speedup of military equipment and parts ordered since the cessation of the U.S.-Yugoslav military aid program. Marko Nikezic, 37, a partisan veteran, was named July 12 to succeed Mates as ambassador to the U.S.

Tito, opening a new highway between Zagreb, the capital of the Croatian Republic, and Ljubljana, the Slovenian Republic's capital, charged again Nov. 23 that east European nations had joined the attempt "to break us and bring us to our knees," but he warned that Yugoslavia would maintain its ties with the West and would travel an independent road to socialism.

1959

Disruptive dissent had declined and the Soviet Union consolidated its control over eastern Europe 3 years after the Hungarian uprising and the Polish disruptions. Besides the intimidating effect of the post-1956 firmness in Hungary, the Soviets' technological accomplishments, particularly in outer space, enhanced respect for Moscow's power.

The Khrushchev regime, in a new mood of self-confidence, sanctioned—albeit with reservations—nonconformist currents in Soviet literature. Elsewhere in eastern Europe the extremes of both repression and "liberalization" leveled off. The Hungarian government began to slow down its actions against participants in the 1956 revolution. The Polish regime, however, stepped up measures intended to discourage opposition by the Roman Catholic Church and by intellectuals.

In Yugoslavia, the vicissitudes of the Moscow-Belgrade relationship promoted unrest. The government acted to strengthen its control over both pro-Soviet sympathizers and advocates of greater liberalization.

DISSENT SUBDUED

Poland

Further deterioration of church-state relations and the persistence of party pressure for agricultural collectivization were foreshadowed by 2 events during the waning winter months.

The Rev. Marjan Pirozynski, a prominent Roman Catholic priest and editor of the church magazine *Homus Dei,* was arrested Jan. 16 with 16 other persons on charges of black-marketeering to obtain paper for the magazine. Pirozynski pleaded guilty to censorship violations Jan. 20 on the ground that it was his "duty to spread the word of God."

U.S. Amb.-to-Poland Jacob D. Beam Feb. 19 denounced as "tragic" a wave of rumors that had resulted in hundreds of eastern Polish peasants descending on the U.S. embassy in Warsaw in the belief that they would receive free emigration to Alaskan farm sites.

Polish Communist leader Wladyslaw Gomulka strengthened his control of the Polish United Workers' (Communist) Party (PUWP) Mar. 19 with the promotion of 3 close aides to the party Politburo and the dismissal of 18 opponents, principally Stalinists, from the 75-member Central Committee. The move, approved Mar. 19 at the final session of the 3d PUWP Congress in Warsaw, enlarged the Politburo from 9 members to 12 with the addition of Marjan Spychalski, Zenon Kliszko and Edward Gierek. 14 of the 18 ousted Central Committee members were adherents of the pro-Soviet Natolin Group, which had opposed Gomulka during the Oct. 1956 upheaval. They included Amb.-to-Czechoslovakia Kazimierz Mijal, ex-Security Vice Min. Waclaw Lewikowski and Frantisek Jozwiak-Witold, former Politburo member for police.

The *N.Y. Times* reported Oct. 28 that Jerzy Morawski, "liberal" aide to Gomulka, had proffered his resignation from the Politburo in protest against Gomulka's tightened economic policies and the appointment of several "hardliners" to important posts. (The naming of Waclaw Tylodziecki to replace Gomulka's long-time liberal intellectual comrade Wladyslaw Bienkowski as education minister was regarded as an instance of such appointments.) Prof. Julian Hochfeld, social historian prominent in the 1956 upheaval, was reported Oct. 29 to have been dismissed as director of the Foreign Affairs Institute in Warsaw.

Hungary

The International League for the Rights of Man charged Apr. 4 that the Hungarian government had jailed, deported or executed 6,000 of the 21,000 Hungarians who had fled abroad during the 1956 revolt but later returned under promises of amnesty. The charges, documented by the Hungarian National Revolutionary Committee in Exile, were presented to UN Secy. Gen. Hammarskjold by League Chairman Roger Baldwin.

Ex-Pres. Zoltan Tildy, 70, a member of the revolutionary cabinet of the late Premier Imre Nagy, was freed from a 6-year prison sentence Apr. 4 under a partial amnesty granted by the Hungarian Presidential Council.

Ex-Prof. Ferenc Merei and the former editor Sandor Fekete of the Workers' (Communist) Party newspaper *Szabad Nep* were sentenced to prison terms of 10 and 9 years, respectively, on charges of organizing an antistate plot with other followers of Nagy.

A report issued in New York Sept. 17 by 3 anti-Communist organizations charged the Hungarian government with increasing the use of terror against industrial workers, students, peasants and the clergy. It was signed by the American Friends of the Captive Nations, the Assembly of Captive European Nations and the Hungarian Committee.

Government spokesmen in Budapest Oct. 17 disclosed the executions of 7 persons in July-August for alleged crimes committed during the 1956 revolt.

Soviet Union

V. N. Sukachev, editor of the Soviet Academy of Sciences' *Botanical Journal,* was replaced Jan. 20 by V. F. Kuprevich, president of the Byelorussian Academy of Sciences, presumably for his criticism of biologist Trofim L. Lysenko's officially supported theories on hereditary transmission of acquired characteristics in plants and animals.

Premier Nikita Khrushchev May 23 suspended the campaign against "revisionism" in literature. In a Kremlin speech at the 3d Soviet Writers Congress, Khrushchev asserted that the "revisionists have suffered full defeat" and must be aided "in their transition from mistaken views to the correct principled positions." Khrushchev specifically vindicated Vladimir Dudintsev, author of the novel *Not by Bread Alone,* asserting that Dudintsev had "noted certain negative features" of Soviet life "in an exaggerated ... form" but "was not against the Soviet system." Khrushchev hinted that First Deputy Premier Anastas Mikoyan had urged him to read Dudintsev's novel because it contained "some observations that sound as if he had been eavesdropping on you [Khrushchev]."

At the congress' opening session the writers May 18 had approved the rehabilitation of Konstantin M. Simonov, condemned for his role in publishing the Dudintsev novel, Ilya Ehrenburg, criticized for his novel *The Thaw,* and Margarita Aliger, a poetess denounced by Khrushchev in 1957 for deviationisn Delegates to the congress voted May 25 to elect Konstantin Fedin to succeed Anatoly A. Surkov as first secretary of the Soviet Writers Union.

3 leading Soviet physicists Nov. 22 denounced, as "vague" and "unscientific," Dr. Nikolai A. Kozyrev's theories that the flow of time produced energy in the universe. Writing in *Pravda,* academicians Igor Y. Tamm, Pyotr L. Kapitsa and Lev A. Artsimovich charged that the Soviet press was guilty of reporting "cheap sensations" and was discrediting Soviet science. They rejected as "nonsense" reports that engineers at a Moscow factory had obtained more energy from a semiconductor than they had applied to it.

Rumania

The London *Times* reported Nov. 3 that several Rumanian Jewish leaders and other Jews who had indicated a desire to emigrate to Israel had been arrested and jailed for espionage. They were said to include Dr. Ernst Horvath, 70, Transylvanian Zionist leader, and Dr. Leo Fried, ex-general secretary of the Rumanian Zionist Organization, both of whom previously had served sentences.

Yugoslavia

The Yugoslav leadership relaxed somewhat the pressure on Soviet sympathizers within the ranks of the League of Communists as 1959 began. At the same time, the regime assured itself of the availability of an expeditious means of dealing with future mischief-makers.

According to reports from Belgrade Jan. 5, Yugoslav authorities had dropped charges of antistate activities that had been filed against 25 prominent pro-Soviet Yugoslav Communists arrested in June 1958. Some of the accused were said to have been released and the remainder jailed for 2 years under "administrative procedures" not requiring court trials. It was reported from Belgrade Jan. 13 that the Federal Assembly, without debate, had reenacted laws providing 2 years' banishment on an Adriatic island for political offenses. Several pro-Soviet Yugoslavs were said to have been sentenced under the law.

Pres. Tito warned in a speech in Belgrade Mar. 7 that his country would take action against the Soviet bloc's "warmongering, hostile and irresponsible" attacks on Yugoslavia. Tito, who had attacked Albanian Communist Party leader Enver Hoxha in a speech in Macedonia Mar. 6, told his Belgrade audience that Yugoslavia would take its complaint to the UN "if this vile campaign does not stop." He denounced Soviet First Deputy Premier Mikoyan for alleging during his U.S. visit that Yugoslavia could be "bought for $100 million."

The Communist Party Central Committee disclosed Apr. 28 that it had appealed to the Soviet Communist Party for "constructive, comradely discussion" to heal the Soviet-Yugoslav rift. The appeal was in answer to a Soviet bid for "rapprochement ... on the basis of Marxist-Leninist principles."

Vladimir Dedijer, ex-aide to Tito disgraced in 1954-5 for his support of imprisoned Milovan Djilas, was reported Nov. 6 to have been granted a passport in order to lecture at the University of Manchester.

Tito warned the world's major powers Nov. 22 that their efforts to regulate the world and act as "guardians" of smaller nations would create "dangerous elements for new conflicts." Speaking in Nis, Serbia, on the Yugoslav-Bulgarian frontier, he said that there was "constant danger" that the Western and Soviet blocs would base coexistence on division of the world into spheres of influence. "Coexistence must be between countries ... not between blocs," he asserted, or "what will happen to those countries that are not inside blocs?"

Wide World

Pres. Tito of Yugoslavia

Tito, in an address made to the Central Committee Nov. 19 and reported Nov. 21, denounced Yugoslav Communists for their growing "lack of discipline." He criticized party leaders and members for "uncontrolled talk and criticism" to non-party members and for "widespread manifestation[s] of localism" and "arbitrariness" in decisions affecting their fellow citizens.

Defections

At least 2 noteworthy figures fled the Soviet bloc in 1959.

The defection to West Germany of Lt. Col. Siegfried Dombrowski of the East German People's Army was revealed in Bonn Jan. 21. Dombrowski, deputy chief of the People's Army Coordination Bureau (an intelligence organization), told newsmen in Bonn Jan. 22 that the East German spy network in the West employed 60,000 agents, 12,000 of them based in West Germany.

The defection of Col. Pawel Monat, leading Polish intelligence agent and chief liaison officer among Polish military attaches abroad, was reported from Vienna Nov. 22 by A. M. Rosenthal, *N.Y. Times* correspondent ousted from Poland. Monat, who had served as Polish military attache in Washington, was said to have turned himself over to U.S. representatives in Vienna. State Department officials confirmed Nov. 23 that Monat and his family had U.S. for political asylum and had been brought to the U.S.

1960

Confrontations between Soviet Premier Nikita Khrushchev and the leaders of Albania marked the beginning of Albania's gradual withdrawal from the Soviet bloc. Previously, Albania had sought Russian support against the Yugoslavs, who had tried to control the Albanian Communist Party and had made allegedly imperialistic claims on Albania after World War II. The Soviet-Albanian friendship remained firm as long as Moscow and Tito were at odds between 1948 and 1955. Khrushchev's actions to cement a reconciliation with Belgrade, however, made it clear that Yugoslavia mattered to him more than Albania. The Yugoslav-Soviet rapprochement, however imperfect, undermined the confidence of the Albanian leaders in Moscow's leadership.

Tito's successful defiance of Stalin provided them with an example to follow. Starting in 1960, they moved toward an alliance with a country — Communist China — that was growing more and more hostile to both the Soviet Union and Yugoslavia.

The continuing deterioration of Sino-Soviet relations complicated Moscow's efforts to maintain control over its east European "satellites." The Soviet leaders took pains to rally them against both the Yugoslav "revisionism" and the Chinese "dogmatism." Regardless of these efforts, diversity in the area increased rather than diminished, and the extent of internal controls differed considerably from country to country. But nowhere did the growing diversity endanger the stability of the regimes. The few manifestations of opposition, particularly in Poland and Yugoslavia, were no exception to this rule. In Hungary, the Kadar regime improved its popular image by cautious but systematic concessions to demands for greater freedom of cultural expression, for the easing of travel restrictions and for economic improvement.

LATENT DISSIDENCE

Initial Friction with Albania

According to the *N.Y. Times* (Western edition, Feb. 18, 1963), the Albanian (Communist) Party of Labor organ *Zeri i Popullit* had published what was alleged to be the secret minutes of a private meeting held in Moscow Jan. 16, 1960 by Khrushchev and Svetozar Vukmanovic-Tempo, a Yugoslav League of Communists official. At that meeting, according to the Albanians, Khrushchev, supporting the Albanians, accused Belgrade of sending terrorists into Albania and other countries.

Zeri i Popullit said that Khrushchev turned on Albania later after it refused to side with his position at the Rumanian party congress in Bucharest in June. The Albanian newspaper reported that Khrushchev invited Albanian leaders to confer with him in Aug. 1960 for the purpose of lining them up against the Chinese in order to obtain a majority for the Soviet side at the forthcoming international Communist congress in Moscow in Nov. 1960. *Zeri i Poppullit*'s account of a series of 4 meetings between Khrushchev and the Albanian officials: "Khrushchev, with arrogance, pressure and threats, tried to impose his own views on our party. And when he became aware that he did not achieve his aim, he provoked the rupture of the talks."

Soviet-Yugoslav Tension

Leaders of 81 national and regional Communist parties meeting in Moscow issued Dec. 6 a manifesto in which they condemned both the revisionist and the dogmatic deviations. In the manifesto the signatory party leaders asserted:

"The Communist parties have ideologically defeated the revisionists in their ranks who sought to divert them from the Marxist-Leninist path. Each Communist party and the international Communist movement as a whole have become still stronger, ideologically and organizationally, in the struggle against revisionism, rightwing opportunism.

"The Communist parties have unanimously condemned the Yugoslav variety of international opportunism, a variety of modern revisionist theories in concentrated form. After betraying Marxism-Leninism, which they termed obsolete, the leaders of the League of Communists of Yugoslavia opposed their anti-Leninist revisionist program to the declaration of 1957; they set ... Yugoslavia against the international Communist movement as a whole, severed their country from the Socialist camp, [and] made it dependent on so-called aid from United States and other imperialists....

"The Yugoslav revisionists carry on subversive work against the Socialist camp and the world Communist movement. Under the pretext of an extra-bloc policy, they engage in activities which prejudice the unity of all the peace-loving forces and countries. Further exposure of the leaders of the Yugoslav revisionists, and active struggle to safeguard the Communist movement and the working-class movement from the anti-Leninist ideas of the Yugoslav revisionists, remain an essential task of the Marxist-Leninist parties....

"The further development of the Communist and working class movement calls, as stated in the Moscow declaration of 1957, for continuing a determined struggle on 2 fronts — against revisionism, which remains the main danger, and against dogmatism and sectarianism....

"Dogmatism and sectarianism in theory and practice can also become the main danger at some stage of development of individual parties, unless combated unrelentingly.

"They rob revolutionary parties of the ability to develop Marxism-Leninism through scientific analysis and apply it creatively according to the specific conditions, they isolate Communists from the broad masses of the working people, doom them to passive expectation or leftist, adventurist actions in the revolutionary struggle, prevent them from making a timely and correct estimate of the changing situation and of new experience, using all opportunities to bring about the victory of the working class and all democratic forces in the struggle against imperialism, reaction and war danger, and thereby prevent the peoples from achieving victory in their just struggle....

"At a time when imperialist reaction is joining forces to fight communism, it is particularly imperative vigorously to consolidate the world Communist movement...

"Communists throughout the world are united by the great doctrine of Marxism-Leninism and by a joint struggle for its realization. The interests of the Communist movement require solidarity in adherence by every Communist party to the estimates and conclusions concerning the common tasks in the struggle against imperialism, for peace, democracy and socialism, jointly reached by the fraternal parties at their meetings...."

Pres. Tito Dec. 26 proclaimed Yugoslavia's support of the USSR despite the denunciation of his regime in the Dec. 6 manifesto. Tito, at a special session of the Yugoslav parliament in Belgrade, declared that Yugoslavia and the USSR followed identical policies on the "most important issues of the day." He asserted that the current aggravation of world tensions was the work of "bellicose people, especially in the West, who still adhere to the position of power policy...." Denouncing the Moscow manifesto's criticism of Yugoslavia as a "rotten compromise" based on "untruths," Tito said: "We know that the main initiators this time were the Chinese delegates." He pledged that Yugoslavia would continue its efforts to develop good relations with Soviet-bloc states.

Polish Unrest

Social dissatisfaction in Poland in 1960 stemmed chiefly from an excess of official zeal in interfering with the free exercise of organized religious worship and from the regime's renewed efforts after the 3d Polish United Workers' Party (PUWP) Congress Mar. 10-19 to collectivize Polish agriculture. Popular feelings found an outlet during the official visit of U.S. Vice Pres. Richard M. Nixon, who received from crowds in Warsaw Aug. 2-5 a welcome and greetings reportedly at least equal in enthusiasm to any received by Soviet Premier Khrushchev there earlier in 1960.

At least 15 policemen were reported injured and 50 persons arrested in rioting begun Apr. 27 in Nowa Huta, steel center near Cracow, by women protesting the removal of a cross from the site of a projected church. Rioters restored the cross, burned the city hall and stoned police. More than 100 persons were arrested in Zielona Gora, western Poland May 29 when 5,000 persons clashed with police during a demonstration against local officials' seizure of a church-operated building.

Controversy was also aroused by government pressures in June for the removal of Msgr. Czeslaw Kaczmarek as bishop of Kielce for preaching against the government in his sermons. The government also attempted to renew a charge, already declared by Poland's Supreme Military Court to be unfounded, that Kaczmarek had collaborated with the Germans during the World War II occupation. The Polish episcopate made a formal complaint July 10 to the Council of State against Religious Affairs Min. Jerzy Sztachelski's conduct in pressing these attacks.

The PUWP Politburo and the presidium of the United Peasants' Party agreed June 25 to the establishment of a state agricultural development fund for the mechanization of agriculture, for the improvement of farmlands and for plant and rural electrification. The Peasants' Party permitted a 7-year extension of quota deliveries of grain, potatoes and livestock by peasant landholders to finance the fund's operations. Both parties noted then that agricultural output had increased 25% in the years 1954-8 (the repressive controls over peasants' disposal of their output during the first postwar years having been abated).

Nevertheless, PUWP First Secy. Wladyslaw Gomulka said Sept. 4 that agricultural production was lagging because of "anti-social" obstructionism by peasants opposed to state efforts to centralize and modernize Polish farming. He asserted that "compulsion and sanctions" were needed against those private farmers hampering the state's "organized collective efforts" to increase farm output.

Maj. Jan K. Szpontak, leader of an anti-Communist Ukrainian guerrilla force, was condemned to death June 25 by a district court in Rzeszow, 90 miles east of Cracow.

Hungary

More evidences of political self-assurance appeared in official circles and public life. The Kadar regime proclaimed a partial amnesty for Apr. 4, cited an increased supply of consumer goods and welcomed open complaints from citizens as a preferable alternative to rankling discontent.

Tibor Dery and Gyula Hay, prominent Communist writers imprisoned for participation in the 1956 revolt, were released under terms of a political amnesty commemorating the 15th anniversary of Hungary's liberation by the Soviet Army. These other intellectuals and backers of the 1956 Nagy regime were released under an amnesty Apr. 4: Ferenc Donath, Ferenc Janosi, son-in-law of the late Imre Nagy, Istvan Eorsi and Miklos Vasarhelyi. The amnesty abolished internment for security reasons and ended the imprisonment of an estimated 4,000 persons serving terms of less than 6 years.

At the Oct. 3d session of the UN General Assembly in New York, Premier Janos Kadar affirmed that ¾ of those jailed for participating in the revolt had been freed and that more than 40,000 refugees who had fled in 1956 had returned; all who had left were welcome to return, he said.

The *N.Y. Times* Oct. 29 cited reports that 3 prominent leaders of the 1956 Hungarian revolt — Istvan Bibo, head of the Peasant Party, and Laszlo Kardos and Arpad Gonc, leaders of the Revolutionary Committee of Intellectuals and the Petofi Circle—were being retried by a Budapest military tribunal in a government attempt to change their sentences from life imprisonment to death.

The sentencing of the Rev. Antal Lotz, a Roman Catholic priest, to 5 years in prison for anti-Communist agitation was reported Dec. 4 by the Budapest newspaper *Nepszabadsag.*

Church-State Conflict in Yugoslavia

The Roman Catholic Church, a minority force among the Yugoslav Federal Republic's Christians except in Croatia-Slavonia and Slovenia, once again found some of its personnel involved in a dispute between the Yugoslav regime and those desirous of more political autonomy in Croatia. Another sore point was the extent of the pope's authority. 2 ranking clergymen and a seminary administrator were convicted of political or economic offenses early in 1960. At the same time, the federal regime and Croatian Communists indicated a desire to improve church-state relations.

2 groups of Roman Catholics were sentenced to prison by Yugoslav courts Jan. 29 and Feb. 8 on charges of anti-state activities and efforts to revive a separate Croatian state. A Zagreb court sentenced the Rev. Rudi Jerak, 37, a Franciscan monk, to 15 years' imprisonment Jan. 29 and gave 13 persons terms ranging from 10 months to 11 years. An Osijek, Slavonia court sentenced the Rev. Ciril Kos, head of a Catholic seminary in Djakovo, Croatia, to 7 years in jail Feb. 8 and gave 5 priests and 2 students terms ranging from $2\frac{1}{2}$ to 6 years. Both groups allegedly had contacts with emigre leaders in Rome and Madrid of the pro-Nazi Ustashi movement, which had governed occupied Croatia during World War II.

Msgr. Smiljan Cekada, the Roman Catholic bishop of Skoplje (Macedonian Republic) and himself a Croat, received an 18-month suspended sentence Mar. 18 for violating Yugoslavia's currency regulations. By his own admission he had accepted more than 14 million dinars (about $35,000) sent from the Vatican and smuggled into the country for the very poor Skoplje and Sarajevo (Bosnia-Hercegovina) dioceses and had used the money for the religious and charitable purposes intended by the Holy See.

The regime was making efforts to better church-state relations, however. 109 Yugoslav Orthodox, Roman Catholic and Moslem priests were decorated by Pres. Tito Jan. 10 for services to the state. This was the first mass award of honors to Yugoslav priests since World War II. Josip Ujcic, Roman Catholic archbishop of Belgrade and also a Croat, was awarded the Yugoslav People's Order of Merit on his 80th birthday Feb. 9 for his work in improving church-state relations.

Vatican readiness to reach a church-state accord with Yugoslavia was expressed by Pope John XXIII in a memorial mass Feb. 17 for the late Alojzije Cardinal Stepinac, who had died Feb. 10 in his native Krasic, northern Croatia. The pope offered "forgiveness and peace" to the Yugoslav government to achieve "civic and religious peace at least sometime in the near future." A new policy toward the Roman Catholic church had been outlined Feb. 15 by Croatian Communist leader Vladimir Bakaric in a Zagreb speech. Bakaric, disclosing that the Communist party had ended its ban on members' attendance at religious ceremonies, asserted: "We have achieved what we sought. We have proclaimed religion a private affair and chased it out of politics, but not from social life."

A demand by Yugoslav bishops for the restoration of Roman Catholic Church properties and rights was reported Oct. 17 in Belgrade dispatches of the *N. Y. Times.* The bishops, who had met in Zagreb, were said to have submitted a memo offering improved church-state relations if the Yugoslav government (1) ended local authorities' interference with religious education, (2) returned some nationalized church buildings, (3) granted increased freedom to the church press and (4) agreed to consult the Bishops Council rather than state-controlled priests' groups.

Refugees

London and Belgrade reports that Gen. Jan Frey-Bielecki, head of the Polish air force, had fled to Yugoslavia were denied Jan. 6 by the Yugoslav government. The reports had linked Frey-Bielecki's alleged defection with Poland's Dec. 1959 expulsion of Col. Nikola Pejnovic and Maj. Svetozar Pazin, Yugoslav military attaches in Warsaw.

An estimated 20,000 East Germans migrated to West Germany and 7,500 West Germans moved to East Germany in the first 2 months of 1960, East German officials told the *N. Y. Herald Tribune* Mar. 2. Spokesmen for the All-German Affairs Ministry in Bonn estimated Apr. 11 that 20,000 West Germans and 30,000 East Germans unable to adjust to life in West Germany had crossed into East Germany in 1959. They asserted that 70% of the West German emigres returned to the West within 2 to 6 weeks and that 10% of the East German returnees eventually made a 2d flight to the West. They reported that 143,000 East Germans had registered as new refugees in West Germany during 1959. East German officials had claimed a total of 63,000 migrants from West to East during 1959.

The defection to the U.S. of First Secy. Ryszard Krolicki of the Polish embassy in Jakarta was reported Mar. 22. Krolicki and his family were said to have fled Indonesia for asylum in the U.S. in February.

The U.S. House of Representatives Apr. 4 passed by voice vote and sent to the Senate a resolution that would permit about 5,000 refugees and displaced persons to enter the U.S. Chairman Francis E. Walter (D., Pa.) of the House Immigration Subcommittee said there were about 22,000 eligible refugees, almost all of them in Europe. But he said they were "largely old people" who did not want to leave Europe.

Jan Cwiklinski, former captain of the Polish liner *Batory,* who had defected in Britain in 1953, was granted U.S. citizenship in New York June 20.

Ex-Soviet Navy Lt. Cmndr. Nikolai Federovich Artamonov, 32, a defector to the U.S., was produced publicly for the first time Sept. 14 at House Un-American Activities Committee hearings in Washington. Artamonov, who said he had defected with his wife in June 1959, while training Indonesian officers in Gdnyia, Poland, testified that "since Feb. 1955, Soviet strategy has been based on the strategy of surprise attack in nuclear warfare." Artamonov, formerly a Soviet destroyer captain, said this doctrine had been established "in a Soviet military publication ... known only to officers of flag rank and above" and "has never been changed." Artamonov told the *N.Y. Times* Sept. 16 that the USSR had at least one nuclear submarine and probably had submarines capable of launching missiles. He said the USSR's submarine fleet numbered 450 to 500 vessels and was the "shock force" of the Red Navy. He asserted that Soviet trawlers seen off the U.S. and in other Western waters were manned by Soviet navy crews, carried sensitive electronic detection equipment and were controlled by Soviet intelligence units.

Other Developments

4 prominent Yugoslavs imprisoned on charges of antistate plotting were released from prison Feb. 28 after serving 2 years of terms ranging up to 8½ years. The 4 were Bogdan Krekic, 72, founder of the pre-war Socialist Party, Aleksander Pavlovic, 75, former Socialist Party vice president, Dragoslav Stranjakavic, theological professor, and Milan Zuyovic, ex-dean of Belgrade University.

Bishop Ladislav Hlad of Czechoslovakia, said to have been consecrated secretly by Pope Pius XII in 1950, was sentenced to 9 years' imprisonment for "secretly performing the functions of a bishop," it was reported in Vienna Mar. 16. Czech newspapers arriving in Vienna Mar. 1 reported that the Rev. Alois Voral, Czech Roman Catholic priest, had been sentenced to 5 years in jail for "anti-state activities."

A parable entitled *A New Year's Tale*, written by Vladimir Dudintsev and published in issues of the Soviet literary journal *Novy Mir* cited Apr. 19 by the *N.Y. Times*, contained what was described as a ruthless characterization of the Soviet Communist Party as "a gang of legitimized bandits."

The newspaper *Sovietskaya Moldavia* of Kishinev reported Apr. 28 that Rabbi Simkhe Teper and 3 religious assistants had been tried and convicted by a public "comrades' court" trial in Faleschti, Moldavian SSR on charges of "teaching students to pray," holding "doubtful" political discussions and misusing synagogue funds.

Boris Leonidovich Pasternak, 70, Russian poet and novelist and the Nobel prizewinning author of *Doctor Zhivago*, died May 30 in the Moscow suburb of Peredelkino of a heart ailment and lung cancer. (In 1954 Pasternak gave the manuscript of *Doctor Zhivago*, which was critical of the Soviet regime, to an Italian publisher, who was to have brought out his edition simultaneously with the Russian one. Permission for the Russian edition, however, was denied. The Italian edition and translations brought Pasternak wide acclaim abroad but vilification at home as a "traitor" and "bourgeois reactionary." After the Nobel Prize committee chose him for the award in 1958, Pasternak cabled it that he was "immensely thankful, touched, proud, astonished and abashed." Later, under pressure by Soviet authorities, he declined the award "in view of the meaning given to this honor in the community to which I belong." After many Soviet writers and officials had petitioned the government to banish him, Pasternak wrote Premier Khrushchev that "leaving the motherland will for me equal death." He was permitted to remain. Pasternak, born of Jewish parents, had joined the Orthodox Church in 1917.)

1961

The erection of the Berlin Wall in August was the most graphic single action against dissent undertaken in eastern Europe in 1961. From the Soviet point of view, the freedom of the East Germans to leave their country for the West with minimal risks had been an anomaly—an unjustified privilege enjoyed by the former enemy over all other nations of the Soviet bloc. In the early years of the Cold War, Moscow accepted this state of affairs, possibly because of doubts about the advantages of a permanent retention of East Germany in the bloc. But after the workers' revolt of 1953, the Russians ruled in favor of that option. By that time, however, the Berlin situation had become so rigid and so much interconnected with other East-West problems that they could not tamper with it without running great risks. They continued to tolerate, albeit with growing impatience, the daily exodus of hundreds of refugees, most of them young, who "voted with their feet" in order to demonstrate their preference for living in the West.

The precedent of the unsuccessful Berlin blockade of 1948 apparently discouraged the Soviet government from attempting a radical solution.

Soviet Premier Khrushchev first tried long-term diplomatic pressure and intimidation: the harassment of the access routes to West Berlin and threats to nullify the Allied rights there by concluding a separate peace treaty with East Germany. In the end, however, the Soviet Union and East Germany suffered more than the West. Khrushchev lost prestige when, having met with determined opposition by the Western Allies, he failed to adopt the threatened unilateral measures. At the same time, the Soviet-induced uncertainty about the future status of West Berlin encouraged more East Germans to take advantage of the escape opportunity while it still lasted. The outflow of refugees reached record heights.

Entire areas of East Germany were depopulated. The severe drain of manpower endangered the very viability of that state of meager resources.

In the short run, the erection of the Wall was a face-saving measure intended to divert attention from the Soviet failure to expel the Allies from Berlin. Afterwards, Moscow quickly ended the confrontation with them and continued to respect the status quo of the western sectors. The long-term importance of the closing of the border, however, lay in its impact on the East Germans. For some time, the killings of refugees trying to force the barrier aroused international indignation although the practice did not differ from what had been commonplace elsewhere along the fortified "Iron Curtain." Later, the demographic stabilization of East Germany created preconditions for its extensive economic take-off in the 1960s. The standard of living improved, and the political regimentation, though still rigid, became more tolerable. Among the countries of the Soviet bloc, East Germany assumed a conspicuous place for its relative prosperity—and for a very low incidence of dissent. There was, however, a noticeably high incidence of and intense collaboration in anti-Communist espionage.

THE YEAR OF THE BERLIN WALL

Refugee Exodus Halted

The East German government Aug. 13 closed off free access between East and West Berlin after more than a month of preliminary moves designed to force Western acceptance of Soviet diplomatic initiatives toward an early conclusion of an all-German peace treaty. The move engendered not only much international tension but also a great deal of fear on the part of about 2 million citizens left in East Germany. It also had the effect of closing an escape route through which more than 2.6 million Soviet bloc refugees had fled to the West between 1949 (when—Oct. 7—East Germany had proclaimed itself a state) and July 1, 1961.

The Pankow regime began the campaign of pressure July 7 by ordering East Berlin residents employed in West Berlin to abide by the stipulations of a hitherto unenforced ordinance requiring all persons working in West Berlin after Jan. 26, 1953 to obtain a *Grenzgaenger* (border crossers) permit from East Berlin municipal authorities or face fines or imprisonment. About ½ of the 53,000 East Berliners employed in West Berlin were thought to have been unregistered before July 7.

The Soviet government brought the next phase of the campaign to a climax Aug. 3 by announcing, in reply to U.S., British and French government notes of July 17 (in which the Allies said they would not recognize any unilateral Soviet attempt to end their administrative rights in West Berlin), that it was prepared "reluctantly" to sign a peace treaty with Germany without the 3 Allied powers' participation. At the same time, the Soviet government said it would "sincerely welcome" a change in the Allies' stance and urged on them "a constructive approach together with the Soviet Union to a German peace treaty."

The U.S., British and French commandants in West Berlin Aug. 3 strongly protested in identically-worded notes to the Soviet commandant, Col. A. I. Solovev, against the Pankow regime's restrictions on the *Grenzgaenger* as a violation of the 4-Power agreement of June 20, 1949 on freedom of movement in Berlin. Solovev rejected the protests.

The Pankow regime opened the next round Aug. 4 by demanding that every *Grenzgaenger* reregister, under penalty of imprisonment at hard labor for failure to do so. It also ordered the *Grenzgaenger* to pay all rent and utility charges in West German marks (DM), then valued on the free market at nearly 5 times the value of the East German marks. The *Grenzgaenger* had been receiving 40% of their pay in West German DM.

In a special broadcast Aug. 13, Radio East Berlin reported that East German authorities had sealed off the border between the western and eastern sectors of the city at 2:30 a.m. local time in accordance with a decision taken by the Warsaw Treaty Organization's political advisory council. Until the conclusion of a peace treaty, the announcement said, the obstructions to free passage would stand "in the interests of peace in Europe and of the German Democratic Republic and the other Socialist states' security." In an official decree, the East German government justified the measure as a precaution taken to prevent the "Adenauer government" from succeeding in overcoming the Pankow regime in "a civil war" and in destroying the allegiance of its citizens by tempting them to spy and by "terroristic persecutions." The government said that East Germans henceforth would need special border-crossing permits "until West Berlin is turned into a demilitarized neutral free city." The border was closed by troops, police, and factory militia of the East German government.

The escape route used by Soviet-bloc refugees ran from East Germany to East Berlin; to West Berlin by foot or the "S-Bahn" elevated railway; by air to West Germany. The border closure was applied only to East Germans; West Germans, West Berliners and Allied military personnel were permitted to enter and leave the Soviet sector through 13 official crossing- or check-points. East Berliners working in West Berlin were halted.

The order effectively stopped the mass exodus of East German refugees, more than 16,000 of whom had registered at West Berlin centers since Aug. 1. More than 4,100 were registered in the last 24 hours the border was open.

2 East Germans were shot and killed as they sought to swim to West Berlin—the first Aug. 24 at the edge of the British sector and the 2d Aug. 29 in the Teltow Canal bordering the U.S. sector. A 3d eluded gunfire and swam across the Teltow Canal to West Berlin Aug. 30.

3 cases were reported of East Berliners who escaped to West Berlin by ramming trucks through the border barriers Sept. 8, 10 and 11. Other escapes were made by East Berliners who slid down ropes from apartments overlooking West Berlin streets, climbed through sewers and swam border canals and rivers.

The 25-mile-long border barrier between the sectors was strengthened beginning Sept. 16 to halt a continuing trickle of refugees attempting to run, jump, swim and batter their way into West Berlin. Additional walls and concrete barriers were installed behind 4 of the 7 Berlin crossing points Sept. 16 to force drivers to zigzag at low speeds when approaching the barrier from the eastern side. 5 cases had been reported of escapees who rammed through the barrier in trucks. The evacuation of houses bordering on West Berlin was begun by East German police Sept. 20.

7 East German refugees cut through the barbed-wire barrier surrounding the U.S. enclave of Steinstuecken Sept. 27. They were flown to West Berlin in a U.S. helicopter.

East Berlin police fired more than 300 shots into Western territory Oct. 31 in an unsuccessful attempt to halt 9 youths who rammed their way through the border barrier on the outskirts of West Berlin in a stolen truck. 16 refugees had escaped to West Berlin Oct. 16 despite a hail of gunfire from East sector police. 5 of the escapees jumped from an East Berlin house into a West Berlin truck filled with fine gravel. 3 East German youths rammed through the border into West Berlin's Staaken district Oct. 17 in a truck they had armored.

East Berlin police fired on several groups of refugees attempting to cross the border barrier Oct. 31 and recaptured 6 persons. Gunfire halted 21 of 30 East Berliners who attempted a mass escape Nov. 5. Despite border gunfire, an estimated 10-20 East Berliners were escaping to the West each night.

The Bonn Press & Information Office *Bulletin,* issued Nov. 14, said that West Berlin Mayor Willy Brandt had reported 268 "incidents" involving refugees escaping over the wall since Aug. 13. 8 refugees were killed and 69 wounded in the incidents. Brandt reported that 201 members of the East German army and East Berlin police had fled to West Berlin during the period.

State Secy. Franz Thedieck of Bonn's All-German Affairs Ministry reported Nov. 25 that more than 400 East German soldiers and police had fled to the West since the construction of the Berlin wall was begun. 25 refugees escaped Dec. 5 aboard a commuter train in which they sped into the British sector from East Berlin. The train was driven by Harry Deterling, 28.

East German Socialist Unity (Communist) Party First Secy. Walter Ulbricht said Dec. 30, in an article in *Pravda,* the Soviet Communist Party daily, that the flight of refugees had cost East Germany's economy the equivalent of $1.5 billion. West Berlin officials announced Jan. 2, 1962, that 207,026 East Germans had fled to the West during 1961, the majority of them before the building of the Wall.

Albania Defies Moscow

The proximate cause of the Soviet-Albanian dispute arose from threats and economic pressure applied by the Soviet leadership in 1960 in an effort to force Tirana to support Moscow in the growing Sino-Soviet rift.

Soviet Premier Nikita Khrushchev had visited Albania in the spring of 1959 and had arranged for massive economic assistance (including the cancellation of a sizable Albanian debt for Soviet deliveries of goods and materials and a long-term credit of up to 300 million rubles) to that Balkan land. It was reported later, however, that First Secy. Enver Hoxha of the Albanian Labor (Communist) Party had charged Nov. 16, 1960 at the international Communist conference in Moscow that the Soviet Union had fomented a revolt in Albania's armed forces and had acquired the enforced services of Mrs. Liri Belishova, an Albanian partisan heroine and then a party Politburo member (before her expulsion in Sept. 1960). Moreover, Hoxha asserted, after Albania had blocked a Soviet move at the 3d Rumanian Party Congress in Bucharest in June 1960 to condemn the Chinese Communist Party for its stand against coexistence, the Soviet leadership had exercised "unbearable pressures" to extort Albanian support. Hoxha gave as an example the Soviet withholding of all but minimal deliveries of grain to drought-stricken Albania in the summer and autumn of 1960.

It was reported in Belgrade Nov. 14, 1961 that the Albanian Labor Party had informed its members that Mrs. Belishova had been expelled from the party and arrested in 1960 as a Soviet spy. Khrushchev had cited her case at the 22d Soviet Communist Party Congress in October in a speech attacking Hoxha's rule. (The real object of the attack was the Communist Chinese leadership, which Albania supported.) Mrs. Belishova was believed to be dead.

According to the Hungarian journalist Paul Lendvai, "the last attempt to prevent an open split" between Moscow and Tirana took place at the 4th Albanian Party Congress in Feb. 1961 in Tirana. (The Albanians had lionized Chinese visitors to the congress "while the Soviet delegates complained that they were being humiliated," Lendvai wrote in *Eagles in Cobwebs,* a 1969 book on postwar Balkan developments.) At the congress, Hoxha asserted that the Albanian leadership had uncovered and forestalled in the fall of 1960 what Hoxha described as a "criminal plot" concocted by "some Albanian traitors and external foes such as the Yugoslavs, the Greeks and the American 6th Fleet" against the Albanian regime. (As Lendvai noted, Soviet bloc accounts ignored this "dramatic revelation," and east European editors, following Moscow's cue, left it out of reprints of Hoxha's speech. The affair exposed at the congress "was widely regarded even at that time as a Soviet plot to overthrow Hoxha," Lendvai reported.)

The Chinese delegation remained in Albania for 2 weeks after the close of the congress Feb. 20 and, in countrywide speaking engagements, stressed the Chinese Communist Party's wholehearted indorsement of Hoxha's foreign and international party policies.

An Albanian firing squad May 31, 1961 executed Rear Adm. Teme Sejku, 39, Soviet-trained former commander-in-chief of the Albanian navy; Tahir Demi, 42, ex-chairman of the Elbasan district party committee; Hajri Mane, 46, a former service officer; and Avdul Resuli, 50, a public official. (Demi had represented Albania at meetings of the Council for Mutual Economic Assistance, or COMECON.) 5 others received prison terms ranging from 15 to 25 years. All reportedly had pleaded guilty to charges of treason dating back as far as 1951.

8 Soviet submarines abandoned their station at Saseno Island opposite Vlore (Valona), Albania in the Adriatic Sea off Albania at the end of May and sailed westward through the Strait of Gibraltar, not to return. (The *N.Y. Times* reported from Vienna Sept. 2, 1963 that a Moscow radio broadcast had charged Albania with an attempt to "seize ... Soviet military property" during the 1961 withdrawal of Russian vessels and sailors from the naval base at Vlore. The broadcast, which said Soviet sailors had thwarted the theft, did not specify what equipment or property was involved. The *Times* reported, however, that the Albanian Defense Ministry newspaper *Bashkimi* had indicated in July that Albania had 3 submarines of unspecified origin. It was presumed that these craft had been part of the Soviet fleet of 8 submarines based at Saseno Island until 1961.)

The expulsion of the Albanian military attache in Moscow and permanent Warsaw Pact representative was reported by the French newspaper *Le Monde* June 9. The paper also reported that 2 Albanian Foreign Ministry officials had been arrested in Tirana Mar. 1 for passing confidential information on Albanian party policy to the Soviet embassy. The 2 were shot May 4 after a secret trial.

Hoxha Nov. 6 accused Soviet Premier Khrushchev of personal responsibility for the Soviet-Albanian rift. Hoxha made his charge in a broadcast marking the 20th anniversary of the Albanian Communist Party. His speech was monitored in the West and reported in the U.S. press Nov. 10. In it Hoxha charged Khrushchev with a "Machiavellian" attempt to impose Moscow's views on the parties of the other Soviet bloc states. Hoxha said: "It is not our party but the present Soviet leadership headed by Khrushchev who have slipped from Marxist-Leninist positions by demanding that other Communist parties submit to the Russian views and obey them"; it was the Soviet Union, not Albania, that was "afraid of imperialism" and had "delayed ... from year to year" the forcing of a Berlin settlement; Khrushchev had violated the basic precepts of Marxism by abandoning the struggle against imperialism in the name of peaceful co-existence.

The *N.Y. Times,* in a summary of the Hoxha speech published Nov. 20, reported that Hoxha blamed Khrushchev's attack on Albania on setbacks suffered by Khrushchev at the Communist meetings held in Bucharest in June 1960 and in Moscow in Nov. 1960. (Khrushchev, Hoxha said, had been rebuffed when he sought to impose the Soviet position on both meetings with only minimal debate.) Hoxha reportedly declared that only 18 foreign Communist parties had joined Khrushchev's attack on Albania, whereas 32 parties had dissociated themselves from the campaign.

Communist Chinese support of Albania was confirmed Nov. 6-16.

The Soviet Communist Party newspaper *Pravda* Nov. 16 reprinted a report on the 22d Soviet Party Congress in which First Secy. Palmiro Togliatti of the Italian Communist Party criticized the Chinese position. Togliatti wrote that "the objection made by ... Chou En-lai to Comrade Khrushchev's criticism of the Albanian leaders ... was unacceptable because public criticism in this case took place after all these questions had been ... discussed confidentially without result."

Albanian Amb.-to-China Reis Malile led his staff Nov. 6 in a walkout from a meeting in Peking celebrating the 44th anniversary of the Bolshevik revolution after Soviet Amb.-to-China Stepan V. Chervonenko had delivered a speech attacking the Albanian stand.

A Chinese Communist Party Central Committee statement issued Nov. 8 congratulated the Albanian party on its 20th anniversary and declared that its leadership was "correct." The statement said that Chinese-Albanian unity "can be shaken by no force on earth." Only 2 other Communist countries issued statements congratulating the Albanians: North Korea and North Vietnam.

An Albanian delegation arrived in Peking Nov. 17 to open talks on a 1962 trade agreement. It was headed by First Deputy Chairman Pupo Shyti of the Albanian State Planning Commission.

Prominent Defectors

Rudolf Nureyev, 23, a star of the Kirov Opera ballet group of Leningrad, fled from the touring group June 16 as it was about to board a plane in Paris for London. He asked for French asylum.

Dr. Mikhail Antonovich Klochko, 59, Ukranian-born winner of the Stalin Prize in chemistry, was granted political asylum by the Canadian cabinet Aug. 16. Klochko had come to Canada as part of a 9-member delegation to the 18th International Congress on Theoretical & Applied Chemistry, held in Montreal earlier in August. After attending the congress, the delegation went to Ottawa, where Klochko presented his asylum plea to the Royal Canadian Mounted Police Aug. 15. Soviet embassy officials were permitted to argue with Klochko for 90 minutes Aug. 16 in a fruitless effort to persuade him to return to the USSR.

Klochko, a member of several editorial boards of Soviet chemistry journals and the author of numerous papers on chemistry, had been a laboratory chief in the N. S. Kurnakov Institute of General & Inorganic Chemistry during 1947-55 and had headed a Moscow chemical laboratory at the time he defected. He was called the most important Soviet scientist to defect. Canadian Justice Min. E. Davie Fulton said in Ottawa

Aug. 17 that Klochko had said he had quit the USSR because "there was no scientific or intellectual freedom" there.

At an Ottawa press conference Aug. 18, Klochko said: "I decided to leave the USSR 5 years ago"; a Communist Party member since 1930, except for a period in 1937, "I was depressed by the lack of contact with the outside world, the falsity of information and the difficulty of self-expression"; "if I stayed in the USSR I would not be able to give to mankind all that I could if I were in a free democratic country"; much of his work had been suppressed in the USSR after he had charged, in 1948, that Soviet scientific historians had distorted facts; a treatise he had written on sea-water use had received international acclaim and had been published in Communist China but suppressed in the USSR; the USSR might be ahead of the West in some scientific fields, but the West led in others, including Klochko's field; "I was not tempted [to defect] by any material considerations but ... [acted] to seek freedom of scientific expression and to save what is left of my human self-respect"; "I could not carry out pure research where the scientist is constantly hampered by political consideration"; "it is the lack of human dignity in the USSR that hurts most."

Nicolai Ivanovich Sereda, 24, an electronics expert from Kiev, was reported Aug. 22 to have received political asylum by the Austrian government after breaking away from a Soviet tourist group in Vienna in July. Sereda's father, Ivan Matveevich Sereda, a member of the Ukranian Academy of Science, was flown to Vienna by the Soviet authorities but failed to persuade his son to return. Sereda, who was flown to West Germany, was said to have opposed Russian rule of Ukraine. The Associated Press reported that Sereda had hinted that an anti-Soviet underground was operating in Ukraine and was in contact with Western refugee groups.

A spokesman for the Yugoslav Consulate in New York reported Oct. 20 that Nenad Popovic, 52, a high-ranking Yugoslav finance official, had defected to the U.S. Popovic, currently teaching at Syracuse (N.Y.) University as a visiting professor of international finance, had left Belgrade in August with his wife and children for a tour of Western Europe. Although due to return Sept. 1, he went on to Britain instead and from there sailed for the U.S.

Soviet Amb.-to-Netherlands Panteleimon K. Ponomarenko and Dutch Amb.-to-USSR Henri A. Helb were ordered expelled from the Netherlands and the USSR, respectively, Oct. 13 as the result of an incident involving defecting Soviet biochemist Aleksei Golub, 35, and his wife, Irena, 32, at Amsterdam's Schiphol Airport Oct. 9. During a tour of Holland, Golub had asked for political asylum, but his wife decided to return to the USSR. She was waiting for a Moscow-bound plane when Ponomarenko and Soviet embassy aides scuffled with Dutch police who had sought to ask her whether she was leaving voluntarily.

(Golub, flew back to Moscow Mar. 27, 1962. A Dutch Foreign Ministry statement attributed his decision to end his political asylum to homesickness. At a Moscow Foreign Ministry interview with 300 Western newsmen Apr. 18, 1962, Golub said that he had been detained and questioned for more than a month by U.S. agents. Freedom to pursue his scientific research had been made dependent on his willingness to divulge Soviet scientific and defense secrets, he said. Nikolai Vokhniakov, 33, a mining worker from the Urals who had left a tour in Rome to seek asylum in the U.S. embassy, made similar charges at the interview.)

Guenther Maennel, 30, chief of the American desk in the East German Foreign Intelligence Department, was reported by the West German Interior Ministry Nov. 28 to have defected to the West.

Other Incidents

Yugoslavia — Ex-Vice Pres. Milovan Djilas, 49, was released from prison conditionally Jan. 20 after serving 4 years for published criticism of the Tito regime and of the Communist system of government. Djilas, a wartime aide of Tito's, had been jailed in Dec. 1956 for denouncing Yugoslav policies toward the Hungarian revolt and had been retried and sentenced to an additional prison term in 1957 following foreign publication of his book *The New Class.* Djilas had been held in Sremska Mitrovica prison, near Belgrade.

Poland — Polish United Workers' Party First Secy. Wladyslaw Gomulka told a Warsaw audience Mar. 18 that Polish Roman Catholic clerics "belonged to Poland with their bodies and to the Vatican with their souls." Denying that his government persecuted the church, Gomulka charged that the Polish church sought to further the Vatican's political aims by assuming a role of "persecution and martyrdom."

Stefan Cardinal Wyszynski, Roman Catholic primate of Poland, replied in a Warsaw church sermon Mar. 18 that "a political system can build streets ... but it cannot administer in the same way the human conscience." In a Lenten church service in Warsaw Mar. 19, Wyszynski accused the government of engaging in "a program of atheization" designed "to free our youth from God." (Wyszynski had warned Poland's 15,000 priests in a pastoral letter issued Jan. 12 and made public Mar. 3 to "prepare for the worst" in their struggle with the Polish government.)

An Education Ministry edict issued Aug. 19 and made public Sept. 8 put severe restrictions on the teaching of Roman Catholicism to children. The decree: (a) barred members of religious orders from teaching catechism; (b) limited religious instruction to 2 hours a week; (c) denied teaching permits to "those priests who have abused the generally accepted principles of behavior ..." by "using religious lessons for reactionary political purposes"; (d) required catechism classes to be registered with local school boards, which were to "exercise supervision" over them.

The Polish Roman Catholic Church was reported Sept. 22 to have protested the government's edict in letters sent to Premier Joszef Cyrankiewicz, Parliament Pres. Czeslaw Wycech and Tadeusz Zabinski, head of the government Office of Religious Affairs. The letters demanded adherence to constitutional guarantees of religious freedom.

Meanwhile, the church's Episcopate, in letters sent to pastors of 8,000 parishes: (1) forbade pastors to sign Education Ministry contracts as catechism teachers; (2) charged that the government's edict was aimed at "the gradual and complete liquidation of the teaching of religion."

Hungary — Security agents Feb. 7 arrested 10 persons, including 8 Roman Catholic priests, on charges of "leading an illegal organization engaged in anti-state activity." Budapest radio identified the leader of the alleged plot as Szilveszter Kormendt, a World War II army captain. A woman identified as Maria Bolzer (formerly Countess Zichy-Domokos) also was arrested.

12 prominent Catholics, including Countess Zichy-Domokos (also known as Marietta Bolza), 5 priests and 3 monks, were given jail terms of 2½ to 12 years by a Budapest court June 19 for "crimes against the state," including plans (a) to "change the internal regime of the Hungarian People's Republic and to restore the bourgeois" regime, (b) to "return the means of production to private owners" and (c) to return to the church its former estates. It was charged that the group had plotted to restore the monarchy and had received "political instructions," propaganda materials and financial aid from abroad.

11 of the defendants were tried in open court, where all but one, Msgr. Odon Lenard, pleaded guilty. The 12th prisoner, the Rev. Istvan Tabody, was tried *in camera,* found guilty of high treason and given a 12-year sentence.

Soviet Union — Rowland Evans Jr. reported in the *N.Y. Herald Tribune* Nov. 6 that the lay leader of the Jewish community in Leningrad and 2 lesser Jewish officials in that city had been tried and convicted about Oct. 9-13 on charges of "criminal contact with the embassy [in the USSR] of one of the capitalist states." The leader of the community, Gedalia Rubinovich Pechersky, 60, reportedly arrested in June, was sentenced to 12 years in prison. The other 2 defendants — Y. S. Dynkin and N. A. Kaganov, both more than 70 years old, were sentenced to 7 years inprisonment. The Soviet newspaper *Leningradskaya Pravda* confirmed the trial and sentences Nov. 11. Tass charged Nov. 17 that the Western press had used the trial of the Leningrad Jews as a pretext for a campaign about "a wave of persecution of Jews in the Soviet Union." Tass said that the arrested Jews had "sold themselves" to Israeli intelligence agents.

U. S. B'nai B'rith Pres. Label A. Katz charged in a statement issued Jan. 7, 1962 that the USSR had instituted new restrictions against the practice of Judaism. Katz said that during June-July 1961:

● A special tax on clergymen of all faiths had been quadrupled and made retroactive for 2 years. This levy was particularly severe on Jews because, unlike other religious groups in the

USSR, Jews were not "permitted to maintain a centralized structure or national federation."

● Rabbi Judah Lichterov had been replaced as Moscow's *yeshiva* (seminary) director.

● The yeshiva's governing council (the *vaad yeshiva*) had been disbanded and placed under the direction of Moscow Chief Rabbi Yehuda Leib Levin.

● The lay chairmen of synagogues had been removed in Kiev, Riga, Minsk, Vilna and Tashkent.

1962

The end of the Berlin confrontation without Soviet diplomatic victory weakened Nikita Khrushchev's prestige. The meager results of his ambitious economic projects and the falling rate of economic growth, caused by the excessive concentration of scarce resources in the costly space technology, further undermined his position. Khrushchev apparently tried to recoup by risky foreign adventures calculated to yield spectacular effects. In the Cuban missile crisis in October, however, he suffered another humiliating setback.

The outcome of the Cuban crisis made the Soviet Union especially vulnerable to hostile criticism by China and its Albanian ally. Their joint verbal attacks reached a climax later in 1962. Moscow encountered difficulties in trying to elicit condemnation of the Sino-Albanian criticism from the east European Communist parties. Opposition trends reappeared among Soviet intellectuals, non-Russian nationalities of the Soviet Union and other oppressed minority groups, especially Jews.

The continued outflow of escapees despite the Berlin Wall was indicative of the continued attraction of the Western way of life for East Germans. The refugees used ingenious methods in order to break through the fortified frontier. Because of improved security measures, however, the incidence of escapes later declined, approaching that in the other countries of the Soviet bloc.

REVIVAL OF DISSENT

Soviet-Albanian Rift

A declaration published Jan. 14 in the international Communist journal *Problems of Peace & Socialism* declared that Albania's leadership had "joined ranks with the enemies of the Communist movement" and no longer could be considered a member of the Socialist bloc. The declaration blamed Albania's deviation on "narrow nationalist egoistic interests" fostered by Albanian Labor Party First Secy. Enver Hoxha and Premier Mehmet Shehu. It called on Albanians to "return their country to the Leninist path."

An Albanian bid for diplomatic relations with Western countries was made in an editorial published by the Albanian Labor (Communist) Party newspaper *Zeri i Popullit* and broadcast from Tirana Jan. 10. It expressed the hope for "diplomatic relations, good trade and cultural relations with all capitalist countries that want this, particularly our neighbors." The only Western countries currently maintaining relations with Albania were France, Italy and Austria.

The Soviet Foreign Ministry publication *International Affairs* charged Jan. 30 that "in inculcating ... the idea that the outbreak of war is fatally inevitable, the Albanian leaders are ... fanning a war hysteria ... which cannot fail to lead to the aggravation of the situation in the Balkans." It declared that Hoxha and Shehu had installed a "regime of terror" in the Albanian party.

The Albanian news agency ATA reported Feb. 11 that protests had been sent to all Warsaw Treaty nations over Albania's alleged exclusion from a Prague meeting of the alliance's defense ministers Jan. 30-Feb. 1.

Shehu, in a speech broadcast Feb. 26 by Tirana radio, called on the Albanian people to "cling to your guns and be ready to fight." Making clear that the enemy he referred to was the USSR, Shehu added: "Nikita Khrushchev turns against Socialist Albania, uttering threats and resorting to the unparalleled methods of a plotter. But all these diabolical ... plans against our party and our people ... will continue to fail." Hoxha, in an address in Tirana Oct. 25, declared that China and Albania were allied in a battle against "the revisionist group of N. Khrushchev." He charged Khrushchev with joining "the most unbridled reactionaries, the colonialists, the imperialists, ... and the revisionist renegades," in a common front against China and Albania, the "true supporters" of Marx, Lenin, and Stalin.

The Soviet-Albanian rift widened after the Soviet withdrawal from the confrontation with the U.S. over Cuba had provoked strong Albanian and Chinese criticism. The Soviet Communist Party Nov. 18 denounced Communist critics of Khrushchev's Cuban policies for "pushing mankind toward thermonuclear war." Communist Party Central Committee Secy. Boris N. Ponomarev, writing in *Pravda,* declared that Khrushchev's actions had been subjected to "unlimited slander." In a reference directed at Albanian leaders but presumed to apply to China as well, he charged that "they have undertaken an especially shameful ... provocative campaign in connection with the crisis in the Caribbean."

Hungarian Socialist Workers' (Communist) Party First Secy. Janos Kadar, opening the 8th Hungarian Party Congress Nov. 20, declared that "we strongly condemn the rebel, Enver Hoxha and ... all the dogmatic-sectarian phenomena making their appearance in other parties of the international Communist movement." Kadar asserted that Communist-bloc unity meant not only a unity of ideals "but also common action in the international sphere on the paramount questions of the revolutionary movement."

The Kadar attack on Albania was criticized Nov. 21 by Wu Hsiu-chuan, leader of the Chinese delegation to the Budapest meeting. Gyula Kallai, the Hungarian party's chief ideologist, and other Hungarian speakers denounced the Chinese, Albanian and Yugoslav parties Nov. 22-23 for deviation from Marxist aims and practices.

The Soviet and Chinese attitudes toward Albania were contrasted Nov. 27 in statements issued on the 18th anniversary of Albania's liberation during World War II. The Moscow statement, published in *Izvestia,* described Albania's leaders as hypocrites and liars and accused them of "plunging into the mire of extreme nationalist and pseudo-revolutionary adventurism." The Chinese statement, in a message to the Albanian government, declared that the Albanian government declared that the Albanian people, "under the correct leadership of the long-tried and tested Albanian Workers' [Communist]

Party, had displayed great heroic mettle in their struggles against domestic and foreign enemies."

Czechoslovak Communist Party First Secy. Antonin Novotny opened the party's 12th Congress in Prague Dec. 4 with a speech in which he accused Albania and, by implication, China of having aided U.S. "imperialism" by attacks on the USSR's Cuban policies. Making clear his reference to the Chinese, Novotny declared that "those who listen to the Albanian leaders or support them in their aggression against the Communist movement put themselves in opposition to the declarations of the world's Communist parties." Party Central Committee Secy. Vladimir Koucky expressed regret Dec. 7 that the Chinese delegation, led by Wu Hsiu-chuan, had failed to join in criticism of Albanian leaders who had voiced "disgusting slanders" against the USSR by alleging its policies had led "in treacherous ways to a Cuban Munich."

Pravda, in an editorial Dec. 9 devoted to the East European and Italian party congresses, alluded to "those who are supporting the Albanian leaders in their splitting activities aimed at undermining the unity of the Socialist countries and the world Communist movement." *Pravda* quoted Novotny as having said: "We cannot agree with the statements of the Albanian leaders and the support which is being given these views by the Communist Party of China." Western observers reported that it was the first time the Russian people had been told directly of the Chinese dissidence.

Opposition in the Soviet Union

The Italian Communist Party newspaper *L'Unita* reported Feb. 6 that Khrushchev had recently escaped an assassination attempt. *L'Unita* offered no details, but the report was considered unusual in view of the close working relationship said to exist between the newspaper and the USSR's Tass news agency. Soviet government spokesmen dismissed the report Feb. 6 as "nonsense," and Brazilian Charge Roberto L. Assumpcao de Araujo reported Feb. 8 that Khrushchev had joked about the report during a meeting in Sochi the previous day.

The *N. Y. Times* reported Oct. 8 that riots leaving 75-500 persons dead had been touched off in Novocherkassk by a June 1 price increase in meat (up 30%) and butter (up 25%). Some observers argued that the disturbances reflected "deeper resentment" over food shortages and work speedups. Novocherkassk, an industrial city (94,000 people) located 20 miles northeast of Rostov and 600 miles south of Moscow, produced locomotives and farm and mining equipment.

The demonstrators included large numbers of women, joined by workers and students assembled in protest against the price rises. The character of the originally peaceful demonstration changed when the local militia, attempting to disperse the crowds, allegedly fired into the air. The volley hit persons who had climbed up trees and on buildings. At that point, the citizens responded with violence. Army troops were reported to have been summoned to help quell the riots.

Similar but less-violent disorders occurred about the same time in smaller cities near Rostov and in Voronezh, 300 miles to the north, in Krasnodar, 150 miles to the south and in Grozny, 400 miles to the southeast. A children's curfew law, passed July 12, forbade all Novocherkassk youths under 16 years of age to appear in the streets and other public places after 8 p.m. in winter and 9 p.m. in summer. Alexander V. Basov, the Rostov regional party first secretary, was removed in August in favor of Vladimir V. Skryabin.

Irina Yemilianovna Ivinskaya, daughter of Mrs. Olga Ivinskaya, friend and aide of the late Boris Pasternak, was reported to have been released from a Soviet labor camp June 13. Mrs. Ivinskaya had received a 3-year sentence in Dec. 1960 for acting as an accomplice with her mother in smuggling into the USSR royalties from the sales in the West of Pasternak's novel *Dr. Zhivago*. Mrs. Ivinskaya had received an 8-year sentence. Soviet author Evgeny Popovkin announced in Stockholm July 25 that publication of *Dr. Zhivago* in the USSR had been authorized by the Soviet government.

Crackdown on 'Economic Crime' Hits Jews

A widespread crack down on such "economic crime" as currency speculation, black-marketing and embezzlement continued throughout the USSR, eliciting charges from

Western sources that the anticrime drive was blatantly anti-Semitic. Western critics pointed out that defendants with Jewish-sounding names frequently received the most publicity and the most severe penalties. Sir Barnett Janner, chairman of the Board of Deputies of British Jews, charged July 15 that the Soviet court proceedings "reveal a distinct anti-Jewish bias." He said that 28 of the 46 persons sentenced to death for economic crimes through June were Jews.

The Soviet government newspaper *Izvestia* reported July 21 that 4 persons (2 of them Jews) had been sentenced to death and other defendants sentenced to prison by the criminal division of the Soviet Supreme Court after a 4-month trial of 50 persons in Frunze, capital of the Soviet Republic of Kirghiz, on charges of embezzling government property, illegally manufacturing and retailing textiles and knitted goods, bribery and currency speculation. The newspaper *Sovetskaya Kirgiziya* reported July 24 that the number convicted in the case was 45 and the number receiving death sentences at least 9 (4 to 6 of them Jews).

2 men (one believed to be Jewish) were reported Aug. 1 to have been sentenced to death and 8 other defendants (several with Jewish names) to have received jail sentences of up to 15 years in Kaunas, Soviet Lithuanian Republic, for illegal currency speculation. 2 men with Jewish names received death sentences and 4 others jail terms of up to 15 years in Khmelnitsky, Ukraine on charges of gold and currency speculation, it was reported Aug. 3.

The U.S. State Department Aug. 8 rejected a proposal of Sen. Thomas J. Dodd (D., Conn.) that Pres. John Kennedy have his ambassador in Moscow return to the U.S. for 2 weeks "for the publicly declared purpose of reporting to the President on the persecution of Jews in the Soviet Union."

(Tass July 18 announced the appointment of Veniamin E. Dymshits, 52, a Jew, as State Planning Committee (Gosplan) chairman and as a deputy premier. Dymshits, who replaced Vladimir N. Novikov as Gosplan chairman, became the first Jew to hold a leading government position since the ouster of the late Premier Joseph Stalin's brother-in-law Lazar M. Kaganovich as a deputy premier in 1957. Dymshits had been first deputy chairman of Gosplan since 1959.)

The Djilas Case

Ex-Vice Pres. Milovan Djilas, 51, of Yugoslavia was arrested at his Belgrade home Apr. 7. The government filed no formal charges, but it was believed the arrest was made in connection with plans for the publication of Djilas' new book, *Conversations with Stalin*. The book was based on talks Djilas held with Stalin prior to Yugoslavia's 1948 ouster from the Soviet bloc. Yugoslav authorities earlier in the week had demanded that Djilas hand over a manuscript copy of his latest work following Western newspaper comments on the book. Djilas was threatened with arrest if the book was published. The author's publisher, Harcourt, Brace & World, Inc. of New York, announced that it had postponed publication pending a study of Djilas' position.

In March the Yugoslav government had banned the distribution of the Italian magazine *Tempo Presente* because it carried a short story, called "The War," written by Djilas while in prison. The government said the story contained "gross slanders" about Yugoslavia's "liberation war, as well as about ... our army."

Djilas had been released from prison conditionally Jan. 20, 1961 after serving 4 years for antigovernment writings. The Yugoslav Information Secretariat asserted Apr. 11 that Djilas had violated the terms of the parole under which he was released from prison.

William Jovanovic, president of Harcourt, Brace & World, Inc. of New York, arrived in Belgrade Apr. 12 in an effort to persuade Yugoslav authorities to release Djilas. Jovanovic met Apr. 13 with Enver Humo, foreign press department chief in the Information Secretariat, but admitted failure and returned to New York Apr. 16.

Humo Apr. 13 released a statement on his meeting with Jovanovic. He said: "For the Yugoslav authorities Mr. William Jovanovic is a private person"; "he concluded a business ... with a Yugoslav citizen who is a convict on conditional freedom"; Yugoslav authorities had nothing to do with "whether Mr. Jovanovic will publish a book or anything else on the basis of the material he received from Djilas"; "if the investigation proves that Djilas committed criminal deeds, which besides that means the breach of the clear obligation that he freely took on himself toward competent authorities [at the time of his parole], all this is the greater since parts of this material already have been used and published in the foreign press."

Jovanovic had said that a Yugoslav Information Office official in New York had told him Apr. 6 that on the basis of the advance articles on Djilas' book, the Belgrade government felt the book would be harmful to Yugoslavia.

Djilas was convicted in Belgrade District Court May 14 of violating the Yugoslav criminal code by revealing official secrets in his *Conversations With Stalin,* which was published in the U.S. shortly thereafter. Djilas was sentenced to 5 years in prison; the court ordered him to serve an additional 3 years and 8 months remaining from a previous sentence from which he had been paroled in Jan. 1961.

The 6½-hour trial was held in secrecy, but the public and foreign newsmen were permitted to attend the opening proceedings and sentencing. As the trial started Djilas demanded in vain that it be held in public, otherwise he would refuse to put up a defense. Reading a statement he had written before entering the court, Djilas charged that he was being "publicly defamed by lies," that the indictment against him had "many fabrications, if not to say it is based entirely on them."

Pres. Tito declared July 23 that his government had "gone too far" in its "very liberal attitude" toward Yugoslav writers. Speaking at the end of a 2-day meeting of the League of Communists' Central Committee in Belgrade, Tito said: "We certainly do not want to teach writers and tell them what they must write, but we will not allow anyone to write nonsense and caricature and distort our social life." Tito also criticized lower echelon party officials for failing to solve the nation's economic ills.

(Vice Pres. Aleksander Rankovic, speaking at the opening session July 22, had said the League of Communists would not tolerate ideological deviations and "liberalist conceptions" within its ranks. Rankovic said it would be "absolutely impermissible" for party members to have "different conceptions and different political attitudes on a single important field of activity or on a big social problem and to put them forward ... without harmonizing them in the forums to which they belong.")

DEFECTIONS

Soviet Agent Flees to West

A high-ranking Soviet intelligence official later identified as Anatoly Dolnytsin defected to the West in early 1962. (His defection was reported by London newspapers July 11 and 13, 1963.) A diplomatic register had listed an Anatolij A. Doilnitsini as having served as a Soviet attache in London during Jan.-Sept. 1961. (The 1963 accounts of the defection and disclosure of the official's identity were published despite the newspapers' receipt of a British government "D" notice [nonbinding] requesting that such news be withheld from the public on the ground that it might be contrary to national interest.)

According to a government source, as quoted in the reports, in early 1962 Dolnytsin contacted officials of the U.S. embassy in a European Communist capital where he was stationed. Dolnytsin escaped to the U.S. and brought with him a great deal of information on the USSR's espionage operations. CIA agents questioned Dolnytsin for several weeks to make sure that he had not been "planted" by Moscow. Dolnytsin was flown to Britain 6 months later and requested asylum.

East German Escapees

According to the West German magazine *Der Spiegel,* more than 600 persons had been spirited out of East Berlin by an underground railway organized by West Berlin students under the name "Travel Bureau, Inc." The network, formed by German and foreign students attending West Berlin's Free and Technical Universities, had been organized immediately after the Communists sealed the border between East and West Berlin Aug. 13, 1961. The students used false papers, secret tunnels and the municipal sewer system to bring escapees past the border. Its existence was reported only after East German authorities had succeeded in uncovering the ring and arresting 146 of its operatives. (The *N.Y. Times* estimated Mar. 28 that

5,000 persons had escaped from East Berlin since it was closed off.)

2 East German construction workers escaped to the French sector of West Berlin Apr. 9 by ramming a heavy truck into the wall and jumping to safety.

A 9-year-old boy escaped Apr. 10 by leaping from an East Berlin rooftop into a net held by West Berlin firemen.

The tunnel escape of 12 East Berliners to the West was disclosed May 18 by Max Thomas, 81, leader of the group. The 12, most of them in their 50s, 60s and 70s, tunneled their way to the West from a chicken coop behind Thomas' home in the East Berlin suburb of Glienicke.

West Berlin police fired more than 100 shots into the Eastern sector May 23 to protect an East German boy of 14 who swam a canal under Communist gunfire to West Berlin. The boy suffered 7 wounds but survived. One East German guard was killed and another wounded in the shooting.

4 bomb explosions tore small gaps in a section of the East Berlin wall facing the French sector of West Berlin May 26. The bombings, the first successful attempts to sabotage the wall, were attributed to anti-Communist activists.

East Berlin guards shot and killed an escapee May 27 as he tried to flee to the West along a railroad line; they killed another East German May 28 as he attempted to swim a canal to West Berlin.

British and East German armored cars were brought to the border June 5 after East German police had shot and killed a man as he attempted to swim the Spree River to the British sector.

14 East Germans seized the 500-ton excursion boat *Friedrich Wolf* June 8 and raced through police machinegun fire to ram the boat into a West Berlin embankment of the Spree. The escapees included 6 members of the vessel's regular crew. They were covered by gunfire from West Berlin police.

2 tunnel escapes and a minor bombing of the wall were reported June 12. 11 persons escaped through one of the tunnels and a larger number—reportedly 22—through the 2d. Up to 54 persons were believed to have made successful escapes from East Berlin during the June 9-10 weekend. West Berlin police disclosed June 15 that one would-be escapee, a boy of 12, had

been killed by People's Police gunfire as he approached the border June 10.

An East German border guard was killed by gunfire from his own unit June 18 as he and other guards fired on a group attempting to enter a tunnel in a house on the East Berlin border. 4 persons escaped; 5 were captured before they could enter the tunnel.

Speaking at a West Berlin rally marking the 9th anniversary of the June 17, 1953 East German uprising, West German Chancellor Konrad Adenauer said that 200,000 persons had been jailed for political reasons in East Germany since 1945 and that 2,027,645 East Germans had fled to the West between June 1953 and May 1962.

Decrees published July 19 and made effective immediately by the East German government closed the country's entire Baltic coast to persons whose presence was not specifically authorized. The measure was aimed at curbing the reportedly growing numbers of refugees attempting sea-escapes to West Germany and Scandinavia.

West Berlin crowds numbering up to an estimated 10,000 persons, most of them youths, staged a series of intensified demonstrations as the result of the slaying Aug. 17 of an East Berlin construction worker, Peter Fechter, 18, as he sought to flee across the Berlin border wall to West Berlin. An 18-year-old companion who fled with Fechter managed to cross the wall and escape, but Fechter, shot by East German guards at 2:10 p.m., toppled back on the East Berlin side of the wall.

In full sight of a crowd of shrieking West Berliners, Fechter was left bleeding to death unattended for more than an hour despite his groans and cries for help. Any Western attempt to go to him was blocked by East German guards, who leveled their machine pistols at the West Berlin crowd and threw tear gas grenades and smoke bombs at them. West Berlin police, in return, threw tear gas grenades at the East Germans, but neither they nor 6 U.S. military police soldiers from the nearby Friedrichstrasse crossing point (Checkpoint Charlie) were able to help the dying youth. The Americans were booed by the West Berlin crowd for not acting. At 3:40 p.m. East German police removed Fechter's body. The East German Interior Ministry said later that Fechter had died in a hospital.

An East German was machinegunned to death Aug. 13 as he tried to escape from East Berlin by swimming across the Werra River to West Berlin.

A uniformed East German guard escaped across the wall into West Berlin Aug. 13, but a 2d guard was caught as he tried a similar escape. A man believed to be a member of the People's Police opened fire Aug. 15 on an East German watchtower in the area bordering on the West German borough of Spandau. 2 tower guards were wounded before their assailant was killed. A teen-aged East German girl crawled through the barbed-wire barrier under a hail of bullets and escaped into Spandau Aug. 18. Although untouched by bullets, she had to be hospitalized for shock. A male companion was shot and captured by the East German guards.

2 East German army corporals fled across the border into West Germany in the vicinity of Fulda Aug. 7. Another soldier escaped to West Germany in the same area Aug. 9 by driving a heavy-tread tractor across a machinegun position, across 2 rows of barbed wire and across the 30-foot "death strip." U.S. Army personnel and West German police blocked East German border police who sought to capture the escapee and recover the tractor.

About 37 East Germans fled from their 550-member delegation to the Communist-sponsored 8th World Festival of Youths & Students for Peace held in Helsinki. The refugees sought asylum in Sweden or West Germany. 8 of the fugitives arrived in Bonn, West Germany Aug. 10. They said security officers had escorted the East German delegation and had warned all delegates "again and again," both before and after leaving East Germany, that the Finnish authorities would return every escapee to East Germany and that "every flight attempt was doomed to fail."

East Germans continued attempts to cross the wall into West Berlin despite the presence of armed border guards.

Hans Dieter Wesa, 19, an East German railway policeman, was mortally wounded Aug. 23 as he attempted to flee to the French sector of West Berlin. Wesa fell and died on the Western side of the border.

An armed East German border policeman leaped the wall into the U.S. sector Aug. 25, but a civilian who tried to swim a canal to the West the same day was picked from the water by a patrol. An East German soldier on night patrol on the wall leaped to the West unharmed Aug. 28 under a hail of bullets from his comrades.

A middleaged man was trapped atop the wall Sept. 4 and was shot to death when he continued to scramble toward the West.

2 workers rammed a heavy truck through East Berlin barriers Sept. 5, climbed a fence and swam a canal to the West under heavy machinegun fire.

Lt. Col. Martin Loeffler, 36, commander of East Germany's First Motorized Infantry Regiment, fled to the U.S. sector of West Berlin Sept. 8. Loeffler, whose defection was disclosed Sept. 15, was the highest-ranking East German army officer to flee.

It was disclosed Sept. 18 that 29 East Germans—men, women and children—had escaped to West Berlin through a tunnel Sept. 14. The group was the largest to have escaped from East Berlin at one time since the wall was built. They used a 400-foot tunnel that had been dug under the wall from the French sector by young West Berlin volunteers. Heinrich Albert, head of West Berlin's Internal Affairs Department, confirmed Sept. 18 that the city government had known of the tunnel project "for a long time" and did not "consider it an illegal act to dig an underground route underneath" the wall. West Berlin authorities said Sept. 19 that 30 other escapees had come through the tunnel in small groups before the mass escape. They confirmed that the tunnel had been discovered and sealed.

East German police uncovered and destroyed an escape tunnel Oct. 3 near the wall's junction with the U.S. sector.

An East Berlin girl was smuggled to the West Sept. 28 strapped under her fiance's car.

An East German miner escaped Oct. 2 by leaping 90 feet from a railway bridge into border canal and then swimming to the West.

East German border guards refused to permit a British military ambulance to enter East Berlin Oct. 6 to aid a West Berliner shot as he helped East Berlin escapees into a tunnel to the Western side of the Berlin wall. This was the first known incident in which East German personnel had prevented an Allied military vehicle from entering East Berlin. According to West Berlin police, the 21-year-old victim was a member of a group that had dug a new branch in an existing escape tunnel and had emerged in a basement shop on East Berlin's Heidelbergerstrasse. The shopkeepers, an aged couple, already had been helped into the tunnel when police burst into the room and shot the West Berliner. The other persons in the tunnel escaped back to West Berlin.

East and West Berlin border police exchanged gunfire along the border Oct. 8 after the Communist guards shot and apparently killed 2 refugees attempting to swim the Spree River to the West. The body of one victim was recovered by East Berlin police the next day while a crowd of West Berlin watchers shouted "murderers!"

All-German Affairs Min. Ernst Lemmer reported in Bonn Oct. 5 that more than 13,000 East Germans, 1,000 of them deserting border guards and soldiers, had escaped to the West since Aug. 13, 1961. He said that 12,316 persons had escaped up to Aug. 11 and nearly 1,000 others since then. The totals included refugees who had crossed the East-West border in areas other than Berlin. (West Berlin police reported Oct. 6 that a man fished alive from a West Berlin canal Oct. 2 was a West Berliner, not an escapee.)

West Berlin Sen. Heinrich Albertz reported Nov. 15 that 41 East German escapees were known to have been killed attempting to cross the Berlin border since Aug. 13, 1961. It was believed that other deaths had occurred on the Communist side of the wall and were not known to the West.

At least 23 East Germans were known to have escaped to West Berlin in the period Nov. 24-27.

8 members of 2 refugee families crashed through gunfire and autobahn barriers in an armored bus Dec. 26 to reach asylum at the U.S. side of the Babelsberg checkpoint near West Berlin.

21,356 East Germans registered during 1962 at the 2 refugee camps maintained in West Germany and at the 3d in West Berlin. Some of the refugees had escaped in 1961 but had not registered until later.

1963

The revival of dissent and the trend toward diversity continued at an accelerated pace in 1963. The appearance of new forms of dissent was indicative of the decline of the police control under Khrushchev. In January, a group of Soviet religious dissenters managed to reach the American embassy in Moscow and ask for asylum. In December, African students protesting racial discrimination touched off the first antigovernment demonstration to take place in the streets of Moscow in decades. Finally, the government's reports on the indictment and military trial of a high officer of the Soviet intelligence, Oleg Penkovsky, accused of supplying extensive classified information to the West, publicized the greatest espionage scandal in Soviet history.

The Soviet regime showed growing uneasiness about the erosion of discipline. In a reversal of his relatively tolerant attitude toward non-conformist writers, Premier Nikita Krushchev opened a campaign against "liberalism" in arts and letters. Meanwhile, official harassment of the Soviet Jews was gaining publicity abroad.

The decline in prestige of the Khrushchev government encouraged the trend toward diversity in the Soviet bloc. The Chinese, seconded by the Albanians, criticized the "de-Stalinization" policy and the Soviet diplomatic failures as the main causes of the diminishing cohesion of the Communist world. In Albania, Chinese influence had replaced entirely that of the Soviet Union. In Czechoslovakia, the regime of ex-Stalinist Pres. Antonin Novotny was accommodating itself to demands for greater intellectual freedom supported by influential voices within the Communist Party itself. Unlike the situation in Czechoslovakia, the new trend in Rumania aimed more at external independence from Soviet control than internal liberalization. The Soviet Union tried to maintain *unity in diversity by taking new steps to improve relations with Yugoslavia, the admired model for the east European dissidents.*

UNREST IN THE SOVIET UNION

Religious Sectarians Flee to U.S. Embassy

32 Siberian Evangelical Christians, charging religious persecution by the USSR, forced their way into the U.S. embassy in Moscow Jan. 3 and asked to be sent out of the Soviet Union. The minority-sect group had arrived by train that day from Chernogorsk, a coal mining town in the Krasnoyarsk Territory, more than 1,800 miles from Moscow. U.S. embassy officials, contending that they had no jurisdiction in the case, turned the group (6 men, 12 women and 14 children) over to the Soviet Foreign Ministry. The sect members were put aboard a train later Jan. 3 to be returned to Chernogorsk.

Before leaving the U.S. embassy building, the evangelicals left petitions charging that the Soviet government had forbidden their group to conduct religious services. The petitions were forwarded to Washington. Embassy officials said the group had expressed a desire to go to Israel or to some other country.

Soviet Foreign Ministry officials denied that the sect had been persecuted. An article distributed among foreign correspondents Jan. 9 by the USSR's Novosti press agency condemned the evangelicals and described them as members of a "Siberian fundamentalist splinter group first formed 10 years ago." (The Evangelical Christians had merged with the Baptist Church in Russia in World War II, but some sect members had refused to join the Baptists.) The article said: The group had gone to the U.S. embassy "to express their desire to settle down on Mt. Zion in Israel where 'Jesus Christ should appear'"; the sect members, conducting "savage rites" and "shady deals," had kept their children "away from ... games and school, forbade them to read books and dragged them along to their tiring meetings"; "the children were brutally beaten for disobedience," and 30 were crippled; sect members, including their leader, Grigory Vashchenko, had been jailed for committing these excesses; "the most malicious of the sect had been deprived of their parental rights, and their children are now being cared for at a boarding school."

Khrushchev Attacks Liberals in Arts

Premier Nikita Khrushchev warned Mar. 8 that his de-Stalinization policies did not mean "the time had come to let things drift, that the reins of government had been relaxed ... and that everyone is free to do and behave as he pleases." Khrushchev uttered this injunction during the 2d day of a closed 2-day meeting of high government and party officials and cultural leaders. His speech was made public Mar. 10. Warning that the Soviet press, literature, fine arts, music, theater and cinema would be expected to conform to the strict party line, Khrushchev said: "There shall never be absolute freedom for the individual, not even under communism"; "under communism, too, the will of one man must be subordinated to the will of the collective."

Khrushchev singled out Ilya Ehrenburg and poet Yevgeny Yevtushenko, 29, in charging that some Soviet writers were ignoring the positive aspects of Stalin's regime while dwelling too much on the late dictator's "instances of lawlessness, arbitrariness and abuse of power."

Khrushchev said that Ehrenburg may be "slipping into an anti-Communist position" by advocating "peaceful coexistence" in the arts with the West. (Ehrenburg was said to have been among a number of intellectuals who had signed and sent to the Central Committee a letter making such a suggestion. A party official said that the letter, disclosed Dec. 17, 1962 by Leonid F. Ilyichev, the party's ideological spokesman, had been retracted by the intellectuals "after careful consideration.") Khrushchev also said that Ehrenburg's defense of modernist tendencies in art was a "gross ideological error."

In his criticism of Yevtushenko, Khrushchev said the poet "didn't show political maturity and demonstrated ignorance of historic facts" in his poem *Babi Yar*. The poem dealt with the World War II slaying of Jews by German soldiers in the Babi Yar ravine in Kiev and with Russian anti-Semitism.

Khrushchev said Yevtushenko should have stressed in his poem that Ukrainians and people of other nationalities, as well as Jews, had been massacred in Babi Yar. Khrushchev said the poem should also have brought out that Russian workers were opposed to tsarist persecutions of Jews.

Ilyichev, at the Mar. 7 meeting, criticized Ehrenburg's "theory of silence" as the code of conduct during the days of Stalin's purges. In his memoirs currently serialized in the literary journal *Novy Mir,* Ehrenburg had written that many Russians knew Stalin's purge victims were innocent but kept quiet. The Soviet official view was that the widespread extent of the purges did not become known until after Stalin's death.

Yevtushenko was severely criticized at the national Union of Writers conference in Moscow Mar. 26-28 for allowing the Paris weekly *L'Express* to publish selections from his *Precocious Autobiography.* He admitted that publishing abroad without clearance from Soviet censors was a "major mistake." He said *L'Express* had distorted the work through cutting and "sensational headlines." (His defense was carried only by Tass' English-language service.) The Soviet press Apr. 2 printed demands that writers not be allowed to travel abroad until they "mature politically." Demands that Yevtushenko be expelled from the Writers' Union were printed in the Soviet press Apr. 12. Yevtushenko canceled a visit to Italy and a lecture tour of American universities, allegedly because of illness.

The literary monthly *Novy Mir,* under attack by government newspapers, continued to publish Ehrenburg's controversial memoirs. The March issue included both Ehrenburg's description of the USSR at the end of World War II and Khrushchev's Mar. 8 criticism of Ehrenburg.

Soviet concert pianist Vladimir Ashkenazy, 25, was granted permission to stay indefinitely in Great Britain, the Home Office announced Apr. 16. A Home Office spokesman said that it was not a case of political asylum but that Soviet authorities had extended the pianist's travel permit and that he planned future visits to the USSR. (It was reported that Mrs. Ashkenazy, an Icelandic-born British citizen, preferred to live in England.)

Revisions of the propaganda apparatus of the Communist Party's Central Committee were reported by Theodore Shabad in the *N.Y. Times* Apr. 6. He said that although changes in the Central Committee were not generally publicized, press releases indicated these changes: a division of the Russian Republic office into urban-rural sectors; the consolidation of the propaganda and agitation departments; the establishment of an Ideological Commission.

The merging of existing artistic groups was urged at the opening of the Soviet Artists Congress in Moscow Apr. 10 by keynote speaker Yekaterina F. Belashova, a sculptor, and Leonid F. Ilyichev, chief ideological spokesman of the Central Committee. Through its journal *Partiinaya Zhizn,* the Central Committee had called for the consolidation of book publishers.

In a speech published in the Soviet press Apr. 26 Khrushchev expressed confidence that hitherto nonconforming writers and artists would "look at life from a new angle" and reaffirm Communist goals as a result of "healthy criticism." He asked writers themselves to join in such criticism. Khrushchev's remarks, delivered at an industrial conference in Moscow Apr. 24, followed continued attacks by party and press on artists considered too liberal. Reorganization plans of cultural units were seen as moves toward tighter ideological control.

The Penkovsky Case

Col. Oleg V. Penkovsky, 43, an ex-Soviet government official, and Greville M. Wynne, 42, of England, went on trial before the Military Collegium of the Soviet Supreme Court in Moscow May 7 on charges of spying for Britain and the U.S. Both were convicted and sentenced May 11. Penkovsky was sentenced to death, Wynne to 3 years in prison and to 5 years in "labor colonies under a strict regime." Penkovsky was reported May 16 to have been executed by a firing squad.

Penkovsky, former deputy head of the Foreign Department of the State Committee for Scientific Research & Coordination, had been arrested Oct. 22, 1962. Wynne, who had travelled frequently in eastern Europe as managing director of Mobile Exhibitions, Ltd., had been arrested in Budapest Nov. 2, 1962.

Penkovsky pleaded guilty to all charges, including high treason, as the trial opened. Wynne also pleaded guilty but "with certain reservations."

Penkovsky testified that during a 17-month period he had transmitted to British and U.S. diplomats in Moscow and to agents in London and Paris information of Soviet rockets and troops in East Germany and of the USSR's preparations for a German peace treaty. He admitted having transmitted secret political and economic data. Penkovsky said: he had transmitted the information in at least 5,000 miniature film clips; he had first contacted British intelligence officers in London in Apr. 1961 through Wynne, whom he had met earlier in Moscow; British embassy aide Roderick Chisholm and his wife, Janet, were the chief recipients of the secret Soviet information passed on directly from him or through Wynne. (The Chisholms had left Moscow in Aug. 1962. 8 British subjects connected with the British embassy in Moscow and 5 U.S. embassy aides were cited during the trial as implicated in the spying.)

In testimony May 8, Wynne confessed that he had acted as a courier between Penkovsky and British intelligence officials for the transmission of letters and packages containing secret data. Wynne said: at first he had not known the contents of the materials he was passing on; when he discovered the nature of the information, British intelligence officers threatened to interfere with his commercial business unless he continued to act as liaison; in Apr. 1961 he received instructions concerning Penkovsky from "a very powerful figure" who he (Wynne) thought was a senior official in the British Foreign Office. (The court identified this official as "the chief of British intelligence.") Wynne said he was informed that Penkovsky was coming to London later that month for what he thought would be meetings of a diplomatic and not espionage nature. Wynne said he later realized that he had been duped and that he had been in contact with British intelligence and not Foreign Office officials.

Penkovsky denied Wynne's assertions and said the Briton had been aware of the contents of the letters and packages he was transmitting to the British.

Izvestia reported May 29 that Chief Marshal of Artillery Sergei S. Varentsov, 62, had been deprived of his title and position as head of tactical and operational rocket forces because he had helped Penkovsky get his post as deputy head of the foreign department of the State Committee for the Coordination of Scientific Research.

The chief prosecutor at Penkovsky's espionage trial, Lt. Gen. Artem G. Gorny, disclosed in the *Izvestia* interview that these 3 men also had been disciplined for having given Penkovsky classified information: Maj. Gen. A. Pozovny; Col. V. Buzinov; V. Petrochenko, a member of Penkovsky's committee. Commenting on Penkovsky's espionage activities, Gorny said: data Penkovsky had given to U.S. and British agents "could not deal any serious damage to the defense potential of the Soviet Union"; the information included "some technical reports by Soviet specialists ... and some scrappy information of a military nature that he succeeded in prying from his friends ... or from classified publications"; "Penkovsky managed to hand over to foreign intelligence ... fragmentary information of old models of rockets that he received when still serving in the army." (Penkovsky had served in the army as a colonel at least until 1956, when he was assistant military attache in Ankara, Turkey.)

A *Pravda* editorial May 26 had warned Russians about accepting invitations to foreign diplomatic receptions in Moscow. It was at such receptions that Penkovsky allegedly passed information to British and U.S. diplomats. The editorial said: "The Soviet people are posing the question—Should we not change our attitude toward certain diplomatic receptions since they have become a meeting place for spies, a place for shady deals bringing harm to peoples?"

Persecution of Jews Charged

World Jewish Congress Pres. Nahum Goldmann charged Sept. 12 that Soviet authorities were applying "exceptional ferocity" against Jews convicted of economic crimes. Goldmann said that according to Soviet press figures, 140 persons had been convicted between July 1, 1961 and July 1, 1963.

Sovetskaya Rossiya had reported July 6 that 5 persons had been executed by firing squad as leaders of a 15-member ring that had profited from the illegal manufacture and sale of razors, fountain pens, buttons and rulers. The 5 had been convicted in Leningrad Feb. 21. The 10 other defendants received prison terms.

A Moscow court July 17 convicted 4 Jews on charges of selling illegally baked *matzoh* (unleavened bread used during Passover) for personal gain. 3 of the defendants were sentenced to 6 months in prison; a 4th was released because of old age and poor health. The first 3 had been imprisoned since their arrest in March. The 4 defendants had been seized shortly after Moscow chief rabbi, Yehuda-Leib Levin, had announced that no *matzoh* would be available from the city's government-operated bakeries.

The Rabbinical Council of America (representing 850 Orthodox Rabbis) was revealed Sept. 22 to have sent Soviet Amb.-to-U.S. Anatoly F. Dobrynin a letter protesting the death sentence imposed on a Soviet Rabbi in August after his conviction on a charge of speculation in foreign gold currency. The letter, dated Sept. 6, was written by Rabbi Abraham N. AvRutick, council president. It charged that the sentence "leaves us with the feeling that a campaign is being waged against religious Jewry in Russia." Asserting that the council, for lack of information, would not comment on the nature of the charge against the convicted rabbi, AvRutick said, "We do feel that the penalty far exceeds the alleged crime."

The Russian Republic newspaper *Sovetskaya Rossiya* Aug. 30 had identified the rabbi as B. Gavrilov and had said that he and 2 other persons had been sentenced to death after a 4-week trial in Pyatigorsk. At least 6 others received jail sentences.

African Students Riot

About 500 African students clashed with Moscow police Dec. 18 in a mass demonstration in Red Square. The students were intercepted by police as they marched on the Kremlin to deliver to Soviet authorities a petition protesting the recent death of a Ghanaian student and alleged racial discrimination against African students in the Soviet Union.

The demonstrators, joined by African students from Leningrad and other Soviet cities, had started their march from the Ghanaian embassy. They dispersed after an official emerged from the Kremlin and announced that Higher Education Min. Vyacheslav P. Yelyutin would meet a student delegation to discuss their grievances. Yelyutin then met with 100 students, who demanded an investigation of the Ghanaian student's death. The students, who had complained of attacks by Soviet policemen, told Yelyutin that their "physical safety was threatened."

The dead Ghanaian student was Edmond Assare-Addo, 29, whose body had been found Dec. 13 at Khovrino, 10 miles northwest of Moscow. The African students charged that Assare-Addo, who was returning from Moscow to his studies at the Medical Institute of Kalinin, had been beaten to death, possibly to prevent his scheduled marriage to a Russian girl Dec. 14. A Soviet autopsy made public Dec. 20 by Tass said Assare-Addo's death had been caused "by exposure to cold [12 degrees below zero] in a state of alcoholic intoxication." A Ghanaian student who had attended the autopsy said Dec. 18 that the body bore bruises and a wound.

Asserting that foreign students were expected "to respect and observe Soviet laws," Tass said Dec. 20 that "anyone who does not like our laws and rules ... is free to leave our country at any time."

The Ghanaian embassy in Moscow said Dec. 21 that the African students who had organized the Dec. 18 demonstration would have to leave the USSR.

GROWING DISSENSION WITHIN SOVIET BLOC

Liberalization in Czechoslovakia

The rehabilitation of the late ex-Czechoslovak Foreign Min. Vladimir Clementis and 5 other imprisoned "Slovak nationalists" was announced by Slovak Communist Party leader Alexander Dubcek at a party meeting in Bratislava June 25.

Clementis had been executed in 1952 with the deposed Czechoslovak Communist Party Gen. Secy. Rudolf Slansky following their conviction on charges of espionage, economic sabotage, Titoism and Zionist conspiracy. The other 5 had been convicted and sentenced Apr. 24, 1954 on charges of participating in a "subversive group of bourgeois nationalists." Dubcek said they and Clementis had been convicted illegally although they had been guilty of "bourgeois nationalism."

The 5 rehabilitated "nationalists" (former sentences in parentheses): Ex-Slovak Education Min. Ladislav Novomesky (10 years); Gustav Husak, ex-chairman of the Slovak National Council (life), accused of heading the "subversive group"; Ladislav Holdos (13 years); Ivan Horvath (22 years); Daniel Okali (18 years). Holdos and Horvath had been jailed in 1951.

The CTK news agency reported Aug. 22 that Slansky had been officially absolved of any treasonable crime. Also officially absolved were 8 other Communist Party officials: Clementis, Bedrich Geminder, Ludvik Freika, Otto Sling, Andre Simone, Evzen Loebl, Joseph Frank and Rudolf Margolis. All except Loebl had been hanged with Slansky Dec. 3, 1952.

Col. Antonin Prchal and Col. Karel Kostal, deputy interior ministers until 1956, were reported by CTK Aug. 22 to have been sentenced to prison terms of 6 years and 7 years, respectively, on charges of "fabricating untrue accusations" and of other violations of "legality" in political trials during 1949-54.

CTK had reported July 20 that Czechoslovakia had released 3 imprisoned Roman Catholic bishops: the Most Rev. Josef Hlouch, 61, bishop of Budejovice (Budweis); the Most Rev. Stepan Trochta, 58, bishop of Litomerice; the Most Rev. Karel Otcenasek, 43, administrator of Hradec Kralove and titular archbishop of Chersoneso di Creta. Trochta and Otcenasek had been freed in 1960, Hlouch recently.

Pres. Antonin Novotny dismissed Viliam Siroky as premier Sept. 21. Novotny also ousted 2 deputy premiers and 4 ministers and appointed 11 new government officials. Siroky and the other 6 ousted men were regarded as Stalinists. Slovak National Council Chairman Jozef Lenart was appointed premier.

The official news agency CTK said Siroky had been dismissed for "shortcomings in his work" and for "mistakes in his past political activity." The latter charge apparently referred to Siroky's role in the 1952 treason trial of "Slovak bourgeois nationalists."

The Vatican newspaper *L'Osservatore Romano* reported Oct. 3 that the Czechoslovak government had released from detention the Most Rev. Josef Beran, 74, Roman Catholic archbishop of Prague and primate of Czechoslovakia. Beran had been placed under detention in 1954. The Vatican announcement said an edict from Prague dated Oct. 2 also had "removed restrictive measures on the personal liberty" of 4 prelates: the Most Rev. Karel Skoupy, 76, bishop of Brno; the Most Rev. Jan Vojtassak, 85, bishop of Spis; the Most Rev. Stanislav Zela, 70, ex-vicar general of Olomouc; the Most Rev. Ladislav Hlad, titular bishop of Cedie.

Khrushchev Visits Yugoslavia

Soviet Premier Khrushchev visited Yugoslavia Aug. 20-Sept. 3 for a working vacation that included intensive political discussions with Pres. Tito. The talks, which were linked to the growing rift between the USSR and Red China, resulted in pledges of closer Soviet-Yugoslav cooperation and of limited Yugoslav participation in the Council for Mutual Economic Assistance (Comecon), the Soviet bloc's economic association. It was Khrushchev's 3d visit to Yugoslavia (previous trips: 1955, 1956).

Khrushchev was accompanied by his wife, Nina, and by a delegation including Yuri V. Andropov, a Communist Party Central Committee secretary responsible for inter-party relations. They arrived in Belgrade by plane Aug. 20. He was welcomed by Tito and by ranking diplomatic representatives of nearly all Belgrade embassies except those of Communist China and Albania. (Red China sent a 2d secretary; Albania sent no one.)

Khrushchev, in his arrival speech, emphasized his hopes for stronger ties with "fraternal" and "Socialist" Yugoslavia; Tito in his reply hailed the USSR's struggle against "reactionary forces" that sought to plunge the world into an "enormous catastrophe."

Visiting the Rakovica automobile and tractor works near Belgrade Aug. 21, Khrushchev lauded Yugoslavia's system of factory management by workers' councils, an institution formerly attacked in the Soviet bloc as "revisionist." He said: "I like the form of the workers' councils. This is a progressive institution," and the USSR would study it. "Our country is now ripe for a democratization of the management of enterprises. We are looking for forms that would not violate the Leninist principle of the unity of leadership. And this is why we are interested in the Yugoslav experience."

Khrushchev and Tito flew Aug. 23 to Montenegro, where Khrushchev boarded Tito's yacht for a ride along the Dalmatian coast. Stopping in Split, Croatia Aug. 24 to visit Yugoslavia's largest shipyard, Khrushchev proposed that Yugoslavia integrate its shipbuilding industry with that of the Soviet bloc. Participation in "the Socialist division of labor" would bring Yugoslav industry greater efficiency, he said.

Khrushchev arrived Aug. 25 at Tito's Brioni Island summer retreat to begin the major political talks of his trip. Daily communiques issued during the talks, which continued until Aug. 27, confirmed that the major subjects discussed were the Soviet-Chinese break and the terms for closer Yugoslav cooperation with the Soviet bloc. A final communique issued Aug. 27 said that the 2 leaders had reached "full agreement" on all matters discussed, but it did not spell out the agreement. Khrushchev, meeting with Western newsmen Aug. 28 on Brioni, made it clear that Yugoslavia would cooperate with the Soviet bloc but was not expected to formally rejoin its institutions.

The 2 leaders left Brioni to tour Slovenia Aug. 30. They traveled Sept. 1 to Zagreb, the Croatian capital, where Khrushchev was conducted through a plastics and chemical plant built with a $23 million U.S. development loan. In a speech in Zagreb later Sept. 1, Khrushchev rebuffed charges that the USSR had sought only its own advantage in its economic dealings with other Soviet bloc states. He asserted that on balance the USSR had lost money on its intrablock trade.

Khrushchev returned to Belgrade and flew back to Moscow Sept. 3. Yugoslav government spokesmen announced after his departure that he and Tito had agreed "in principle" on Yugoslavia becoming an associate member of Comecon. The announcement said that Yugoslavia would get observer status rather than formal membership. (Yugoslavia had sought a limited association with Comecon, but the USSR formerly had refused to grant it less than full membership.)

Rumania's Self-Assertion

Soviet bloc news reports indicated that Rumania had balked at Comecon plans—pressed by the USSR—for more centralized economic planning and industrial specialization for the Soviet Union and the nations of Eastern Europe. The Comecon program had been hailed by Khrushchev and other Soviet leaders as a step toward a "Socialist division of labor" in the Communist world.

Rumania's opposition to these plans had been made known Mar. 9, when, in an announcement of the Central Committee of the Rumanian Workers (Communist) Party, it was disclosed that Vice Pres. Alexander Birladeanu would go to Moscow to affirm his government's intention to proceed with heavy industrialization. Under the Comecon plan, Rumania had been asked to concentrate on the development of its raw materials resources to feed the industries of the more-developed East European countries. Rumania, currently enjoying an industrial boom, instead had announced plans to speed the development of its iron, steel, petroleum and chemical industries.

An attempt to persuade Rumanian leaders to moderate their position was made by Nikolai V. Podgorny, member of the Soviet Communist Party Presidium, in 2 weeks of Bucharest talks concluded June 5. Accounts of Bucharest addresses made by Podgorny and Communist Party First Secy. Gheorghe Gheorghiu-Dej (published by Moscow's *Pravda* June 5) showed, however, that the Rumanian leaders had insisted that economic and political relations among the Soviet bloc states be based on "strict observance of sovereignty and independence."

Evidence of Rumania's intention to demonstrate its independence was seen in the publication June 22 by the Rumanian Communist Party newspaper *Scinteia* of a 60,000-word letter in which the Chinese Communist Party Central Committee attacked Khrushchev's ideology and policy. The letter's 25-point agenda proposal for projected talks in Moscow touched on all the major Sino-Soviet differences. (No other Soviet bloc newspaper had published the Chinese letter at that time.) Gheorghiu-Dej was absent from a Communist-bloc "summit" meeting in East Berlin June 30 despite Bucharest reports that Khrushchev had flown to Rumania June 24 to confer with him secretly on the Rumanian-Soviet differences.

Tito and Gheorghiu-Dej in Belgrade Nov. 30 signed an agreement providing for the joint construction of a $400 million hydroelectric plant on the Danube River. The project also called for raising the water level in the area to ease navigational problems. Tito and Gheorghiu-Dej said in a communique that their 8 days of joint talks in Belgrade showed "identity or similarity of views on basic international questions."

Albanian-Soviet Antagonism

At the 18th UN General Assembly session in New York Sept. 27, Albanian Foreign Min. Behar Shtylla charged that the Moscow treaty to limit nuclear tests was a "hoax" designed to perpetuate the U.S.-British-Soviet monopoly on nuclear weapons and to deny Communist China equivalent modern weapons of defense. "The Moscow treaty doesn't serve the cause of peace, but it threatens it," he declared.

China Criticizes Disintegration

Communist China charged Sept. 6 that the USSR's leaders had "pushed Sino-Soviet relations to the brink of a split and have carried the differences in the international Communist movement to a new stage of unprecedented gravity."

The Chinese statement, published in the Chinese Communist Party newspaper *Jenmin Jih Pao (People's Daily)* and in the theoretical journal *Hung Chi (Red Flag)*, contended that the denunciation of Stalin had opened the rift within the Soviet bloc. The statement said:

"The whole series of differences of principle in the international Communist movement began more than 7 years ago. To be specific, it began with the 20th Congress of the Communist Party of the Soviet Union [CPSU] in 1956. The 20th Congress ... was the first step along the road of revisionism taken by the leadership of the CPSU....

"The criticism of Stalin at the 20th Congress ... was wrong both in principle and in method. Stalin's life was that of a great Marxist-Leninist, a great proletarian revolutionary. For 30 years after Lenin's death, Stalin was the foremost leader of the CPSU and the Soviet government, as well as the recognized leader of the international Communist movement and the standard bearer of the world revolution. During his lifetime, Stalin made some serious mistakes, but compared to his great and meritorious deeds his mistakes are only secondary....

"It was necessary to criticize Stalin's mistakes. But in his secret report to the 20th Congress, Comrade Khrushchev completely negated Stalin, and in doing so defamed the dictatorship of the proletariat, defamed the Socialist system, the great CPSU, the great Soviet Union and the international Communist movement....

"The errors of the 20th Congress brought great ideological confusion in the international Communist movement and caused it to be deluged with revisionist ideas.... Most striking among the events which took place during this period were the incident in Soviet-Polish relations and the counterrevolutionary rebellion in Hungary.... The leadership of the CPSU made grave errors in both [events]. By moving up troops in an attempt to subdue the Polish comrades by armed force it committed the error of great-power chauvinism. And at the critical moment when the Hungarian counterrevolutionaries had occupied Budapest, for a time it intended to adopt a policy of capitulation and abandon Socialist Hungary to counterrevolution.... In the face of this situation, the Chinese Communist Party and other fraternal parties ... insisted on the taking of all necessary measures to smash the counterrevolutionary rebellion in Hungary and firmly opposed the abandonment of Socialist Hungary...."

Riots in Poland

The Polish government's seizure of a Roman Catholic school for church organists in Przemysl Oct. 2 reportedly led to 2 days of street riots. Other church education properties were said to have been seized in Warsaw, Nova Miasto, Rokitno and Cracow.

Roman Catholic Church sources reported Nov. 2 that the Polish authorities had ordered seminary students, hitherto exempt from military service, to report for army duty. The seminaries affected were in Warsaw, Poznan, Tarnow and Przemysl.

East German Refugees

A woman swam the Spree River to the U.S. sector Jan. 1; this escape provoked a gun duel in which West Berlin police wounded a Communist guard.

4 East-Berliners were reported Jan. 9 to have made their way under the wall through a sewer. 3 more persons escaped through a barbed wire barrier in a Berlin suburb Jan. 17, and 2 Communist border policemen defected to West Berlin Jan. 19. (Several bombings were reported, among them a blast that tore a small hole in the Berlin wall Jan. 10 and another said to have occurred in East Berlin's governmental area Jan. 21.)

2 East German policemen, both aged 19, escaped undetected into West Berlin Jan. 24 while on anti-refugee patrol duty by jumping from the roof of a 3-story border building.

A grandmother, 51, led her grandson and 5 other boys, aged 12-16, over the Berlin wall undetected Jan. 28. Horst Klein, 36, an East German circus tight-rope walker, Feb. 1 reported his escape the night of Dec. 27, 1962 by inching across the wall on a 50-foot high-tension power line, which he thought was "live" but was not. After a 100-yard trip in 12 degree cold, he fell into West Berlin, suffering 2 broken arms and other injuries. 2 men, aged 19 and 28, swam the icy Havel River to West Berlin.

2 East German policemen on guard duty walked with their tommyguns across the Oberbaum Bridge over the Spree River into Kreuzberg Feb. 2. (Shots and cries for help were heard Feb. 19 in the French sector's Leubars district as Communist police reportedly foiled an attempted mass escape.)

Among other defectors from East Germany to West Germany were: a 21-year-old policeman and his fiancee near Bad Neustadt Apr. 13; Wolfgang Engels, 19, a civilian mechanic for the East German Army, who crashed into the Berlin wall Apr. 17 and was shot by East German border guards, but escaped; 4 East Germans who escaped Apr. 28 by crashing an army truck into the wall and 4 more who scaled the wall into West Berlin; Heinz Meixner, 20, an Austrian working in West Berlin, who brought his fiancee and her mother from East Berlin May 5 by running a small car under a 5-foot barrier on the east side of Checkpoint Charlie.

12 young East Germans failed May 12 in an attempt to escape to West Berlin by crashing a steel-plated airlines bus through the wall at Sandkrug Bridge in the British sector.

1964

Diversity within the Soviet bloc continued to increase amid signs of growing unrest among intellectuals, particularly in Poland, Czechoslovakia and the Soviet Union. Moscow's preoccupation with China encouraged defiance among the east European nations. Albania demonstrated it most openly by seizing the Soviet embassy buildings in Tirana in February. Rumania remained neutral in the Moscow-Peking controversy, exploiting it to assert an independent national course. It advocated liquidation of the Warsaw military alliance and rapprochement between the Western and Eastern blocs. The trend toward diversity convinced the U.S. of the advisability of building "bridges" to those nations of eastern Europe that showed a greater degree of independence from Moscow and liberalized their domestic policies.

This loosening of discipline in the Soviet bloc precipitated the downfall in October of Soviet Premier Nikita Khrushchev and his replacement by a new regime led by Leonid I. Brezhnev and Aleksei N. Kosygin. The diverse response of the foreign Communists to this sudden change was indicative both of their surprise and of their uneasiness about the future course of Soviet policy. Their misgivings about Moscow's qualifications for leadership of the Communist world had already been nourished by the publication in September of a posthumous tract by the Italian party chief Palmiro Togliatti; the Togliatti document was sharply critical of Soviet centralism and intolerance. As a result, dissatisfaction with Moscow's domination in eastern Europe increased rather than diminished after the expulsion of Khrushchev.

DOMESTIC OPPOSITION

Czechoslovak & Polish Youths & Intellectuals

31 youths, including 5 girls, were arrested May 1 after an estimated 3,000 youths, some of them reportedly university students, clashed with police in Prague during a May Day demonstration. Those arrested were accused of being the ringleaders and of disturbing public order. The demonstrators allegedly protested "political indoctrination" at the universities and economic difficulties.

In a public warning to dissenting writers, Jiri Hendrych, a Czechoslovak Communist Party Presidium member and Central Committee secretary, criticized the nation's newspapers, magazines, and television stations May 7. He warned in a Prague speech of severe measures "against those who, regardless of the meaning of party decisions, apply different interests in their realization."

Melchior Wankowicz, 72, a Polish-American writer and lecturer, went on trial Oct. 26 and was convicted in Warsaw Nov. 9 of distributing "false and slanderous" material against the Polish government in Poland and abroad. He was given the minimum jail sentence of 3 years, which was immediately halved under a 3-month-old general amnesty. Wankowicz, a Polish-born U.S. citizen, had been arrested Oct. 5 following a Warsaw Writer's Union meeting at which some intellectuals reportedly rebuked Polish Party leaders for censorship and harassment. Wankowicz was one of 34 intellectuals who had petitioned the government in March for a more liberal cultural policy.

Soviet Dissidents & Defectors

Mrs. Olga V. Ivinskaya, an assistant of the late Soviet writer Boris Pasternak, was reported Nov. 1 to have been released from prison after serving 4 years of an 8-year sentence for accepting 800,000 rubles ($200,000) in royalties from Italy for Pasternak's novel *Doctor Zhivago.*

Iosif Brodsky, 24, a nonconformist Leningrad poet, was reported Nov. 3 to have been released after serving 7 months of a 5-year compulsory labor term for being a "social parasite." Some Soviet intellectuals had charged that Brodsky, a Jew, had been convicted by a prejudiced court. The transcript of the trial had been smuggled out of the USSR and published in Western periodicals.

Yuri Asseyev, 35, an associate professor of philosophy at the University of Leningrad and a research student at Harvard University since Sept. 1963, was granted U.S. asylum by the State Department Jan. 4. Asseyev, at Harvard under the cultural exchange treaty, said he had fallen from a 3d-floor apartment window in Cambridge Jan. 2; he was in a Cambridge hospital. (Asseyev was reported to be the first Soviet defector under the U.S.-USSR cultural exchange program, which had started in 1958 and had brought some 150 Russians to the U.S.) It was reported in Cambridge, Mass. Apr. 11 that the State Department had decided to turn Asseyev over to the Soviet government. He was put in MacLean Hospital, a mental institution in Belmont, Mass., after he had been pulled from the edge of a subway platform in Cambridge Mar. 2.

The State Department announced in Washington Feb. 10 that Yuri I. Nossenko, a staff officer of the Soviet secret police, had defected and requested political asylum in the U.S. The announcement said that Nossenko, 36, normally assigned to the Moscow headquarters of the Soviet KGB (Committee of State Security), had been on temporary duty with the Soviet delegation to the Geneva disarmament conference when he defected. According to members of the Soviet disarmament delegation, Nossenko apparently had disappeared from his hotel Feb. 4. Semyon K. Tsarapkin, the USSR's chief disarmament negotiator, notified Geneva police of the disappearance Feb. 8 and asked their help in finding Nossenko. Soviet sources in Geneva conceded Feb. 10 that he probably had defected to the West.

Nossenko had arrived in Geneva Jan. 20 as the 7th ranking member of Tsarapkin's delegation. He was listed as a legal expert on disarmament. According to the State Department, he had been scheduled to return to Moscow Feb. 4, the date of his defection. It was believed that he had been spirited out of Switzerland by U.S. agents. Nossenko reportedly left a wife and 2 children in Moscow.

Tsarapkin charged Feb. 12 that Swiss authorities had shown lack of interest in finding Nossenko and that Switzerland had failed to provide sufficient security for delegates to conferences on its territory. He demanded that the Swiss government take steps to end the "provocative activity" of foreign agents in Switzerland. Swiss Foreign Min. Friedrich T. Wahlen rejected Tsarapkin's allegations later Feb. 12 at a news conference in which he noted that foreign delegations always had expressed appreciation for the absence of Swiss interference in their affairs.

Nossenko told a Soviet diplomat and a Swiss diplomat who were allowed to visit him in Washington Feb. 14 that his defection had been voluntary. Soviet Foreign Min. Andrei A. Gromyko had protested to U.S. Amb.-to-Russia Foy D. Kohler in Moscow earlier Feb. 14 that Western intelligence agents might have been involved in Nossenko's disappearance.

Escapes from East Germany

As East Germans continued their risky efforts to flee to the West, reports reaching West Berlin Jan. 2 said that a group of East Berlin workers had demanded in their plant newspaper that the Berlin wall be removed and free travel restored in all of the city.

3 East German girls escaped to West Berlin Jan. 7 through a 450-foot tunnel dug under the border wall. The tunnel, the first one completed successfully in 6 months, was discoverd by Communist border guards and destroyed Jan. 9.

A 17-year-old East German youth was saved by West Berlin police Jan. 19 after he had become entangled in barbed wire atop the Berlin wall and had been shot in the foot by border guards. The West Berlin police at the scene aimed their weapons at the East German guards and warned they would fire if another shot was aimed at the youth. The refugee was removed safely and taken to a West Berlin hospital.

2 East Berlin families consisting of 4 adults and 11 children ranging from one to 11 years of age successfully escaped to West Berlin Sept. 9 in a meat delivery truck driven by Erich Ross, 32, father of one of the families. Ross, a Communist party member, told newsmen that he had picked up the 14 other persons on the *autobahn* outside West Berlin and had driven them through the Communist checkpoint into the city. The truck, usually used to deliver meat to West Berlin under the

city's trade agreement with East Germany, had been given only a cursory inspection at the checkpoint.

A U.S. soldier helped a wounded East German cross the Berlin wall into the city's Western section Sept. 13 despite Communist gunfire, returned by West Berlin police. The refugee, identified as Michael Meyer, 21, a jockey, was removed to a West Berlin hospital with 5 bullet wounds. Meyer was shot by East German border guards when he approached the wall about 900 yards from the Friedrichstrasse crossing point, manned by a U.S. Army patrol. Sp. 4/c Hans Puhl, 22, of East Weymouth, Mass., summoned to the scene, pointed his rifle at 2 East German guards near Meyer. Puhl, a recent German immigrant to the U.S., shouted at the guards to retreat; when they refused to do so, he threw a tear gas grenade, and they backed away. Puhl then had himself lifted to the top of the wall, where, despite gunfire from nearby East German posts, he supervised the cutting of a barbed wire barrier and the lowering of a rope to the wounded escapee. Puhl dragged Meyer across the wall to the West after the East German fainted.

The West Berlin city government disclosed Oct. 5 that 23 men, 31 women and 3 children from East Germany had crawled through a narrow tunnel under the Berlin wall in groups of 2 and 3 to safety in West Berlin Oct. 2-5. This was the largest such escape since the wall was erected. About 30 West Berlin students who built the tunnel said they had been working on it since Apr. 29. It ran 500 feet from a cellar under a closed bakery shop at Strelitzerstrasse, East Berlin, to 97 Bernauerstrasse in the French sector of West Berlin.

East German border guards discovered the tunnel Oct. 5 just as the last group of refugees, aided by West Berliners, was crawling through it. An East German corporal was killed by gunfire as he and other border guards were checking the tunnel entrance. ADN, the official East German Communist news agency, charged that the corporal had been killed by "aimed shots" fired by "West Berlin agents." It said that "the murderers came through an agents' tunnel dug and built with the permission and active support of the West Berlin police." But spokesmen for West Berliners helping the escapees said they had been unarmed and that the slain guard might have been hit accidentally by a bullet fired by another East German guard.

4 East Berlin factory workers dug a hole in the wall under their work bench at the West Berlin border and after 3 weeks escaped through the hole to the French sector Oct. 21.

In 1964 a total of 3,155 East Germans escaped to West Germany (according to a West German Refugee Ministry report Jan. 7, 1965). This brought the total number of such escapes since the Berlin wall was erected in 1961 to about 21,000. Escapees included persons who climbed over or tunneled under the wall to West Berlin as well as those who escaped at other points along the East-West German border. 63 persons were reported to have been killed since 1961 in attempts to escape across the Berlin wall, and 58 escapees were killed at other border points.

Yugoslav 'Plotters' Sentenced

A 5-member Yugoslav tribunal in Rijeka, Croatia, sentenced 9 alleged terrorists Apr. 18 to prison terms ranging from 6 to 14 years. They were charged with trying to overthrow the government. Ilija Tolic, a leader of emigrant Yugoslavs, and Josip Oblak, Croatian Revolutionary Brotherhood leader, received 14-year terms.

DISUNITY IN EASTERN EUROPE

Rusk on Changes in Soviet Bloc

Speaking at a world affairs conference sponsored by the AFL-CIO, State Secy. Dean Rusk said in Washington Feb. 25 that U.S. policy toward communism had altered because "in recent years an important new trend has been perceptible: some of the Communist governments have become responsive, in varying degrees, ... to the aspirations of their subjects.... The Communist world is no longer a single flock of sheep following blindly behind one leader."

Rusk cited several proofs of his thesis:

(1) The USSR and Communist China were engaged in a "deep and comprehensive quarrel" over "how best to promote the Communist world revolution." The USSR had begun to

understand that there was "an irresolvable contradiction between the [Chinese] demands ... and the needs and interests of the Soviet state and people."

(2) "Yugoslavia is an independent state," sometimes siding with the U.S., sometimes with the USSR, sometimes following a totally neutral policy, largely because of U.S. aid after Pres. Tito's 1948 break with Stalin.

(3) "For some years we have treated Poland ... differently from other Soviet-bloc states. A good deal of the national autonomy and domestic liberalization which the Poles won in 1956 persists."

Albania Seizes Soviet Embassy

The Soviet government newspaper *Izvestia* reported Feb. 24 that Albanian authorities had seized the Soviet embassy in Tirana. The embassy had been occupied only by caretakers since 1961, when the 2 nations had recalled their ambassadors from each other's capitals. *Izvestia* said that the 3 caretakers had been harassed by Albanian authorities and finally had been asked Dec. 27, 1963 to leave Albania. The embassy compound, consisting of an office building and 2 residential buildings remained vacant except for embassy possessions. According to the newspaper, Albania seized the buildings Feb. 24. It said that the buildings had been built at Soviet expense on land donated by Albania.

A statement broadcast by the Tirana radio Feb. 28 said that Albania had seized the buildings because the USSR had refused to pay for them.

Rumania Seeks Independent Course

A Rumanian Communist Party delegation led by Premier Ion Gheorghe Maurer held political talks with Chinese leaders in Peking Mar. 3-11, reportedly on the ideological differences between China and the USSR. The Rumanians were believed to have gone to China in an effort to avert an open break between Moscow and Peking. Their mission was described officially as devoted to Chinese-Rumanian relations and to "the unity of the Socialist camp," a euphemism for measures to end the Russian-Chinese rift. The Rumanian Communist Party had backed the Soviet leadership on most major ideological matters, but it recently had pursued an independent line within Comecon, the Soviet-bloc economic organization, and had maintained a measure of amity in its relations with China.

Maurer and the Rumanian delegates conferred with a Chinese delegation headed by Pres. Liu Shao-chi. They also met with Party Chairman Mao Tse-tung and other Chinese officials concerned with party and trade matters. A final communique issued Mar. 11 by China's Hsinhua news agency said only that the talks had been carried out "in a friendly atmosphere"; no mention was made of any decisions taken at the meeting.

The pace of Rumania's international activities intensified at once:

● A report on the Rumanian-Chinese talks was given to Soviet Premier Khrushchev by Maurer at their meeting Mar. 15-16 in the Georgian Soviet Republican thermal resort of Gagry on the Black Sea. A communique issued Mar. 16 through the Soviet news agency Tass said the Khrushchev-Maurer conference dealt with the "struggle" for "a strengthening of the unity and cohesion among Socialist countries."

● The Rumanian official press agency Agerpress and Bucharest radio announced Apr. 22 that an "enlarged plenum" of the Rumanian Communist Party Central Committee had concluded a week-long meeting that day and had unanimously approved actions taken by the Rumanian Party Politburo in connection with the Sino-Soviet dispute.

● Rumania announced Apr. 26 that it had proposed to act as mediator in the dispute between Moscow and Peking. A government statement published in the Rumanian party newspaper *Scinteia* said that the USSR had agreed to "examine" a Bucharest plan submitted in March to have Moscow and Peking join Rumania in a 3-nation commission to prepare the groundwork for a world meeting of Communist party leaders. China, the newspaper said, had not replied.

● The U.S. and Rumania June 1 signed trade and political agreements at the conclusion of bilateral talks that had started in Washington May 18. A joint communique said Rumania would be permitted to buy "most commodities" in the U.S. without individual export licenses, and the Rumanians were granted U.S. licenses for "a number of particular industrial facilities in which the Rumanian delegation expressed special interest." The 2 nations also agreed to elevate their respective legations to the level of embassies. Representing the U.S. at the talks: State Undersecy. (for political affairs) W. Averell Harriman. Representing Rumania: Deputy Premier Gheorghe Marin, chairman of the State Planning Committee. (The U.S. Commerce Department July 14 formally lifted license restrictions to clear the way for shipment of diverse commodities to Rumania. Licenses were still required for shipment of about 1,300 other products, including advanced machinery.)

● Deputy Premier Alexandru Birladeanu disclosed June 14 that his government had released 7,674 political prisoners in the past 3½ years. 74 had been released in 1961, 2,300 in 1962, 2,900 in 1963 and 2,400 thus far in 1964. Birladeanu said a general pardon was being granted to "practically all" political prisoners in August. Conceding that there still were differences of opinion between Moscow and Bucharest, Birladeanu said "there is no shadow over the relations between our people and the peoples of the Soviet Union."

● A Rumanian delegation headed by Premier Maurer held ideological and economic talks with Soviet officials in Moscow July 6-14. A joint communique issued at the conclusion of the conference indicated that both sides had discussed Soviet-Rumanian relations, Communist China, and economic cooperation within Comecon.

● Deputy Premier Gheorghe Apostol said July 7 that Rumania had its differences with other Communist countries but was in complete agreement with them on major international issues. Apostol criticized Comecon for not including all Communists as members (a reference to the exclusion of Communist China) and he suggested that non-Communist states be permitted to join.

● The government radio July 8 announced that a new Rumanian-Chinese trade agreement had been signed in Bucharest that day at the conclusion of a 9-day conference of officials of the 2 countries. Under the agreement, both nations were to exchange scientific and technical information in the petroleum, chemical and food industries. Rumania was to receive from China minerals, steel, alloys, industrial chemicals, textiles and consumer goods.

● A Franco-Rumanian agreement on scientific and technical cooperation was signed in Paris July 31 at the conclusion of bilateral talks that had started July 27. The pact, signed by

Deputy Premier and Foreign Min. Cornelius Manescu and
French Foreign Min. Maurice Couve de Murville, provided for
an exchange of students and relevant publications. Premier
Maurer, who headed the Rumanian delegation, said after the
signing that "the agreement and the exchanges we have had
here in Paris ... have ... afforded opportunities to study ways
and means of developing even closer ties." During his Paris
stay, Maurer had conferred with Pres. Charles de Gaulle and
Premier Georges Pompidou.

An unidentified Rumanian government official said in an
interview published in the *N.Y. Times* Nov. 20 that his
government would continue to pursue a policy of independence
in the Soviet-Chinese ideological dispute. Although Rumania
was a member of the Warsaw pact, the official said, "our policy
is directed against military pacts." "We are for general and
complete disarmament," he declared, "and this implies
liquidation of pacts. Using prudent and moderate means, we
are trying to assist a *rapprochement* between the blocs."

Other points made by the Rumanian: Bucharest would
send a representative to a proposed world Communist
conference only if all parties attended; Rumania had "the best
relations" with all Communist countries of differing ideologies;
"at the same time we are improving relations with the countries
of the West."

Premier Maurer was reported Dec. 17 to have indorsed
China's detonation of its first nuclear device Oct. 16. Maurer's
support was expressed in a reply to Chinese Premier Chou En-
lai, who had notified world leaders Oct. 17 of the atomic test
and had proposed a ban on all nuclear weapons.

KHRUSHCHEV DEPOSED

Brezhnev Heads Party

Nikita S. Khrushchev, 70 was stripped of his positions of
leadership in the Soviet government and Communist Party Oct.
14-15. Khrushchev was deposed unexpectedly and without
outward disruption of Soviet public life. His removal was
announced to the Russian people and the outside world in a
communique dated Oct. 15 and issued shortly after midnight.

Leonid I. Brezhnev, 57, a member of the Communist Party Central Committee's Secretariat, replaced Khrushchev Oct. 14 as party first secretary, considered the most powerful post in the Soviet hierarchy. Aleksei N. Kosygin, 60, a first deputy premier in the Soviet government, succeeded Khrushchev Oct. 15 as chairman of the USSR Council of Ministers, equivalent to premier.

The announcement of Khrushchev's removal gave no political reasons for the change; it said only that he had asked to be relieved of his party and government responsibilities because of his "advanced age and deterioration of health." The brevity of the announcement and its failure to praise Khrushchev made it clear that he had been ousted in disgrace.

Full text of the Soviet announcement as distributed by the Soviet embassy in Washington Oct. 15:

"A plenary meeting of the Central Committee of the CPSU [Communist Party of the Soviet Union] was held on October 14, 1964.

"The plenary meeting of the CPSU Central Committee granted Nikita S. Khrushchev's request to be relieved of his duties as the First Secretary of the CPSU Central Committee, Member of the Presidium of the CPSU Central Committee, and Chairman of the Council of Ministers of the USSR in view of his advanced age and deterioration of his health.

"The plenum of the CPSU Central Committee elected Leonid I. Brezhnev First Secretary of the CPSU Central Committee.

*

"The Presidium of the USSR Supreme Soviet met on October 15 this year with Comrade Anastas I. Mikoyan, President of the Presidium of the USSR Supreme Soviet, in the chair.

"The Presidium of the USSR Supreme Soviet discussed the question of chairman of the USSR Council of Ministers.

"The Presidium of the USSR Supreme Soviet granted the request of Nikita Sergeyevich Khrushchev that he be relieved of the duties of Chairman of the USSR Council of Ministers in view of his advanced age and deterioration of health.

"The Presidium of the USSR Supreme Soviet appointed Comrade Alexei Nikolayevich Kosygin as Chairman of the USSR Council of Ministers, releasing him from his duties of First Vice Chairman of the USSR Council of Ministers.

"The decrees by the Presidium of the USSR Supreme Soviet on the relief of Comrade Nikita S. Khrushchev of his duties as Chairman of the USSR Council of Ministers and on the appointment of Comrade Alexei N. Kosygin as Chairman of the USSR Council of Ministers were adopted unanimously by the members of the Presidium of the USSR Supreme Soviet.

"The members of the Presidium of the USSR Supreme Soviet warmly congratulated Comrade Alexei N. Kosygin on his appointment to the post of Chairman of the USSR Council of Ministers.

"Comrade Alexei N. Kosygin heartily thanked the Central Committee of the Communist Party of the Soviet Union and the Presidium of the USSR Supreme Soviet for the confidence shown him and gave the assurance that he would do his utmost to discharge his duties."

The first public indication of the reasons for Khrushchev's removal was given in an editorial published Oct. 17 in the Soviet Communist Party newspaper *Pravda*. Without mentioning Khrushchev by name, it attacked him for "harebrained scheming" and "hasty decisions" and made it clear that the USSR would both continue to seek peace with the West and begin to work for the reconstruction of Soviet-bloc ideological and political unity.

Excerpts from the *Pravda* editorial:

"The monolithic unity of the party and its unflinching loyalty to Lenin's behests were demonstrated with new force by the plenary meeting of the Central Committee of the CPSU held on Oct. 14....

"The Leninist party is an enemy of subjectivism and drifting in Communist construction, harebrained scheming, immature conclusions and hasty decisions and actions divorced from reality. Bragging and phrasemongering, commandism, unwillingness to take into account the achievements of science and practical experience are alien to it....

"The life and activity of the party are determined by the principles and standards which were worked out by V. I. Lenin, tested, confirmed and enriched by the historical experience of many decades. Collective leadership is one of the most important of these principles, a well tried weapon, the greatest political asset of our party....

"It is only on the basis of the Leninist principle of collective leadership that it is possible to direct and develop the growing creative initiative of the party and all people. It is only on the basis of this principle that it is possible to analyze the situation correctly, to evaluate the successes achieved soberly, objectively, without conceit, to see the shortcomings and eliminate them in time and completely...."

Details on Ouster

Western sources in Moscow reported that Khrushchev's ouster appeared to have been meticulously prepared but that the final move against him apparently had not been undertaken until Oct. 12, while the then-premier vacationed at his villa outside Gagry, near Sochi, on the USSR's Black Sea coast.

Khrushchev had gone to Gagry Sept. 30 for what appeared to be a brief and routine respite from his official duties.* While

---

* According to the Oct. 26 edition of Newsweek magazine, Khrushchev's vacation in Gagry had been ordered by the party Presidium on the ground that he needed a rest. The report, unsubstantiated, implied that the anti-Khrushchev faction had lured Khrushchev away from Moscow in order to begin the process of deposing him.

there, he received visitors and continued to participate in Soviet public affairs. The day the coup against him was believed to have been launched—Oct. 12—Khrushchev was televised as he spoke by radio with 3 Soviet cosmonauts sent into orbit earlier that day. He was seen by millions as he congratulated the cosmonauts and promised to welcome them on their return to Moscow. Soviet Pres. Mikoyan was with him and was introduced to the cosmonauts by Khrushchev with the prophetic quip: "Here is Comrade Mikoyan. He is literally pulling the telephone from my hands...."

That same day, Oct. 12, all the members of the Presidium of the Communist Party Central Committee were in Moscow, with the exception of Khrushchev and Mikoyan. Brezhnev had returned Oct. 11 from a visit to East Germany. Other Presidium members had also converged on Moscow; Nikolai V. Podgorny came back from Moldavia. The Presidium reportedly began discussion that day of proposals that Khrushchev be replaced. According to the *N.Y. Times,* it had reached a firm decision to remove him by early Oct. 13. Mikoyan, who had left Gagry shortly after his televised conversation, reportedly returned to Moscow late Oct. 12 or early Oct. 13 and was given an ultimatum to cooperate. He agreed and became the group's spokesman in its ouster of Khrushchev.

The Presidium called a meeting of the Central Committee for Oct. 13 to ratify its decision. Khrushchev, still apparently uninformed of the moves against him, was scheduled to spend Oct. 13 in Gagry conferring with Gaston Palewski, visiting French state minister for atomic and space research. But their talks were cut short when Khrushchev received a message and excused himself, saying that he had to return to Moscow. Khrushchev immediately flew to Moscow, reportedly arriving in the capital the afternoon of Oct. 13. (According to some rumors, Khrushchev already was under guard and returned to Moscow in the company of 5 secret policemen.) He was said to have gone directly to the Kremlin, where he was met by the other members of the Presidium and informed of their action against him.

The key confrontation between Khrushchev and his opponents was reported to have taken place at the Central Committee meeting begun later Oct. 13. The session was said to have been opened with a 5-hour denunciation of Khrushchev by

Mikhail A. Suslov, considered the party's chief ideologist. Although Suslov was reported to have devoted himself to Khrushchev's alleged mishandling of foreign and Soviet-bloc affairs, particularly in the widening rift with Communist China, he was also said to have attacked Khrushchev personally, charging him with nepotism and the creation of a new type of "personality cult."

Khrushchev was reported to have defended himself against the charges. Speaking immediately after Suslov, he was said to have denounced his attackers abusively. Some reports described Khrushchev as insulting virtually the entire membership of the Central Committee. Khrushchev's address was said to have been followed by one in which Dmitri S. Polyansky attacked him for his failure to solve the USSR's economic and agricultural problems.

The Central Committee vote depriving Khrushchev of his post of first secretary and his membership on the Presidium was reported to have been taken early Oct. 14. Khrushchev was said to have accepted the outcome. His associates then, by unanimous vote, elected Brezhnev his successor as party first secretary.

The Presidium of the Supreme Soviet was convened the following day, Oct. 15, to complete the shift by removing Khrushchev from his governmental duties. With Pres. Mikoyan presiding, the Presidium ratified the ouster of Khrushchev as premier and the election of Kosygin to succeed him.

It was reported from Moscow Oct. 16-19 that Khrushchev apparently was under house arrest.

It was learned that some of Khrushchev's close personal aides, particularly those responsible for publicity and propaganda, were removed from office with him.

Aleksei I. Adzhubei, 40, Khrushchev's son-in-law, was dismissed Oct. 16 as editor of the Soviet government newspaper *Izvestia.* Vladimir I. Stepakov was named to replace him.

Mikhail A. Kharlamov was dismissed Oct. 17 as chairman of the USSR State Committee for Radio & Television. He was replaced by Nikolai N. Mesyatsev. 3 members of Khrushchev's personal staff were reported to have been dismissed Oct. 16: Oleg A. Troyanovsky, son of a former Soviet ambassador to the U.S., Khrushchev's English translator and informal expert on American affairs; Vladimir Lebedev, chief of Khrushchev's personal secretariat; Aleksandr Shuisky, his personal advisor on agricultural affairs.

Mixed Response to Khrushchev Ouster

The reaction of the east European Communist parties to Khrushchev's ouster ranged from outright approval to reserve and skepticism and to praise for Khrushchev.

The Bulgarian Communist Party Central Committee Oct. 18 officially approved the Soviet government changeover. It was the only East European Communist party to do so. Albania hailed Khrushchev's loss of power as "a heavy blow" to U.S. imperialists and to "the modern revisionists who are faithfully serving their purposes."

Yugoslav Pres. Tito Oct. 17 congratulated the new Soviet Communist Party leader, Leonid I. Brezhnev, and expressed the hope that "friendly ... relations ... between our parties and countries will continue and develop in the common interest." The Yugoslav League of Communists' newspaper *Borba* Oct. 17 reprinted *Pravda's* Oct. 16 editorial report on Khrushchev but deleted a critical reference to Khrushchev as a "harebrained" schemer and braggart.

Polish Communist Party leader Wladyslaw Gomulka and Hungarian Premier Janos Kadar, who was visiting Warsaw, proposed jointly Oct. 17 that a world Communist meeting be convened to restore Communist unity.

Gomulka lauded Khrushchev for his "immense achievements" in building Soviet power and in the "struggle for peace." Asserting that there were "many reasons" for the Soviet power shift, Gomulka said it had a "purely internal character."

Kadar said Oct. 18 that Khrushchev had "very great merits in the fight against Stalin's personality cult and in the maintenance of peace." The Hungarian people, who had welcomed Khrushchev on a recent visit to their country "as the tireless fighter for peace," "did well in so doing and need have no afterthoughts about it," Kadar declared. A statement published Oct. 25 by the Hungarian Central Committee expressed "understanding" of the need for Khrushchev's ouster but repeated Kadar's praise of Khrushchev as a leader of "significant merit in his fight for peace and his fight for international security."

A statement drawn up by the East German Politburo Oct. 17 and released Oct. 18 had said: "The news of the release of ... Khrushchev['s] functions has caused deep emotion within our party and our peoples." The statement urged Moscow's new leadership to press "for the honorable fulfillment" of the Soviet-East German friendship pact signed June 12. It was rumored in Berlin Oct. 24 that East German Pres. Walter Ulbricht had gone to Moscow for talks on the unrest reported to have been aroused in East German party circles by the Soviet shift. East German leaders were reported to have conferred in East Berlin Oct. 21 on how to deal with bitter reaction said to have been shown by members of local party units when officials attempted to justify Khrushchev's ouster.

A statement by the Czechoslovak Communist Party Oct. 18 expressed approval of Khrushchev's "struggle to accomplish the policy of peaceful coexistence" and his "disclosure of the erroneous methods in the period of the cult of personality."

The foreign parties were disquieted at the sudden shift and at the new Soviet leadership's repeated assertions of its intentions to restore Soviet-bloc unity. Khrushchev had been credited personally with ending the Stalin-era domination of foreign Communist groups by Moscow and with permitting limited but real divergence of views on policy.

Gomulka announced Oct. 28 that his meetings with Brezhnev and new Soviet Premier Aleksei N. Kosygin had "convinced" him that there were "justified grounds" for Khrushchev's ouster and that the Soviet leadership changes "took place according to Leninist principles of interparty unity." Gomulka's statement, backing the new Soviet leadership, was made in Warsaw at a Mongolian-Polish friendship rally in honor of visiting Mongolian Communist Party First Secy. Yumzhagin Tsedenbal. The discussions held by the Soviet and Polish party leaders had disclosed "full unanimity" of views between the 2 parties, Gomulka declared. He expressed "full satisfaction" with the Soviet assurances "that the general line of the Soviet party as defined by the 20th and 22d Soviet party congresses will be upheld, and that it fully agrees with our [the Polish] party, our government, our country." Gomulka urged the leaders of the Soviet and Chinese

Communist parties to "undertake the needed and necessary steps" to reestablish international Communist "unity."

Togliatti's 'Will'

The Italian Communist Party Sept. 4 published an extensive memo in which its late leader Palmiro Togliatti had criticized the USSR for its clumsy handling of world problems. He especially scored the growing Soviet split—with Communist China, the Kremlin's efforts to prevent the growth of freedom in Soviet-bloc and Western Communist parties and its continued toleration of Stalinist practices in Soviet life.

In the 4,500-word memo, which excited widespread interest in eastern Europe, Togliatti declared that every Communist party should be free "to act in an autonomous manner relevant to its national problems and without submission to central control. He criticized Khrushchev's earlier plans for a December Moscow conference of 26 Communist parties, called to prepare joint action against Communist China's ideological dissidence. He made clear, however, that the Italian Communist Party rejected the "unbridled and shameful campaign" conducted by Peking.

The memo, known popularly as "Togliatti's will," was regarded as the Italian Communist Party's declaration of independence from Soviet tutelage.

Togliatti apparently had prepared the memo as a basis for pending discussions with Soviet Communist leaders. He had completed it a few hours before he was felled by a stroke Aug. 13. Togliatti wrote the draft of the memo by hand, and it was typed for him in its final form at Yalta while he lay critically ill. Luigi Longo, who succeeded Togliatti, carried the memo home to Italy Aug. 22 on the plane that bore Togliatti's body.

In an introduction to the document, Longo wrote: "The text [of the memo] was to be typed while Comrade Togliatti went to Artek to visit the International Pioneers Camp. On his return he had intended to revise the typewritten manuscript.... But we believe ... that we can regard the text left to us as the precise expression of his thoughts on the problems it deals with. The direction [Political Committee] of our party took cognizance with deep emotion of the document.... It recognized that 'in it are repeated with great clarity the views of our party regarding the present situation of the international Communist movement' and adopted it as its own. We are therefore publishing the memorandum of Comrade Togliatti as a precise expression of the position of the party on the problems of the international workers and Communist movement and its unity."

Longo told Italian Communist Party members at Genzano near Rome Sept. 8 that the memo's criticism of the Soviet Communist Party did not signify any new split in the world Communist movement. "The ties that bind us to the Communist Party of the Soviet Union and to all brother parties," Longo declared, "spring from our very nature as a workers' revolutionary party that fights for socialism, spring from the unconditional support we give to the orientations expressed in the 20th Party Congress and to their implementation on the part of the Soviet party and, in particular, of Comrade Khrushchev."

Although Brezhnev, then a secretary of the Soviet Party Central Committee, reportedly had urged the Italian Communist Party to suppress the memo, by late September it had been printed in every party organ in the Soviet bloc except in Bulgaria. Yugoslavia was the first country in Eastern Europe to publish it, and the Soviet Communist Party newspaper *Pravda* published it Sept. 10 with no comment.

Excerpts from the Togliatti memo:

"... The plan we [the Italian Communist Party leadership] had proposed for an effective struggle against the erroneous political lines and against the splitting activity of the Chinese Communists was different from that effectively followed. In substance, our plan was based on these points:

● "Never to interrupt the polemic against the positions of principle and the political views of the Chinese.

● "To conduct the polemic, contrary to what the Chinese do, without verbal exacerbations and without generic condemnations, on concrete themes, in an objective and persuasive manner and always with a certain respect for the adversary.

● "At the same time to proceed by groups of parties to a series of meetings for a profound examination and a better definition of the tasks presenting themselves today in the different sectors of our movement (Western Europe, the countries of Latin America, ... 18 of the 3d world ... etc.). ...

"Only after this preparation, which could take a year or more of work, could one have examined the question of an international conference that could truly be a new stage for our movement, its effective strengthening on new and correct lines. In this way we would also have been able better to isolate the Chinese Communists, to face them with a more compact front, united not only through the use of common general definitions of the Chinese line, but also because of a more profound knowledge of the common tasks of the entire movement and those concretely facing each one of its sectors.

"Furthermore, once the tasks and our political line had been well-defined, ... one could also have renounced the international conference, if this were to appear necessary, in order to avoid a formal split.

"A different line was pursued and I do not consider the results as altogether beneficial....

"It is not correct to refer to the Socialist countries (including the Soviet Union) as if everything were always going well in them. This is the mistake, for instance, in that section of the 1960 declaration dealing with these countries. In fact, there continually arise in all the Socialist countries difficulties, contradictions and new problems that must be presented in their effective reality.

"The worst [thing to do] is to give the impression that everything is always going well, whereas suddenly we find ourselves faced with the necessity of referring to difficult situations and explaining them....

"The criticism of Stalin ... has left rather deep traces. The most serious thing is a certain degree of scepticism with which also some of those close to us greet reports of new economic and political successes.

"Beyond this must be considered in general as unresolved the problem of the origin of the cult of Stalin and how this became possible....

"There is an attempt to investigate what could have been the political errors that contributed to giving rise to the cult. This debate is taking place among historians and qualified cadres of the party.

"We do not discourage it because it helps toward a more profound awareness of the history of the revolution and its difficulties. However, we advise prudence in coming to conclusions and the taking into account of publication and research in the Soviet Union.

"The problem that claims greater attention, one affecting the Soviet Union as much as the other Socialist countries, however, is, today, especially that of overcoming the regime of restrictions and suppression of democratic and personal freedom introduced by Stalin.

"Not all the Socialist countries present the same picture. The general impression is that of a slowness and resistance in returning to the Leninist norms that insured, within the party and outside it, a wide liberty of expression and debate on culture, art and also on politics.

"This slowness and resistance is for us difficult to explain, above all in consideration of the present conditions when there is no longer capitalist encirclement and economic construction has had tremendous successes...."

INDEX

O

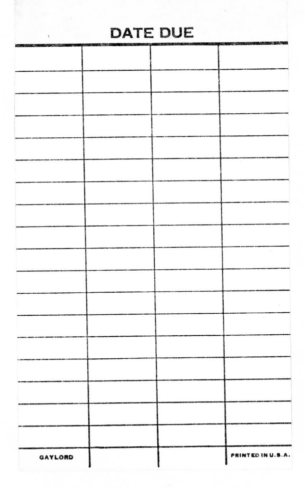

DATE DUE

GAYLORD   PRINTED IN U.S.A.